An October in Catalonia

An October in Catalonia
Paradoxes of the independence movement

Josep Maria Antentas

Resistance Books, London
and the International Institute for Research
and Education, Amsterdam

"This book does a wonderful job of dissecting the Catalan independence movement, analysing its victories, defeats, and the broader implications of its strategic decisions. We are provided with profound insights into the interplay of internal weaknesses and state repression, whilst offered a nuanced critique of both leadership choices and institutional crises. A timely exploration of political dynamics, and enduring challenges, this book is essential for understanding Catalonia's past and envisioning its future."
Andrew Dowling, Reader in Contemporary Spanish History, Cardiff University

"Antentas has written a magisterial analysis of the failure of the Catalan struggle for independence, a defining political event of the 2010s. If the Left across Europe is to recover its strategic bearings, it needs to be familiar with his account of class, nation, state, sovereignty, and internationalism in Catalonia."
Costas Lapavitsas, SOAS, University of London

"This is perhaps the most important analysis from a Marxist perspective of the October 2017 events in Catalonia. It brings forward both the dynamic and the contradictions of the pro-independence movement, situating it in the broader context the deeper hegemonic crisis of the Spanish State. And it underscores the crucial challenge of how to rethink the very notion of the people at the intersection of class, nation, gender and race, and as way to revisit the question of a potential subaltern hegemony. A must read for anyone interested in contemporary questions of radical left strategy."
Panagiotis Sotiris, Hellenic Open University

Resistance Books
resistancebooks.org
info@resistancebooks.org

The International Institute for Education and Research
iire.org
iire@iire.org

An October in Catalonia – Paradoxes of the independence movement is Issue No.79 of the Notebooks for Study and Research published by the International Institute for Research and Education. It was first published in Spanish by Editorial Sylone, Barcelona, in 2019, with the title *Espectros de Octubre (per)turbaciones y paradojas del independentismo Catalan*. This edition published 2025 by Resistance Books (London) and the International Institute for Research and Education (Amsterdam).

Design by
Michael Wallace
Gareth Lindsay

Typefaces used
Karrik by Jean-Baptiste Morizot and Lucas Le Bihan
Cardo by David Perry

ISBN: 978-1-872242-30-9 (pbk)
ISBN: 978-1-872242-17-0 (e-pub)

Acknowledgements

Resistance Books is grateful to Iain Bruce and Brian Anglo for the translation, James Ryan for his help by correcting the manuscript, Fred Leplat who organized the production, and Michael Wallace and Gareth Lindsay who designed the book. Without their contribution, it would not have been possible to publish *An October in Catalonia – The paradoxes of the independence movement*.

Resistance Books is also grateful to Editorial Sylone, Barcelona, who published the first edition in Spanish and granted the permission for this edition in English.

Josep Maria Antentas is a sociologist, professor at the Universitat Ramon Llull (URL) in Barcelona. He is member of the editorial board of the journal *Historical Materialism* and of the Advisory Council of the journal *Viento Sur*. He has written extensively on Spanish and Catalan politics and social movements. He is co-author with Esther Vivas of *Planeta Indignado* (2012) and *Resistencias Globales – De Seattle a la crisis de Wall Street* (2009).

Contents

Foreword to the English edition
13

1. Contexts and Background
15
Origins
15
Instabilities
21
Independence pure and simple
27
Sovereignties
36
The internationalism of the 99% and the Procés
40

2. The October Crisis (I)
52
The referendum and its former lives
52
Dual legittimacy
55
Tribulations without a strategic plan
63
Irresponsible responsibility
70
Strategic self-deception
78
Disruptive powers
82
A coup d'état by the state itself
88
Dilemmas of the left hemisphere
92
Contradictions, paradoxes and (im)purities
97

3. 'A Single People?'
105

Divorces and marriages
105

Spectres of the 'Emperor of the Paralelo'
107

Worker and popular dilemmas
111

Alliances for 'a single people'
118

Transitions and dislocations
122

Tensions and articulations
126

The legacy and spectre of Pujol
131

Language wars
141

Emergence of the orange people
151

Cracks in 'a single people'
153

Images of the nation
160

Spectres of the (im)migrant nation
164

4. The October Crisis (II)
173

Strategic collapse and foundational limitations
173

Diverging paths on the left
180

The potential of the purple people
187

Eurocommons?
193

Legitimism
197

Diverging mirrors
202

The reformulation on hold
205
Resistance
215
Splits on the Right
223
An unexpected replacement
228

5. **Strategic Spectres**
234

6. **Epilogue: A Long Strategic Crisis**
239
Lawfare
240
Protracted strategic crisis
243
Complexities
247
Amnesty
250
Perspectives
251

Political Chronology (2000–2024)
256
Glossary of Organisations
298
Acronyms
311

Foreword to the English edition

This book analyses the Catalan pro-independence political cycle that erupted in 2012 and peaked in October 2017. It sets it in relation to the broader political and social crisis that broke out in the Spanish state after the 2008 crisis and, in particular, the rise of the 15-M movement in 2011.

It is an essay that attempts to discuss in strategic terms the strengths and weaknesses of that phase. It also contains some reflections on previous processes in the history of Catalonia and Spain, the consideration of which is useful to understand the Catalan independence process and the Spanish contemporary crisis.

The book has a somewhat peculiar format, with a traditional structure divided into chapters and sections, but with a structure of paragraphs that in many cases function as autonomous reflections. Hence, each paragraph contains a number. This expository style has no particular pretensions. It is the result of how the book was conceived, since it was born from fragmentary notes that I wrote to clarify my own ideas.

The book was published in Spanish in early 2019 and written during the second half of 2018, when the impact of October 2017 was still near. Many years have already passed. I have chosen to keep the original content intact in this English edition with no desire to correct statements or assessments that the passage of time may have discredited as I consider that, in general terms, the strategic reflection written then is still of interest. However, I have added an epilogue, written in the summer of 2024, to update the content and assess the period 2017–2024, marked by a progressive strategic decomposition of Catalan independence movement and, also, a decline of the left (whether pro-independence or not) in Catalonia and in Spain, reborn in the heat of the 15-M.

To make things easier for the English-speaking reader, the book contains a social-political chronology of the Spanish state from the year 2000 to the summer of 2024. It also includes a glossary of the acronyms used in the book and another appendix with a brief explanation of the organisations mentioned in the text.

Barcelona, August 2024

1
Contexts and Background

Origins

1.

From the viewpoint of its historical significance, the Catalan crisis - at once constitutional, institutional, political and social - has laid bare all the limitations of the '1978 State' as codified in the Spanish constitution of that year in terms of its national identity, its democratic political structure and its internal architecture. To appreciate these limitations to their full extent, however, they must be seen in relation to those which emerged at the time of the Indignados movement, more commonly referred to in Spain as the '15-M'. It is in the synthesis of 15-M 2011 and October 2017 that the true nature of the second Bourbon restoration, the *Transición* (the 'Transition') process that brought it into being and its insertion in the neoliberal model of global capitalism appears in its entirety. In particular, the mass movement that burst onto the scene on 11 September 2012 and was to be the start of the Catalan pro-independence Procés (the Process)[1] that culminated in October 2017 must be understood as the result of a triple accumulative dynamic: the legacy of the reaction to the aggressive Spanish nationalism of the second Aznar government (2000–04), the consequent failure of the reform of the Catalan autonomy statute, spectacularly topped off by the Supreme Court verdict in June 2010 declaring key parts of it unconstitutional, and the impact of the economic crisis and the turn to hardline austerity policies in March 2010.

2.
The October crisis was, at bottom, the ultimate expression of the 1978 regime's inability to overcome the historical failure of a Spanish nation-building attempt that attracted limited support from below due to its deficiencies, and which never managed definitively to gain legitimacy throughout the whole of Spain. To do so would have required the development, at the time, of a plurinational conception of the country. But that was not the path taken during the Transition, when, paradoxically, a weak idea of Spain in the context of a deep crisis of Spanish nationalism and the superficial acceptance of plurinationalism by the left-wing forces in Spain as a whole existed alongside, and complemented, each other.

3.
The 1978 State recognised Spain's plurality, but, de facto, not its plurinationality. It reserved the term 'nation' for Spain alone and denied the right of self-determination to the ambiguously named 'nationalities' situated on its periphery. Although this term could be construed as a synonym of nation, its real scope was severely curtailed by the assertion, in the Constitution, that national sovereignty belongs to the Spanish people and that the Constitution itself is based on the 'indissoluble unity of the Spanish nation', whose identity is regarded as having been in existence prior to it. This formula at most entailed cultural, but not political, national plurality.[2]

4.
The development of the Spanish state as a 'State of Autonomies',[3] resulting from the generalisation of the model of autonomous communities in the early 1980s, was directly dependent on Catalonia, whose demands set the tone for all the others. It ended up intermingling, in internal tension, a decentralising overall model of territorial organisation of the state – permanently under construction, and to a large extent

unplanned – with a limited form of recognition of its national plurality. It had an internal competitive logic, at one and the same time an integral feature of the model's very nature and a factor tending to destabilise it. As an inseparable aspect of its capitalist modernisation and integration into Europe in the eighties, the 'State of Autonomies' superficially and relatively put off dealing with its long-standing, fundamental problems and they remained unresolved.

5.
However, as a consequence of its intrinsic limitations, it eventually succumbed to the combined process of Aznar's reactivation of exclusionary Spanish nationalism beginning in 2000 and the collapse of the modernising-Europeanising narrative following the 2008 crisis. The first factor meant the revival of the intolerant Spanish nationalism associated with Francoism and with it the re-emergence of old and apparently forgotten spectres. The second entailed the collapse of the entire political and economic project implemented since the Transition linking together neoliberal restructuring, modernisation, Europeanisation and democracy. This had been the material basis supporting not only the integration of the subaltern classes (by way of their illusory transformation into middle classes, driven by consumerism), but also the identity of Spain as a country that was to be plural and based on autonomous communities, but not plurinational; that was to be administratively decentralised, but with a centralised, mono-national sovereignty. It was not only the economy that collapsed, but a certain idea of Spain and its place in the world.

6.
Spain's post-Franco national identity was tied to the 'consensus' of the Transition and associated with 'normalisation', construed as the absence of internal antagonisms, limited plurality within proper channels and a distorted relation to its own history,

beginning with Spanish culture in exile which was only integrated into the post-Franco national narrative once it had been depoliticised and removed from its context.[4] It combined an unstable, variable balance between a guarantee of the absolute unity of the Spanish nation and an internal plurality in which the Catalan, Basque and Galician national identities were subordinated in the hierarchy to Spanish national identity. This precarious balance was completely upset by Aznar's turn, the most consummate expression of the historical failure of Spanish nationalism to create a legitimised, accepted and inclusive project.

7.
The non-Spanish nationalisms were always seen as factors destabilising the national narrative, if only to a limited extent, with the exception of the *abertzale* movement in the Basque Country (which at the same time was utilised for the purposes of inner cohesion as a real, yet functional, adversary). Their existence was never integrated into a truly plurinational project, which would have meant accepting a diversity of political subjects, the de-hierarchisation of identities and the end of the association between Spanish nationalism and the state itself. The historical osmosis between Castilian and Spanish identity generated an asymmetrical relation among Spain's different nations, cultures and languages based on taking a part for the whole (Spain as the nation of all rather than one of the nations of a shared, plurinational state) and the absence of reciprocal plurinationality and pluriculturality (the existence of Spanish identity, culture and language in Catalonia, the Basque Country and Galicia, and a rigid cultural and historical indifference in the rest of the state in regard to these nations' languages and cultures).

8.
In historical terms, the present 'Catalan crisis' is another episode, with particular characteristics, of a recurrent, long-drawn-out

crisis of the Spanish national project and the perpetuation of Spain as a state with a failed national project (which is undoubtedly different from regarding it as a failed state), which it has not given up. Persevering with a failed model has generated a permanent identity crisis to which Spanish nationalism has traditionally responded at critical moments by exacerbating its most exclusionary features and, consequently, the fundamental reasons for its own failure. The official legal and institutional definition of Spain and its political and national reality is structurally dysfunctional and characterised by discord. Historically this has varied in magnitude, but the State of Autonomies failed to resolve it. It provided a temporary consensus (except in the Basque Country) and a broad, consensual legitimacy, but it always had limitations and insurmountable 'design flaws', and never won full acceptance. The contemporary 'Catalan problem' is in fact an apparent reflection of the 'Spanish problem'. It is the historically problematic nature of Spain that the Catalan crisis has brought out into the open.

9.
Spanish nationalism has been characterised by its lack of an 'awareness of particularity', connecting its own identity to a project of universality whose historical lever was the imperial project.[5] An outwardly expansive universality, whose correlate is its inwardly uniformising drive, which since the 1898 crisis has been characterised by a strong 'reactive' component[6] in regard to the peripheral nationalisms viewed as the enemy within, in the context of a notable existential historicist pessimism. The sublimation of the Castilian language at the beginning of the early 20th century as a constitutive element of the Spanish national project, as a reaction to the advance of Catalanism[7] and as a pillar of Hispanoamericanism,[8] was a central component of this *españolista* (literally 'Spanishist' or pro-Spanish) universalism that was already well aware of its own decadence.

10.

As a state nationalism and a dominant nationalism, Spanish nationalism has the structural privilege of being taken for granted and being able to be invisible, even of presenting itself, when it wants to, not as a nationalism, but as mere common sense, and denouncing the peripheral nationalisms as nationalist. However, as a result of the failure of Spanish nation-building, it did not achieve sufficient internal normalisation to become fully, in Billig's well-known expression,[9] a 'banal nationalism', that is to say an everyday nationalism manifesting itself through internalised habitual practices enabling reproduction of the national identity. It became banal in so far as it was able to go unnoticed and become naturalised. But it did not do so completely because of its relative lack of legitimacy on account of not being entirely reconciled with itself and with society. The traditional identification of Spanish national symbols exclusively with the right is a clear example of this, although symbols of national identity have recently been used in a naturalised way without explicit ideological connotations, for example during the period of the Spanish national football team's successes at Euro 2008, the 2010 World Cup and Euro 2012.

11.

The incomplete banalisation of Spanish nationalism has gone hand in hand with the virulent activation of a reactive attack type of self-assertiveness at times when it perceives itself as being threatened. From the 1898 crisis to the October 2017 crisis, history has been punctuated by such episodes. But the nature and function of this current aggressive variant of Spanish nationalism cannot be understood without seeing it in relation to its banalised aspect. Unless one is aware of the latter, the structural causes of the former cannot be properly grasped. It is its incomplete naturalisation that requires a combative nationalism whose definitive victory, if it were to go beyond mere coercive imposition, would be the once-and-for-all banalisation of Spanish nationalism.

Instabilities

12.
During Aznar's second term, the Spanish right adopted, as an integral part of its strategic project, a hard-line Spanish nationalism based on a rigid, scarcely plural view of Spain that clashed head-on with Basque and Catalan nationalism, and a project of administrative recentralisation of the state. This new Spanish nationalism developed in an atmosphere of political and intellectual euphoria arising out of economic growth and joining the Eurozone in 1999, the official propaganda emblem of the country's definitive modernisation and putting its age-old backwardness behind it. The neoliberal euphoria at the end of the millennium stood in contrast to the pessimism at the close of the 19th century, but both moments bore witness to the rebirth of Spanish nationalism, reactive and pessimist in one case, offensive and triumphalist in the other.

13.
Aznar's reactionary expansionism signalled a change in regard to the preceding governments under the PSOE (in power from 1982 to 1996), whose national project and idea of Spain combined a defence of 'plural Spain' with the prevalence of a strong Spanish nationalism, which was the real vector of its conception of Spain, but without it being too suffocating for Catalan or Basque nationalism. Faced with a past that was seen as having failed, the PSOE's national project had been constructed by linking it to a project aimed at a future of modernisation and Europeanisation.[10] For Felipe González's PSOE, the nation appeared to be at the service of the stabilisation of the state, which necessitated a certain superficial pluralism in its conception, whereas for the Aznar-led right the nation was to become a goal in itself which, because of its exclusionary logic, ended up putting the state under strain and destabilising it. The inconsistency of its model of the nation, hidden behind its offensive and intolerant façade, eventually made the state more fragile.

14.
Aznar's project sought to construct a new Spanish nationalism that was relaunched by using the anti-ETA consensus to drive forward an aggressive Spanish nationalism employing the enemy within as a lever to reaffirm its own identity. The murder of Popular Party politician Miguel Ángel Blanco by ETA in 1997 was to mark a decisive turning point and facilitated the creation of a media and institutional bloc that paved the way for this Spanish neo-nationalism. In gestation during his first term, when Aznar, short of an overall majority, headed a relative-majority government supported by right-wing Basque and Catalan nationalists, this project would emerge fully fledged following his re-election in 2000. After winning an overall majority on 12 March and being sworn in as prime minister on 26 April, one of his first decisions was to hold the official Armed Forces Day parade on 28 May for the first time in Barcelona since 31 May 1981. These two events had very different meanings. The first, very shortly after the attempted coup of 23 February, was staged as a reification of the 'consensus' surrounding the Transition, linking parliamentary monarchy, constitutional stability and internal plurality, and attended by the head of the Catalan government.[11] The second, on the other hand, appeared as an affirmation of hardcore Spanish nationalism and identity, in the face of which the Catalan government was patently uncomfortable, while a street demonstration was held against the parade.

15.
The Popular Party destroyed part of the Transition 'consensus' in the name of this very consensus by offering an extremely restrictive version of its political and cultural framework. But the fact that it could so easily be crushed (or reinterpreted so rigidly) and that the PSOE could be dragged along in this process without much difficulty is yet another indication of its original limitations and the permanent fragility

on which it rested. Its dismantling by the right should not lead us to invoke it again, as some moderate voices in the political centre sometimes do, but, on the contrary, to deepen criticism of the Transition process, its results and the structural violence that presided over it. It is the very nature of the state that crystallised in 1978 that explains its later reactionary regression, including what happened after October 2017. These are not anomalies, but rather possibilities in the regime's DNA and there is no break in continuity with the less retrograde versions and interpretations of the constitutional framework.

16.
At the beginning of the present millennium, exclusionary Spanish nationalism was transformed into the Spanish neocons' main instrument to unite and mobilise their social base, and became a constituent part of their project. Although it was carried out in the name of the Spanish constitution and the Transition myth (a feeble substitute for the founding anti-fascist myth of many European state nationalisms after 1945),[12] and an attempt was made, without much success, to legitimise it by enlisting Habermas' 'constitutional patriotism',[13] it actually put forward a particularly centralist and homogenising interpretation of the ground rules and a reactionary national project of socially crushing dissidence and national diversity. Useful in the short term for winning votes outside Catalonia and setting the political agenda, Aznar's was a 'scorched earth' policy that laid the basis for the growing hostility of large sectors of Catalan society towards the Spanish state. This approach was governability by means of crisis and permanent conflagration, a mechanism for legitimisation via conflict by way of a paradoxical legitimation that engendered delegitimisation and consolidated a project of unstable stability. Although seemingly strong and solid, this option actually expressed an inability to generate a stable hegemony (or at least a relatively stable one, insofar as

no hegemony is entirely stable and long-lasting). It was also a reflection of a particular feature of the imperfect Spanish two-party system: the structurally destabilising nature of one of the two legs it stood on.

17.
The process of reforming Catalonia's autonomy statute, formulated for the first time by Pasqual Maragall in 2001 and the key goal of the 'tripartite government' (Socialist Party, Republican Left of Catalonia and Initiative for Catalonia) formed in 2003, was the Catalan left's response to both the end of the government cycle under right-wing nationalist Jordi Pujol and the Aznar project. The reform proposed two very basic aims, both very moderate and compatible with the constitutional framework in place: first, to render the Catalan autonomous government's powers ironclad, that is to say ensuring them some kind of irreversibility that would not leave them exposed to the neoconservative recentralisation of the state already underway and, secondly, to achieve symbolic recognition of Catalonia's 'identity' as a nation. What happened is well known: despite its superficiality, the reform of the statute unleashed an extremely intense campaign of agitation by the Spanish right throughout the country (repeating, in a very different context, an approach already used during the campaign for Catalan autonomy in 1918–19 and in the process of the adoption of the 1932 statute). In Catalonia the reform process was experienced in contradictory fashion: on the one hand, it had the effect of mobilising (and then disappointing) the most Catalanist part of Catalan society, whilst on the other, it was met with a certain indifference by a large section of the working classes originating, directly or indirectly, from the rest of Spain, and with opposition from a social minority linked to Spanish nationalism.

18.

The removal of sections of the statute by the Spanish parliament in March 2006 and, above all, the verdict of the Constitutional Court on 28 June 2010 declaring fourteen articles of the remaining text unconstitutional, created the feeling in a large part of Catalan society that greater self-government was not possible within the Spanish state and that Spain was an irreformable project. This happened three months after Zapatero's Spanish government had made a harsh turn to austerity policies, thereby bringing together in time two events that would cause a double crisis of legitimacy of the state and contribute to the emergence of a double political, social and national crisis against a shared background of democratic malaise. The upheavals of 15 May 2011, with the explosion of the Indignados movement, and 11 September 2012, the occasion of the first huge demonstration explicitly in favour of independence, were just around the corner.

19.

The rise of the pro-independence movement must be placed in a context in which the worsening of living conditions as a result of neoliberal restructuring and austerity policies, the relative decline of Catalonia's economy, the generalised political crisis and identity insecurity in the face of globalisation and authoritarian reactionary Spanish nationalism are mingled together. Its sudden growth saw a change in the historical goal that the majority of Catalanism, in its different variants and senses, had had since its appearance in the late 19th century: the reform of the Spanish state. At the same time, the contemporary pro-independence movement operates in a different context from the one Catalanism had acted in throughout most of its history. It came onto the scene at a time of economic weakness following forty years during which Catalonia had been particularly vulnerable to all the economic crises that had affected Spain. Although it retained a considerable industrial base, Catalonia's economy had increasingly turned towards services, tourism, property speculation and the generalisation of low-skilled and poorly paid jobs. Barcelona's transformation, with the 1992 Olympic Games as a lever, into a post-industrial city heavily oriented to mass tourism was the key element in this shift.

20.
Madrid's growth as a financial and industrial pole in conjunction with its status as the country's political capital put an end to the dissociation between the geographical location of political and economic power characteristic of 19th and 20th century Spain. This changed the meaning and role that historical Catalanism had taken on from the 19th century onwards. Avoiding falling definitively behind in a highly competitive global world, rather than taking part in reforming Spain in order to modernise the country under Catalan leadership, became the Catalan political elite's strategic horizon. And the demand for its own state, either with a view to actually obtaining it or as a means of achieving an advantageous position in Spain and the European Union, became its strategic perspective. It is this contradictory situation as an economically privileged region in partial decline that must be taken into account in order to understand the mutual incomprehension between a large part of Catalan and Spanish society.

Independence pure and simple

21.
Born following the demonstration on 11 September 2012, the mainstream independence movement's common sense has been based on the primacy of the national question as the framework of a shared identity ('Catalans must unite because we have common interests') and the strategic primacy of possessing one's own state as a means of deciding what kind of country ('without our own state we can't do anything'). These two ideas tend simultaneously to underestimate the

class contradictions inherent in all social formations and the class nature of state institutions themselves. This double emphasis – on the national and on state questions above all else – was rounded off in the case of the pro-independence left by a certain stagist perspective ('first independence, then we'll fight over everything else'). With meagre results in innumerable historical episodes, stagism usually fails to take into account that the end result of any transition process is heavily determined by whoever controls the parameters of that transition.

22.
The strategy for independence pure and simple involved a fetishisation of the state in which it appears as guarantor of another society, ignoring its real, concrete functions. It suffered from a particular form of what Gramsci, applying the concept to a very different situation, called 'statolatry': confusing the state with the whole of society and the nation, and casting it as the fundamental lever of change and the embodiment of the collective will. The state as an absolute took precedence over the real state, its historical nature and its contemporary role. Thinking of the Russian revolution, Gramsci held that 'statolatry' was normal in social groups that had not had a long, independent intellectual and moral evolution. But he added that this could not go on forever and as such had to be criticised.[14] Similarly, it is understandable that the movement of a stateless nation should overemphasise the virtues of having a state without questioning its nature, but this does not mean passing over in silence the weaknesses of such a position. The struggle since 2012 for its own state was thus waged in the absence of any debate whatsoever on what a state is and what its functions are, or on how it interacts with international institutions and European integration. This reflected a sort of instrumentalist voluntarism that extolled the state without tackling the question of its class nature and its role in the current historical phase.

23.

With these premises as the starting point, independence appeared as the promise of a new beginning, a new course in history, similar to the one Hannah Arendt identified as constituting modern revolutions.[15] But it was presented officially as the overall solution to current problems and at the same time as a future project devoid of any concrete content. As a project without any substantive content beyond itself, it had clear limitations, but this was also the paradoxical source of its across-the-board attraction. It was seen as a guarantor and the possibility of setting a new course, of breaking out of the historical stalemate, but without defining the new road to be taken.

24.

The movement came into being from the very start with the wrong strategic approach on a key question: the social alliances and social base to which it addressed itself. The independence movement's great founding strategic obsession was how to push the Catalan nationalist right onto the pro-independence path, but, in contrast, it failed to consider a more decisive strategic problem: how to attract the left, which had a Catalanist but not pro-independence tradition, and those sections of the working class most indifferent to Catalanism. In other words, it did not pose the question of how to link up with the legacy of the Indignados movement of 2011. The entire strategy designed by those who sincerely built a movement for independence was conceived with the aim of not losing the Catalan right, in power since 2010, on the way and making it as easy as possible for it to come on board. The path chosen was to delink the demand for 'independence' from any specific criticism of its austerity policies. By contrast, this meant that the independence movement was unable to offer a concrete connection between its project and a way out of the crisis favourable to those who had most suffered from it, other than the generic promise that things would be better with a state of one's own. Any serious strategic debate on what social bloc needed to be built was held in abeyance.

25.
In a unilateral way without any social content, the cause of independence was framed in terms of an accumulation of its own forces and a bilateral confrontation with the state, dissociating itself from any broader prospect of the fall of the regime on an all-Spain level. This unilateralism expressed both a legitimate and necessary starting point (the self-emancipation typical of any collective) and lack of a strategic perspective (the failure to understand the need for allies) inseparable from its own founding framework.

26.
All this shaped a movement based on major strategic fallacies, but also with a democratic project that clashed head-on with the institutional framework of the 1978 regime. It was impossible, therefore, to be neutral in this battle. In the collision of legitimacies between the state and the Catalan government and pro-independence movement, on one side there was a reactionary, authoritarian proposal, and on the other a democratic demand. It is from the standpoint of support for its legitimacy and its trial of strength with the state that criticisms of the independence movement's founding limitations should be formulated.

27.
Has there been, in the Procés, a strong element of a mere split between elites? No doubt. Has this break-up had vigorously theatrical elements about it, employed according to the parties' respective electoral requirements? Of course. But can the Procés be reduced to that? Therein lies the fundamental strategic question. What has happened in Catalonia since 2012 represents a tectonic shift of a considerable part of Catalan society with the unprecedented rise of a mass

pro-independence movement. Moreover, these masses are not mere puppets subject to the machinations of the political elites which can interfere, more or less consciously, in their plans. The ruptures at the top can unleash dynamics which end up with those who have set them in motion losing control. Ritualised standoffs can lead to material clashes and these can become considerably affected by the strength and noisiness of the masses' entry onto the scene. The events of 1 October had a lot of this about them.

28.

Neither naïve readings of the Procés that accept its founding narrative and strategic framework, or at least agree to act entirely within it, nor dismissals of it in toto, which end up becoming self-fulfilling prophecies through inaction, are of much use in founding a political strategy capable of operating in a complex scenario such the one existing after 2012. Accepting the democratic legitimacy of the pro-independence movement's proposition, while at the same time stressing its limitations and carefully assessing both its drawbacks and the opportunities it opens up, is a much better and more nuanced option. This approach translates into an orientation that is both inside and outside the Procés, a political strategy that is also strategic politics.

29.

The series of informal votes on independence, known as 'consultations', in different towns and villages all over Catalonia that began in Arenys de Munt in September 2009 and culminated, following successive waves, in Barcelona in April 2011, was the immediate precedent for the start of the Procés after 11 September 2012. These 'consultations' were significant not only because of their demand for independence, but because they attested to a form of political action combining grassroots involvement, a challenge to the political institutions and voting. They synthesised the civic, democratic, citizen-driven culture on which the independence movement has based its legitimacy and its conception of political change. The movement's strategic strengths and weaknesses were already there in embryo: great stress on mass mobilisations, building majorities, the need for democratic legitimacy and an integrating civic culture, but also heavy dependence on representative politics and political institutions, and a lack of what might be called insurrectional spirit. So, once the Procés was underway, street mobilisations, seen as an instrument for putting pressure on a friendly political power to which the political management of the movement's demands is then delegated, have been the chief means of achieving electoral legitimacy and a political majority by a movement that has always based itself on the logic of representation and delegation.

30.
The majority of the independence movement has been enormously moderate, both because of its own conception of political action and the tasks necessary to achieve its aims, and because of its drastic decoupling of its proposal for an independent state from any explicit criticism of austerity policies. Actually, although this has been accepted matter-of-factly, as one outside observer has pointed out,[16] it is quite surprising that a movement such as this should be established in the midst of an economic crisis without any criticism of the present economic order except insofar as the relationship between Catalonia and Spain is concerned. Nevertheless, in spite of its scant radicalism, the paradox is that it has also been the bearer of a demand – for independence – which clashed with the very nature of the 1978 constitutional framework and Spanish national identity, and was therefore unacceptable to the state.

31.
Although the independence movement shares the democratic frame with all the other protest movements arising during

the crisis, it has actually had little contact with other social realities and organisations, and, in fact, has been characterised by wanting to dissolve all other grievances to do with the crisis in the idea of having one's own state. The Procés has not sought synergies with other processes existing in Catalan society, in particular with the 'other Procés' going from the Indignados to Ada Colau's victory in the local elections in Barcelona and En Comú Podem (In Common We Can) winning more votes than any other party in Catalonia in the general elections on 20 December 2015 and 26 June 2016. Its aim, on the contrary, has been to dissolve or subordinate all other realities, a decisive mistake that strengthened the right within it and moreover encouraged and provided arguments for those who, from outside the independence movement, did everything possible to avoid entering into any dialogue with it. From 2012 onwards it promised a forward-looking overall solution to the problems – having one's own state – but offered no concrete response to any of the contemporary anti-austerity struggles and grievances. It was based more on subsuming them into the cause for Catalonia's own state than on strengthening them and driving them forward. Furthermore, such a policy permanently absolves the Catalan government and institutions of all responsibility, a factor that clashes with the everyday direct experience of those who have been in the front line facing cuts and austerity measures.

32.
The independence movement grew due to a combination of pragmatic and instrumental reasons (the idea of getting away from the Popular Party, the feeling that Spain was a failed project, etc.), and deeper reasons concerning national identity. Although Catalan national identity is an important variable in determining support for independence, there is not a mechanical relationship between them and, when support for independence began to grow quickly from 2010 on, the gap between the curves tracing their development

widened. In other words, support for independence not primarily connected with national identity increased among people defining themselves as both Catalan and Spanish. Political preferences changed more quickly than identities. Aware of this, part of the independence movement has tried to distance itself from nationalism and sketch out instrumental arguments in favour of their cause not based on identity. However, the 'instrumental' nature of its proposal was self-limited due to the presence of a neoliberal party mired in corruption scandals at the head of the Catalan government and the delinking of the project of its own state from any concrete social agenda.

33.
From the very beginning, the contradiction between the promise of a bright future through independence and a dismal present administered by some of those who were vouching for this rosy future placed a structural strain on the independence movement's strategic perspective. It implied suspending the present to bring about the advent of the future, always a high-risk operation, as the coming of the latter is directly connected to the content of the former. The birth of tomorrow cannot be detached from the contemporary conditions of its gestation. Rather than ignoring the present in order to transfer political action to the future, the key lies in strategically connecting intervention in the present to the aspiration for another future; changing the present to have another future; thinking of another future as the strategic horizon for the struggles in the here and now; in short, inserting the aspiration to independence into the day-to-day fight for survival at a time of endless austerity. But the path chosen was a different one.

34.
In retrospect, without indulging in the nostalgia of what might have been and was not, it is useful to consider the

question of how things would have turned out if in 2012 the movement had accompanied the 'independence' slogan with a basic social emergency and regeneration of democracy programme. The answer is clear: the Catalan nationalist right and Artur Mas's government would have felt even more uncomfortable with the pro-independence tsunami, but they would not have been able to dissociate themselves from it and support for the Procés would have spread among the popular and working classes. The traditional left-wing political organisations (and, from 2014, those newly arrived on the scene) as well as the trade unions would have had to take part in the movement in one way or another, and this would have transformed the very nature of the Procés. Counterfactual thinking does not solve the problem, but in hindsight it can point to the roads not taken and help to clarify strategy. It creates possibilities in the past that can be projected into the future and therefore adopted in the present to open up doors not yet glimpsed.

35.
In 2012, with the historical workers' movement and its social base fossilised and in a state of decomposition, and the Indignados' upheaval having failed to crystallise into a clear political or organisational form, the independence movement thought that, without a precise project and political horizon, the left-wing camp would gradually adapt more or less to it, and that its social base would either swing over to the idea of Catalonia having its own state or would remain passive, like an object in decay and not an active political subject. Between 2012 and 2014 the founding strategic limitations of the Catalan independence movement did not seem to be an insurmountable boundary and its promoters could ignore them relatively easily in a context in which the movement's social base and strength was advancing and expanding. But following the simulated referendum on 9 November 2014, this growth came to an end and its

support levelled out while the social malaise was politically taking shape in another direction, a direct inheritor of the driving force of the Indignados and the 'social tides': the sudden appearance of Podemos in Catalonia in the 25 May 2014 European Parliament election and, after that, the project headed by Ada Colau of standing in the local council election in Barcelona launched in June 2014 under the name of Guanyem Barcelona (Let's Win Barcelona).

36.
The lack of strategic reinvention and the strategy of non-reinvention was to mark the period following the 9 November simulated referendum and the path leading to the 1 October referendum. The independence movement's founding strategic constraints proved to be as deep-seated as its inability to rise above them. For their part, the new political expressions arising out of the potential opened up by the Indignados movement turned out to be as insensitive to strategic collaboration with the independence movement as it was with them. A case of strategic isolation on both sides? Ever since then Catalan politics and society have been haunted by the spectre of heading towards two different horizons, two different promises of the future. Two ways out of an unbearable present vied with each other. The outcome was mutual competition and reciprocal annihilation. Establishing synergies was doubtless difficult. Failing in the attempt would not have been problematic. Not having tried certainly was.

Sovereignties

37.
Globalisation has brought about a reshaping of sovereignties. A new hierarchy of states has emerged. Far from being passive victims, these must be seen as active agents of globalisation and promoters of a process serving international capital that eventually leads to their own sovereignty being weakened,

although in different ways depending on their position in the world order. The states' business-friendly turn has brought about a radical divorce between the interests of the financial elite and the majority of the population in each country, and a drastic reorganisation of class and power relations within each state. At the same time, the other side of the virulence of this market-driven universalisation, together with the decomposition of the workers' movement, has been outbreaks of identitarian panic and the assertion of differences and particularities expressed in movements of diverse and/or opposing kinds. Although it had already been in motion since the nineties, this whole dynamic was brutally exacerbated by the 2008 crisis, causing the breakup of the mechanisms of institutional representation and the hijacking of politics by finance. However, the reorganisation of the system of states, the transformation of sovereignties and the subordination of the political system to the financial world happened while the territorial integrity principle remained intact. It is at this complex juncture that the rise of the Catalan independence movement must be located. It expresses a democratic, though skewed and superficial, aspiration. It points towards certain solutions, but ignores others.

38.

The right of self-determination and the struggle for national liberation run through the entire history of the 20th century during which social revolution existed in a complex dialectic with the national dimension. Understood as the 'collective right, or right of a differentiated group, to freely decide a particular political "status" that can be claimed by national communities without a state of their own and a particular territorial domain in which to exercise their sovereignty',[17] it enjoyed its glory days after the end of the First World War with the crisis of the old Austro-Hungarian, Ottoman and Russian empires, and attained its heroic peak and its most socialistic expression in the decolonisation period following the Second World War. After the fall of the Berlin Wall, the proclamation of the new world order and the rise of neoliberal globalisation, there was another wave of national movements and nations achieving independence or attempting to. But by now they were mostly lacking the generically proto-socialist dimension, whether moderate or radical, which their counterparts had had in the previous period, and found themselves in a situation in which the meaning of their exercise of independence was less amenable to a single interpretation than in the past.

39.

The right to decide, as a reformulation in democratic terms of the classical right of self-determination, has been the democratic desire common to many social and political struggles of our era, but their main strategic and emancipatory deficiency has been their confinement to the national question. As a result, a mutilated right to decide, shorn of its full potential, has been shaped, unconnected to other battles in the present. The democratic aspiration links the independence movement to the Indignados movement. Rigidly restricting its meaning and trying to confine it within a neoliberal framework dramatically distances it from the Indignados. The contemporary desire for democracy is a reaction to the implosion of the mechanisms of institutional participation and representation subordinated to the interests of finance capital. In other words, the dispossession of all real sovereignty. Therefore, democracy and sovereignty must be linked to each other. The latter helps to ensure the former has substantive content. And democracy enables sovereignty to be conceived in non-reactionary, non-exclusive terms, distancing it from the reactionary defence of sovereignty that is on the rise in Europe.

40.

The independence movement defined sovereignty in exclusively national terms, without connecting national sovereignty to popular sovereignty and without linking formal political sovereignty to real sovereignty in regard to finance capital. But independence, within the framework of democracy restricted to national sovereignty and the acceptance of an economic framework that removes all popular sovereignty – and a part of national sovereignty too – ends up stripped of sovereignty. It may lead to a paradoxical independence project devoid of real sovereignty in pursuit of a formally independent state in a subaltern position within the European Union, in favour of international agreements such as the Transatlantic Trade and Investment Partnership and with policies serving the major multinationals. This would represent a sort of change without change that can only go beyond its limitations if it is capable of coupling the national with the popular and defining the latter in oppositional terms and making it revolve around the working class. All this does not take away the independence cause's legitimacy, but it does show up its inconsistencies as far as emancipation is concerned.

41.

The independence movement has been a democratic movement standing for national sovereignty, but has not had an agenda for creating people's power. Elections, referendums, representative democracy and expressive mass mobilisations have been its strategic and conceptual foundations, but not self-organisation and the real deepening of democracy in the sense of putting forward a different relationship between representatives and those they represent, a different relationship between economic power and political power, and questioning private economic power. In short, it has been a movement in favour of a democratic political change through the building of a broad political and electoral majority, but not a movement defining itself in terms of the 99% vs the 1% or people power vs the financial oligarchy.

42.
If it is to be used to leverage collective empowerment, a number of internal shifts need to be made in the concept of sovereignty. It must be understood as people's and not national sovereignty. At the same time, 'the people' needs to be understood in class terms, not by schematically counterposing class and people, but rather defining the people in terms of class instead of as an undifferentiated amorphous mass. This does not mean positing a black-or-white opposition, first, between national and popular sovereignty, and then between people power and class power, but seeing that the national must be at the service of the popular, and that the latter's strategic and conceptual mainstay must have the working class – understood in a broad, non-reductionist sense – and all the subaltern subjects at its core.

43.
Sovereignty must be understood as part of a people's power project encompassing every aspect of social life and standing in close connection to the struggle against all forms of oppression and exploitation. When construed in this way, it links up with the basic idea of exercising control over one's own life and with the concepts of self-emancipation, self-organisation and self-determination. Extending sovereignty's scope is a way both of making it effective and freeing it from its national and state straitjacket without ignoring either aspect. Sovereignty's scope needs to be broadened in order to go beyond its own conceptual limitations. The politics of sovereignty for those who are subordinated should not mean the political subordination of sovereignty. The claim to sovereignty must serve to transcend it, linking it to democracy and opposition to all domination, widening its scope to dissolve its contradictions.

44.
The fundamental question is how a politics of national sovereignty can shift to a politics of people's sovereignty and how this can be taken forward as a politics of class independence in the framework of a plurinational and pluricultural, non-reductionist conception of the working class. Any appeal to sovereignty is hollow unless it takes on an oppositional popular dimension linking political to economic sovereignty. And any call for sovereignty in terms of democracy must be coupled with an approach of internationalism and solidarity, firstly, in order to survive in the context of globalised capitalism and, secondly, so as not to fall into the trap of an illusory and dangerous policy of national precedence based on national and popular class corporativisms. Class, people and nation interact with each other and must be redefined within the framework of the transformations of global capitalism and the current crisis. Such a redefinition can only be effective in the context of a strategic radicalisation of internationalism.

The internationalism of the 99% and the Procés

45.
Popular movements have traditionally understood internationalism as solidarity and an alliance between subaltern groups and classes across state and/or national borders. The internationalism of the subalterns, that is the 99%, is governed by a strategic geography based on a dialectical relation between spatial scales and planes: the local, the national, the state level (when this does not coincide with the national), the regional-continental and the worldwide. It does not counterpose all these levels of action in binary fashion, but seeks to combine them on the organisational, operational and theoretical terrain through what Daniel Bensaïd called a 'sliding scale of spaces'.[18]

46.
Internationalism also has a domestic dimension by way of a paradoxical intra-state and, to some extent, intra-national dimension. This has been a common meaning in the political context of the United States marked by the diversity of the society's origins, ethnic groups and languages. But it has taken on strategic importance in contemporary Europe, as it is increasingly racially mixed and heterogeneous, ravaged by xenophobia and racism. This inward-facing internationalism means thinking about the nation in a plural and open-ended manner through a dialectic between universality and difference, which requires not confusing unity with homogeneity or difference with fragmentation. Understood in this way, internationalism consists of a strategic game of breaking down walls of prejudice and building bridges of horizontal solidarity, a project that can only be conceived of in conjunction with a programme of social mobilisation. There is no way of joining all this up without the experience of struggle, a horizon that can be reached by two partly different, partly complementary routes: on the one hand, by broadening the conception of the national – in this case of what it means to be 'Catalan' – radicalising and extending the old slogan of 'whoever lives and works in Catalonia is Catalan' to an ethnically, linguistically and culturally ever more plural sociological reality; and on the other, again following Daniel Bensaïd, by decoupling citizenship from nationality, prioritising social over national citizenship by way of a 'secular citizenship that organises a pluralism of routes, trajectories and subjectivities'.[19]

47.
The internationalism of the 99% must be distinguished from liberal cosmopolitanism and post-national democracy's siren calls. That approach, championed by centre-left authors, is indebted to the Kantian tradition and its commitment to an international anti-war alliance guaranteeing perpetual peace

and cosmopolitan law.[20] Its main limitation is that it ends up by merely offering an insufficient democratic and social correction of neoliberal globalisation and/or European integration in the name of a modernising discourse and a naïve Europeanism. It is, rather, an abstract humanism that dodges a robust strategic reflection on its contradictions and class or national dividing lines, and on the function of the state and the nature of the international system of states. The universal republic and international fraternity appear disconnected from any strategic itinerary rooted in the contradictions of the real world.

48.
Although generally construed in moderately left-wing terms, there also exists a radical variant of rootless cosmopolitanism based on a dismissal of the national question in the name of a denationalised class (thereby joining with those workers' movement traditions that were always opposed to the right of self-determination and saw the national conflict as merely a strategic nuisance) or in the name of an anti-statism taken to such an extreme that, either putting itself forward as a localism without borders or advocating a geographically indeterminate space of struggle, takes the liquidation of the state for granted and regards any political demand centring on it as irrelevant. This does not allow for a really operative policy with regard to either the emergence of national movements of stateless nations (such as the Catalan independence movement) or demands made by popular and social movements opposed to austerity for the recovery of national or state sovereignty in the face of globalisation or European integration. Hastily outflanking them all on the left, such an approach runs the risk of being cut off from real – albeit insufficient and contradictory – democratic processes and movements.

49.
Cosmopolitanism is not the problem. The problem is the content of its traditional liberal meaning or its abstract radical version. In fact, cosmopolitanism and internationalism are not opposing concepts. In the time of Marx and Engels, for example, they did not have very different precise meanings and neither author counterposed them, although the latter concept did eventually become more associated with the concrete politics of the workers' movement, its day-to-day tactics and its cross-border organisational forms.[21] Various authors, including Harvey[22] and Sousa Santos,[23] advocate a cosmopolitanism of the subaltern similar to what we have called the internationalism of the subalterns. The advantage of this latter term is that it makes it easier to link up with the historical internationalist tradition, avoids conceptual confusion by distancing itself from liberal-progressive approaches and is associated with a more concrete practice. It has greater strategic strength, although less epistemological scope. That is why it is best to operate with a dialectic between the two. Put another way, the internationalism of the 99% requires a cosmopolitan mentality and cosmopolitanism of the 99% requires an internationalist practice.

50.
A policy of national sovereignty based on 'recovering the state', however, involves a symmetrical mistake to that of liberal or radical cosmopolitanism. When it is formulated from within a nation-state without any internal national conflict or from an all-state perspective in the case of states with unresolved national questions such as Spain, it is limited to calling for sovereign re-appropriation of some of the state's levers in pursuit of a neo-Keynesian logic. When linked to republican formulations of democracy, of the republican political nation, it often runs the risk, as happens with much left-wing, nationalist republicanism in France, of idealising the nation-state tradition, which runs up against its colonial,

homogenising ghosts of the past and the spectres of a more and more racially mixed and pluricultural present and future. Or it simply embraces a republican tradition that, despite its inclusiveness and its political and citizen dimension, moves away from any tradition of emancipation from below.

51.
The politics of national sovereignty may be reduced to an impossible neo-Keynesianism in a single country or, at best, to a strategic inter-nationalism that, unlike internationalism, focuses its entire outlook on the nation-state arena and grants a subsidiary role to the others, thus reproducing all the strategic limitations of the workers' movement of the Second and Third Internationals and their trade union variants of the last century.[24] In its worst versions, it can mean failing to identify the need to oppose the xenophobic nationalism of the far right head-on and allowing itself to be carried away by the mirage of its anti-globalisation or anti-EU rhetoric in the name of an economistic class corporativism construed according to reductionist national criteria.[25]

52.
The Catalan independence movement embodies a politics of national sovereignty formulated from the position of a stateless nation and is based on a legitimate democratic aspiration, namely to have its own state. It cannot be contested in terms of legitimacy; to do so implies an antidemocratic refusal of collective rights. There is a need, however, to reflect strategically on the limitations of its dissociating formal political sovereignty from real economic sovereignty and its exclusively national, non-popular dynamic. Going along with the logic of globalisation and European integration, it expresses the illusory desire to be able to fare better within it through a state of its own, either aspiring to a competitive neoliberal capitalism facilitated by a commodifying state (the 'Massachusetts of Europa' sometimes touted

by Artur Mas and those in or around the right-wing Catalan nationalist party Convergència) with a consolidated welfare state protected by its own state (the 'Denmark of Europe' according to an expression also used by the pro-independence right when it has needed to stress its social dimension, but fitting in well with the outlook of Esquerra Republicana de Catalunya (Republican Left of Catalonia – ERC) and a large part of the movement's social base. The founding strategic contradictions of a movement that delinked its legitimate democratic aspiration to its own state from any criticism of austerity policies or the nature of European integration have veered between these dreamed-of competitive advantages in a global world and the longing for a future of wellbeing.

53.
The dichotomy between liberal cosmopolitanism and a retreat-into-the-nation-state is strategically sterile. They are both failed perspectives. To overcome them it is necessary to adopt a coherent internationalist approach. This breaks with all politics of sovereignty understood as implicit or explicit nostalgia for the 20th century, without falling into the trap of either the liberal cosmopolitan illusions of post-national democracy supported by the international institutions, or a radical policy of post- or anti-sovereignty ignoring the state arena and the national dimension, whether it be in the name of a localism without borders or an indeterminate space of struggle. It does not counterpose solidarity to sovereignty, but links them to each other and connects any project for sovereignty to cross-border alliances, projecting sovereignty outwards in pursuit of another global order.

54.
The internationalism of the subalterns is a perspective opposed to both liberal cosmopolitanism and radical abstract cosmopolitanism as well as inter-nationalism, whether it be in the form of a national or state-level retreat nostalgic for

Keynesianism or harking back to the idea of socialism in a single country. Leaping over states in the name of a rootless cosmopolitanism, appealing from below to a localism without borders or enclosing oneself within one in pursuit of national sovereignty led to skewed strategies that weaken any popular movement. The sliding scale of spaces must be expanded into a true sliding scale of concepts, a sliding scale of one's own spatial and conceptual strategy.

55.
Nationalism as a way of approaching the world from the standpoint of the nation as the priority vector precludes a correct understanding of the nature of capitalism and its relation to the different forms of oppression. The national viewpoint obscures other much more fruitful readings. But nationalism is not a homogeneous socio-political phenomenon. There exist nationalisms of many kinds and it is necessary to distinguish the different variants. From a strategic perspective there are five essential criteria to be taken into account: whether it is the nationalism of a state or of a stateless people; of a dominant or a dominated nation; culturally and ethnically exclusionary or inclusive; the nature of its social and class composition; and its relation to the social question in general. It is on the basis of such a characterisation of each nationalist movement that we must decide what attitude to take towards it and what its role is in regard to a project of emancipation.

56.
Often, more in the Spanish than the Catalan left, defence of stateless peoples' national rights has been considered contradictory to internationalism. In fact, it is its structural precondition. There is no solidarity or joint action unless it is based on mutual recognition, which, in the case of movements and organisations belonging to the central nation of a state, requires their acceptance at all times of the stateless nations'

right of self-determination (which does not necessarily mean agreeing with the choice of opting for separation), and that they distance themselves from the nationalism of their own state, in both its combative and its banal dimensions.

57.
Criticism of the nationalism of others, unless it is accompanied by acceptance of their right to decide, tends in fact to conceal acceptance of one's own nationalism, whether it be in terms of an explicit project of domination or in the shape of an unconscious internalisation of a national narrative that has condensed into the form of common sense. And when the criticism is made in the name of an abstract international solidarity, it ends up playing into the hands of one's own state. Without a stance of solidarity towards the stateless nation, one winds up accepting a nationalist cultural and ideological framework that makes it easier for the dominant classes to manipulate and instrumentalise the popular classes in a reactionary direction against minority nationalisms.

58.
'The proletariat must demand the right of political secession for the colonies and for the nations that "its own" nation oppresses. Unless it does this, proletarian internationalism will remain a meaningless phrase' wrote Lenin in April 1916.[26] His classic distinction, already present in Marx, between nationalism of the dominated and the dominators is a useful reference point for finding one's way in national conflicts and debates on the right of self-determination. At least it is an elementary political compass that usually works as a starting point and avoids treating colliding nationalisms generally as equal, which, in the Spanish case, would mean failing to see the unequal historical function performed by Spanish nationalism and the 'peripheral' nationalisms respectively, the former having an authoritarian role and denying the others' rights. However, the distinction between nationalism of the

dominated and nationalism of the dominators in favour of the former should not be taken as a universally valid abstraction. In a generic sense, it would be possible to imagine a triumphant democratic, left-wing Spanish nationalist project or an ultraconservative Catalan nationalism reacting to a left-wing majority project in Spain as a whole. It is therefore a matter of taking the distinction as a criterion that has to be put to the test of a specific, concrete analysis, and in the history of the Spanish state it has passed the test with ease.

59.

In Spain's case, two political points need to be clarified in applying the distinction between these two types of nationalism. The first concerns the qualified nature of the relation of national oppression when referring to the post-Franco period. However, in broad historical perspective, the exhaustion of the autonomous communities model and the current political crisis clearly reveal the existence of a structurally asymmetrical relationship within the Spanish state. The second is that a strategic understanding of the unequal function of these two types of nationalism, the Spanish and the peripheral, must in turn be accompanied by taking one's distance from any reductionist project in the fields of culture and identity such as those advocated by some variants of the latter kind in the way they understand their respective nations. This does not detract any legitimacy from their national demands, but does pose the challenge of thinking about them in another way.

60.

The national liberation movements more or less inspired by Marxism, whose Catalan equivalent would be the Candidatura d'Unitat Popular (Popular Unity Candidature – CUP), have developed a nationalist internationalism. Although their supporters often reject the adjective 'nationalist' in view of its negative connotations, arguing that theirs is an option for political and strategic independence, they must be regarded as such insofar as they grant strategic and conceptual centrality to the nation. At all events, theirs is a nationalism that is part of an emancipatory project. It is an internationalism of national liberation, an internationalism of 'nation-peoples' in which these peoples constitute the subjects in alliance, and which tends to seek solidarity among movements of stateless nations and anti-imperialist campaigns. The positive part of this approach is its historical capacity for aggregation, using national identity as cement. But its negative consequence is the cross-class pressure this generates, the adoption of a nationalist cultural outlook and the displacement of the spatial axis of struggle to the national arena alone to the detriment of the state and international planes.

61.
The internationalism of the subalterns, on the other hand, sees itself as the joint, mutually supportive activity of the exploited and the oppressed, as an organic, strategic alliance of those below, in which the national facet is just another dimension, not the basis for its strategic grouping. If the internationalism of national liberation has independence as an explicit goal and its ultimate destination, internationalism of the subalterns stands for separation or free federation, depending on the conjuncture. It seeks a dialectical relation between the two options (such as, for example, voluntary union following free separation) and, when independence is the rallying cry to be adopted, it does not disconnect it from the possibility of a future federation while maintaining, albeit generically, a horizon of emancipation without borders. If the internationalism of national liberation is organised only on the scale of its own nation and does not form part of any state-wide project, internationalism of the subalterns also has organisational links on an all-state level. And, finally, if the first limits internationalism merely to forms of mutual

solidarity among oppressed peoples with their respective struggles, the second attempts to build cross-border organisational frameworks and carry out political action based on a dialectic between the different spatial scales. In short, one is a radical variant of inter-nationalism, whereas the other is an internationalism.

1   The Process (Procés) has been the usual name in the media and in the political milieu to call all the political pro-independence dynamic that went from September 2012 to October 2017 (Translator's note).
2   See, for example: Jaime Pastor, *Los nacionalismos, el Estado español, y la izquierda*, Madrid, La Oveja Roja, 2012.
3   'State of Autonomies' is the name given to the constitutional arrangement by which the Spanish state includes 17 autonomous regional governments and two autonomous cities.
4   Luisa Elena Delgado, *La nación singular*, Madrid, Siglo XXI, 2014.
5   Ibid., p. 83. It is no coincidence that the reclaiming and whitewashing of historical imperialism have recently re-emerged as part of Spanish nationalism's general rearming. The clearest example is to be found in: María Elvira Roca Barea, *Imperiofobia y leyenda negra*, Madrid, Siruela, 2016. I discuss the question of the Empire and also the V Centenary of 1992 in: Josep Maria Antentas, 'Spain: The State, the Regime Crisis and the National Question', *Socialism and Democracy*, 2021, Vol. 35, No. 1, pp. 51–78.
6   José Álvarez Junco, *Mater dolorosa. La idea de España en el siglo XIX*, Madrid, Penguin Random House, 2001, pp. 601–607.
7   Catalanism (*Catalanisme*) appeared in the late 19th Century and has been the name given to the broad movement, which has had several ideological strands, defending the national rights of Catalonia (Translator's note).
8   Xosé Manoel Núñez Seixas, *Suspiros de España. El nacionalismo español 1808–2018*, Barcelona, Crítica, 2018.
9   Michael Billig, *Banal Nationalism (Theory, Culture and Society)*, London, SAGE Publications Ltd, 1995.

10 Sebastian Balfour and Alejandro Quiroga, *The Reinvention of Spain: Nation and Identity since Democracy*, Oxford, OUP, 2007.
11 Xosé Manoel Núñez Seixas, op. cit.
12 Sebastian Balfour and Alejandro Quiroga, op. cit.; Xosé Manoel Nuñez Seixas, op. cit.
13 Jürgen Habermas, *The Postnational Constellation*, Cambridge, MA, MIT Press, 2001; Jurgen Habermas, *The Inclusion of the Other. Studies in Political Theory*, Cambridge, MA, MIT Press, 1998. The term is originally due to Dolf Sternberger, who formulated it in 1979. It was reinterpreted and promoted by Habermas in the context of the so-called 'historians' dispute' in the 1980s over the nature of Nazism and its memory's place in the Federal Republic of Germany, which pitted him mainly against the conservative historian Ernst Nolte.
14 Antonio Gramsci, *Prison Notebooks, Vol 3*, New York, Columbia University Press, 2007; Q 8 §130. Following the established international criteria, quotations from Gramsci's *Notebooks* are given by indicating the number of each notebook (Q) and the number of the note (§).
15 Hannah Arendt, *On Revolution*, London, Penguin Classics, 2009.
16 Andrew Dowling, *The Rise of Catalan Independence*, London, Routledge, 2018.
17 Jaime Pastor, op. cit., p. 35.
18 Daniel Bensaïd, *Éloge de la politique profane*, Paris, Albin Michel, 2008, p.262.
19 Ibid., p. 258.
20 Immanuel Kant, *Perpetual Peace: A Philosophical Sketch*, London, Allen & Unwin, 1903. Available at: www.oll-resources.s3.amazonaws.com/titles/357/0075_Bk.pdf

21 Michael Löwy, *Fatherland or Mother Earth?* London, Pluto Press, 1998. Gilbert Achcar, *Marxism, Orientalism, Cosmopolitanism*, Chicago, Haymarket, 2013.
22 David Harvey, *Cosmopolitanism and the Geographies of Freedom*, New York, Columbia University Press, 2009.
23 Boaventura de Sousa Santos, *Sociología jurídica crítica*, Madrid, Trotta, 2009.
24 For a consistent defence of 'internationalism' as 'inter-nationalism' see: Frédéric Lordon, 'L'internationalisme réel, c'est l'organisation de la contagion', *Ballast*, 2016. www.revue-ballast.fr/frederic-lordon-organiser-la-contagion/
25 This is the case of the position held by Héctor Illueca, Manuel Monereo and Julio Anguita in '¿Fascismo en italia? Decreto dignidad', *Cuartopoder*, 5 September 2018. Available at: www.cuartopoder.es/ideas/2018/09/05/fascismo-en-italia-decreto-dignidad/; among the many critical responses see, for example: Miguel Urbán and Brais Fernández, 'Decreto dignidad: ¿Fascismo en Italia? Una respuesta', *Cuarto Poder*, 7 September 2018. Available at: www.cuartopoder.es/ideas/2018/09/07/decreto-dignidad-fascismo-en-italia-una-respuesta/; and the rejoinder by the authors: Héctor Illueca, Manuel Monereo and Julio Anguita '¿Todos los gatos son pardos?', *Cuartopoder*, 14 September 2018. Available at: www.cuartopoder.es/ideas/2018/09/14/ anguita-monereo-decreto-dignidad-italia/
26 V.I. Lenin, 'The Socialist Revolution and the Right of Nations to Self-Determination (Theses)', 1916, Available at: www.marxists.org/archive/lenin/works/1916/jan/x01.htm

2
The October Crisis (I)

The referendum and its former lives

62.
The referendum on the independence of Catalonia announced for 1 October came five years after the pro-independence process was formally launched following the gigantic demonstration on 11 September 2012 (11-S). It returned to the stage, first as a spectre and finally with an existence of its own, marked by its three former lives: first, as the movement's official horizon in 2012–14; second, in the form of the Catalan parliamentary election on 27 September 2015 (27-S) transmuted into a plebiscite following the consultation on 9 November 2014 (9-N); third, as a result of its reappearance as the proposal for a referendum agreed with the Spanish government in the framework of a new constituent political majority put forward by En Comú Podem (In Common We Can, loosely referred to as Els Comuns or The Commons) and Unidos Podemos (United We Can) in the campaigns for the general elections on 20 December 2015 and 26 June 2016. The referendum eventually obtained a new and unexpected life from September 2016 onwards following the Catalan government's commitment to hold it no matter what by the end of 2017. It was reborn as a consequence of the ghostly incompleteness of its three former lives: the unattained horizon of 2012–14, the imposture of its plebiscitary version and the impossibility, in the short term, of a majority in Spain favourable to a referendum (an impossibility that was, however, paralleled by the great evocative power of the proposal launched by Els Comuns, which for a time destabilised Catalan politics).

63.
The November 2014 consultation marked the end of the movement's first phase which had begun in 2012. Half way between a legitimised consultation and an act of head-on institutional and civil disobedience, the 9-N was ultimately a disobedient detour that eluded both a capitulation to the impositions of the state and a direct institutional confrontation. The Spanish government was not able to stop a mass democratic event from being held, but neither was the independence movement able to go ahead with an act of explicit institutional rupture that would decisively speed up events. It opted for a last-minute feint and squeezed a goal just inside the post allowing it to easily overcome the challenge of carrying out an activity that was not merely a token gesture, but failed to usher in an unequivocal future scenario.

64.
Failure to convey an indisputable political message, due to the extremely high proportion of Yes-Yes votes (1,861,753 on a turnout of 2,305,290 for Catalonia to become a state and for this state to be independent) coupled with the consultation's hybrid nature (neither a recognised referendum nor an open institutional confrontation), meant that the 9-N was paradoxically both the perfect formula for holding a referendum without doing so and not holding one by doing so. In this way, while being an unquestionable political and social success, it was also a serious strategic mistake, as it led to a peculiar impasse and pushed the independence movement into adopting a new roadmap that would always be based on an internal contradiction. The same movement that, when faced with the first legal ban on one of its initiatives, did not dare to disobey it, now set its sights on a second stage that would require greater social strength, mobilising power and confrontational capacity: launching a process towards independence in 18 months following the transformation of the Catalan parliamentary election into a plebiscite on this proposal.

65.
By taking this diversion via the 9-N alternative and the plebiscitary election, the Catalan government, supported by the pro-independence social organisations, gained time, but at the price of a detour along paths that, sooner or later, would have to bring it back to a situation not very different from the one in autumn 2014. Without having passed the test of the first challenge, it went on to the second phase riding on a fragile uncertainty. Eventually the strategic incoherence of the route mapped out to justify the 27 September plebiscitary election became evident and, a strategic rewind being impossible, it again embraced the original goal of the 2012–14 period – a referendum. This reflected the intrinsic exhaustion of the policy of permanently stretching out time pursued since 2012.

66.
Implicitly, without ever acknowledging it, the Catalan government and the independence movement amended their own roadmap laid out in 2014. Those who had claimed then that conditions were not ripe for a referendum backed an alternative consultation and turned the Catalan parliamentary election into a plebiscite, offered no explanation whatsoever, nor did they draw up a serious public political balance sheet of the strategic mistakes they had made in those three years (2012–15). At the end of this, they were back to square one, though in different conditions; back to the need for a referendum as the triggering and catalysing moment of a democratic confrontation. The lack of such a balance sheet and a self-examination of the strategic limitations of the movement born in 2012 explain to a large extent the improvisation on the way to 1 October and the subsequent fiasco.

67.
The decision to go for the referendum meant getting away from the independence-in-18-months fantasy, now redundant,

and posing once again the need for a truly democratic moment. However, it did not mean going beyond the illusory strategy of disconnection and transition from-one-law-to-another that had shaped the Procés's conceptual framework. In other words, the referendum was a tangible, material objective that, in this sense, had a non-Procés -style component, but it was designed and argued for within the scope of the Procés's strategy and narrative in order to give it a fresh boost.

Dual legitimacy

68.
After five years of a seemingly eternal Procés, in which its actors' grandiose gestures were proportional to the extraordinary slowness of events and their dogged determination to avoid a clash with the state, in September 2017 the moment of truth finally arrived. It wasn't the film's final scene, but it was certainly a key passage in determining its outcome. 'The Procés is over, now the party begins,' was the felicitous expression with which the CUP summed up the changed situation at the time. A party that, let us not forget, should have started in 2014 if Artur Mas's government had not pulled up at the first hurdle in November of that year when he decided not to try to hold the referendum ('consultation' in the language of the period) following the ban by the Constitutional Court. It was the wrong choice which, surprisingly, at that time met with hardly any resistance from the other major actors in the Procés (with the brief exception, at the beginning, of ERC).

69.
The passing of the Referendum Law on 6 September 2017 marked a critical point of no return. From then on Catalonia officially entered a situation of dual legitimacy – two legitimacies (and two legalities) on a collision course – which, by its very nature, could last only until the balance came down definitively on one side or the other. This created a situation

with a highly asymmetric, unsteady and unequal institutional dual power (the power of the Spanish institutions and that of the Catalan institutions that had placed themselves, together with the street, outside the former's legality). The description of this state of affairs as 'highly asymmetric, unsteady and unequal' must be strongly emphasised in order to understand the conjuncture properly and not think that what happened was a clash between two equivalent or similar powers. The disparity between them was huge.

70.

'Between equal rights, force decides' wrote Marx in chapter 10 of the first volume of *Capital* dedicated to analysing the working day.[1] Forgetting this would lead to naïve and illusory views on the nature of the state (not the Spanish state in particular, but the modern capitalist state in general). At the same time, it must be pointed out that 'force' cannot be separated from the legitimacy of the power employing it and the political context in which it operates. Legitimacy and context determine the degree to which the power in question can use it. And neither of them is fixed; they evolve as events unfold. Brute force and political force in a wider sense permanently intermingle. This determines what a state can and cannot do when there is a crisis of legitimacy, itself a variable that is always open-ended and whose actual outcome depends on specific political factors.

71.

Any movement must be able to define the world and situations in terms favourable to its interests, convey confidence in its possibilities of victory and in the belief that its goals are achievable. In the independence movement's narrative, the term 'disconnection' was habitually used to depict the process of unilaterally achieving independence. The concept has a pleasant, agreeable ring to it, far removed from any shrillness or tension. It drives away any sensation of conflict or insecurity. In this sense it probably played an important part in making the strategic horizon of independence credible, but at the price of enormously simplifying the analysis of the complexity of its project and what it means to confront a state.

72.

The idea of disconnecting conjures up an image of painlessly unplugging an electric circuit. There is a well-known scene in the 1968 Stanley Kubrik film *2001: A Space Odyssey* that illustrates very well how to 'disconnect' from a superior being. It comes in the 'Jupiter Mission' segment, set in the year 2001, when the spaceship *Discovery* is heading towards the giant gaseous planet. When they detect anomalies in the behaviour of HAL 9000, the supercomputer in charge of controlling *Discovery*, the astronauts Dave Bowman and Frank Poole plan to disconnect it. Following Poole's death as a result of HAL's action, Bowman manages to enter the room where the machine's process or core is and begins deactivating the computer, which gradually loses its higher functions, regresses to childhood and ends up, before being completely turned off, singing a children's song, 'Daisy Bell'. The great Leviathan that controlled the spaceship, a humanised supercomputer, has died.[2]

73.

Contrary to this image, it is not actually possible to 'disconnect' from a state. It is perhaps feasible to break with it following a confrontation. The idea of 'disconnection', although quite different, paradoxically reminds us in this respect of Hardt and Negri's 'exodus' theories,[3] which were all the rage in the previous two decades, but in this case it is a matter of advocating an 'exodus' not to create liberated non-state spaces and abandon the Empire, but to create another state. However, there is no such thing as a pleasant disconnection from a state against its will. Apart from cases settled by a military clash, a break can occur as a consequence of an intense tussle and decisive mass political and social confrontations combined with a favourable international geopolitical situation forcing a state to accept a democratic outcome to the conflict against its interests. But all this has very little to do with the strategic imaginings the independence movement operated with until October consisting of a paradoxical anti-strategic strategy permanently swallowed up by short-term tactics and calculations, along with rhetorical conjuring tricks; hence the paramount importance of what happened in September and October 2017 and how fundamental it was that the referendum took place as a result of the impetus of the mass mobilisation.

74.
The Catalan independence movement seemed to think that the force of reason alone was sufficient, ignoring its powerlessness in the face of the reason of force. It appeared to define the struggle more in terms of legitimacy than of force, without clearly assessing the chances of coming out on top in its clash with the state, dissolving the very idea of a clash by artificially constructing the concept of disconnection. In some of its more serious formulations, this concept was associated with the need for a trial of strength, but in a way that subordinated this to the creation of its own legality. For example, the political analyst Ferran Requejo, a member of the National Transition Advisory Council, defined the situation in these terms: 'When the transition law is passed, there will be two governments and two powers wanting to impose their legality. And the million-dollar question is whether we will be strong enough to uphold our legality without paying heed to the other one.'[4] The terms in which the strategic dilemma was couched, however, themselves raise some of the problems the movement would exhibit during the decisive month of October. It regarded the adoption of a law of one's own as equivalent to the construction of a power of one's

own, and saw this as entering into a logic of dual power. In reality, the adoption of its own legality implied a dynamic of dual legitimacy, but this would have to be combined with a dynamic of popular self-organisation from below and institutional resistance from above in order to transform itself into a situation of dual power. The schema 'first we pass the law, then we meet the challenge of upholding it' ignores the fact that the combined process of adoption of a new legality/ bottom-up self-organisation/institutional disobedience/ materialisation of a new political-institutional-legal scenario needed to be understood in an integrated fashion and not as a sequence of separate events.

75.
The 'from one law to another' transition strategy also brought with it an unnecessary legalistic mess with the passing, on 7 September, of the so-called Transition Law, laying out all the legal steps that would be taken in the event of a Yes victory in the referendum. Intended only for show and to convey the false sensation that everything was planned, its adoption was entirely unnecessary, all the more so since those who passed it never thought they would have to implement it. The idea of delivering a message of calm, of giving an assurance that in the event independence were to win this would not produce a political vacuum, was not in itself negative. However, providing a false solution by passing a law to regulate what could not be regulated (a carefree transition from Spanish legality to a new Catalan legality) only served to furnish the referendum's opponents with arguments by conveying the feeling that the result of the poll was taken for granted in advance.

76.
The 1 October ballot had a strange temporality. It was scheduled and yet untimely. It displayed an unusual combination of planned and disruptive temporality in which the destabilising

emergence of mass mobilisation mingled with the government's blandness. Marked on the calendar as 'D-Day', half propaganda, half real, it led to a speeding up of time that outstripped its protagonists. The untimeliness of 1 October smashed to pieces the clockwork mindset and fictitious rhetoric of 'state structures'; the conception of a break with the Spanish state as merely a matter of prior institutional planning (which is different from conscious preparation for a political confrontation) and of a calm legal transition disintegrated.

77.
The pro-independence process that began in 2012 was able to formulate its objective as a specific utopia that provided a perspective and a future. It gave concrete form to a future that generally appeared uncertain and dark. In a definition that enjoyed considerable success, Marina Subirats[5] described it as an 'alternative utopia', able to channel the wishes for a better future in a situation where utopias associated with the left were singularly lacking. It was the 'available utopia' that could fill the void of a better future. A utopian dimension is necessary in any movement for change. In today's world 'there is no alternative to utopia', as Fredric Jameson[6] reminds us. But utopia is ambiguous and contradictory. To be effective it needs to shed its fanciful elements and strengthen its strategic side; in other words, any utopia must be strategised. The independence movement, however, did the opposite. Instead of strategising its utopia, it turned its strategy into a utopia, formulating a utopian strategy of the most fantastical kind (the 'from one law to another' disconnection), an illusory strategy that collapsed in the face of the reality of the state and power relations.

78.
Every emancipatory movement needs a 'guiding strategic horizon'.[7] This has two interrelated foundations: the destination and the path to get there. Not having one of these, or formulating it wrongly, throws the whole strategy off balance.

Getting the route and/or the destination wrong means getting lost at some point on the way. This double guiding perspective has today vanished from the political and strategic imagination of most contemporary movements. With it the very notion of transition disappears. A fundamental question in the classical discussions on strategy in the history of the workers' movement, the 'transition' problem has been key in the social and political movements bearing a project for the future. Following the defeats of the 20th century and the collapse of all perspectives of social change, the very idea of 'transition' seems to have faded away, with some exceptions such as the debates on climate change and energy transition or the discussions about 'transition towns'. 'Change' remains, then, imprecise in its objectives and/or vague as to its itinerary. The absence of a final destination and/or a clear route weakens the emancipatory potential.

79.
The independence movement had the merit of setting a clear destination (independence) that served as a mobilising tool, but it sketched out an illusory and insubstantial route to reach it (the 'disconnection from one law to another' and 'first independence, then everything else') which did away with the real problems of the transition, including the social bloc that needed to be built and the strategic priorities. To have set out a coherent route would have involved a reflection on the goal of independence itself and a search for common ground with the other, federal and confederal movements in opposition to the '78 regime, as well as linking the independence project to the criticism of austerity policies.

80.
The metaphor of the journey has been a constituent part of the independence movement's utopian imaginary. Doubtless the most important one refers to the voyage to Ithaca, which was already used by Artur Mas in March 2012 at

the 16th Congress of Convergència Democràtica de Catalunya (Democratic Convergence of Catalonia – the main conservative Catalan nationalist party and senior partner in many Catalan governments). It subsequently became a commonplace among the metaphorical images of the Procés, a cultural reference associated in the Catalan popular imagination with Lluís Llac's 1975 album, Viatge a Ítaca (Voyage to Ithaca), whose title and main song are based on the poem Ithaca, a reinterpretation of Homer's Odyssey written by the Greek poet Konstantin Kavafis in 1911. The voyage of the Procés, however, was always envisioned as a journey that would be solemn but not dangerous, epic but with the risks kept carefully under control, with rather pleasant, conflict-free paths to travel along. State structures, electoral legitimacy and disconnection all within 18 months indicated a relatively linear, anodyne vision that had little to do with the twists and turns and calamities endured by Ulysses on his tortuous journey to Ithaca, his homeland, after the end of the Trojan war. The Procés's strategic conception was always anti-Homeric.

81.
In his updating of the classic, Kavafis heightens the significance of the voyage in itself so that it becomes the meaning of life and the most important thing about it. In this sense, the Procés and its tendency to go on endlessly, to constantly lengthen its route, might at first sight appear to bear a connection with the poet's verses. However, a close reading reveals a decisive difference between the Procés's and Kavafis's voyage to Ithaca. For him, the journey is a permanent source of learning from the experiences he has lived through. The Procés's ability to learn, by contrast, has been severely limited by the way it has handled the problems and challenges it has met with on its journey. Instead of confronting them, it permanently chose to go around them (like its 9-N sidestep) and take detours to nowhere (for example the

plebiscitary election and the aim of disconnection in eighteen months) that only put off addressing face to face the journey's real dangers. More skilful at dodging around obstacles than overcoming them, the Procés-style independence movement's ability to learn has been decidedly limited. The 'lessons of October' (it is hard to resist a pun on the title of Trotsky's famous 1924 pamphlet[8] of the same name) are still waiting to be drawn; as are the lessons of the path leading up to October. The nature of the route mapped out became both a strategy of non-experience (or limited experience), in which rhetoric took precedence over facts, and a non-strategic experience (or one of reduced strategic impacts) in which permanent tactics and illusionism prevailed.

Tribulations without a strategic plan

82.
October demonstrated a spatial and temporal mismatch between the Catalan crisis and the crisis of the governmental regime in Spain as a whole. The national, territorial and peripheral dimension of the crisis reached its high point at a time when its social and popular dimension was waning and social struggles and Unidos Podemos had come to a relative standstill. It evinced, in Bensaïd's language, a 'discordance of times and spaces';[9] there was a segmented spatialisation of the crisis (focused on Catalonia) and a desynchronised temporality (the outbreak of the national-territorial crisis and the impasse of the social-popular crisis). This lack of synchronisation between the social crisis and the national crisis echoed other decisive moments in Spain's history, such as October 1934 (when an uprising in Asturias was left relatively isolated), and was a reminder of the complex centre–periphery and national–social dialectic of Spanish politics. This structural desynchronisation was the backdrop to the strategic trials and tribulations of October 2017. It was an instant when the temporalities condensed, as they do at every moment of political crisis, but against a background

where the temporality (and spatiality) of the wider crisis of the political regime in which October was embedded was itself falling apart.

83.
Without a plan; this is how the Catalan government's strategy after 1 October can be summed up. Let us recapitulate: the government was formed following the election on 27 September 2015 with an unrealistic roadmap for 'disconnection' from the Spanish state – by passing successive laws and creating new 'state structures' – within 18 months. Faced with the vacuousness of this plan, the government, to a large extent thanks to the CUP's insistence, agreed in September 2016 to hold a referendum on independence by the end of 2017. Without ever acknowledging it, it thus amended the roadmap it had itself drawn up in autumn 2014 when it refused to try to hold the referendum scheduled for 9 November which had been declared illegal by the Constitutional Court and instead opted for a non-binding citizen consultation as a preliminary step to turning the September 2015 autonomous regional election into a plebiscite. After going all round the houses it was right back where it had started: with the referendum – a referendum that concealed the strategic void that had put it once again on the horizon.

84.
As the date for the poll drew nearer, the executive headed by prime minister Carles Puigdemont continued to go ahead with the preparations, even though in private it was convinced that it would not be able to go through with it and that, at some point on the way, it would be abruptly stopped short by the intervention of the state. The rivalry between ERC and the Partit Demòcrata Europeu Català (Catalan European Democratic Party – PDECAT, a pro-independence liberal party founded in July 2016 to succeed the Democratic Convergence of Catalonia) meant that neither of them

wanted to be the first to pull out, each one waiting for the other to throw in the towel, trying to hang on as long as they could. Finally, the government ended up going much further than it had ever imagined or prepared for. This was both a success and a failure – a contradictory situation, where the failure's success prepared the success's failure.[10]

85.
From 20 September onwards, when a large crowd gathered to protest against a search by the Civil Guard for referendum-related information at the Catalan Economics Ministry, there began to take shape for the first time a space in favour of a rupture that wasn't contained within the Procés. It encompassed pro-independence and non-pro-independence sectors, including the CUP, Podem, minority currents within Catalunya en Comú (Catalonia in Common) and social movement and alternative trade union activists. Student protests and the newly formed Committees in Defence of the Referendum (CDR) became the most visible expression of this dynamic. It was this informal bloc that played a decisive role in the days leading up to 1 October and on the day of the referendum itself, forcing de facto the Catalan National Assembly (ANC), the large pro-independence organisation founded in 2012, to go further than it had intended. The referendum took place, not because of the careful planning by government or the ANC, but because of the dynamic of self-organisation-from-below that began in the wake of the repression set in train on 20 September and accelerated in the days prior to the referendum with the occupation and defence of the polling stations. Both the government and the ANC were satisfied with just opening the voting centres and distributing the ballot boxes and the voting slips. They assumed the Spanish police would prevent people from voting and their aim was to get the 'photo' of long queues of citizens outside the polling stations closed by force. As we know, things turned out differently.

86.
The decision by Puigdemont's government on 10 October to suspend the planned declaration of independence and not even to proclaim it formally before revoking it was, as all the reports and accounts of the hours prior to his intervention in the Catalan parliament attest, the result of pressure from the economic powers-that-be and the European Union, and fear of the consequences of an escalation of the repression by the state. This pressure particularly made an impression on certain sectors of his own party, PDeCAT, which had for some time been uneasy about the way the independence movement was going. The improvised nature of what was done on 10 October, including major errors of internal and external communication, as subsequently became clear, mean that the decision taken cannot be put down to a well-thought-out, calculated tactic, but to a complete absence of strategy amid sharp divisions within the government.

87.
However, once the partial retreat had actually taken place, the Catalan government, and, above all, some of its supporters, rationalised what they had done, thinking that if, in spite of everything, the Spanish state reacted heavy-handedly, it would serve, first, to win over part of Catalan public opinion that had doubts about the independence project, in particular the Comuns' social base, and, second, to furnish itself with supplementary arguments in dealing with the international press. Although in a certain sense suspending the declaration served to reaffirm the Catalan government's preparedness to talk, in fact it was basically an exhibition of enormous weakness at a decisive moment, which foreshadowed what was to happen in the days to come, and fostered serious confusion in the pro-independence ranks as they were left unarmed at the crowning moment and without any short- or medium-term perspective for action. This disarray would only increase thereafter and was merely the prelude to a strategic collapse in the making.

88.
From its emergence in 2012, the independence process sought a sort of suspension of time in the midst of a huge earthquake, in which a day-to-day epic was combined with a lumbering, slow-motion march. It was not a movement that was prepared for generating rapid crises, seasoned in disrupting time scales and making strategic decisions at the critical moment: rather it was forged in designing gentle roadmaps and proceeding at cruising speed, trying to project an unlikely, leisurely, linear temporality that would avoid the upheaval that was coming. 20 September marked a change in the speed at which events were unfolding and required a different strategic management of time – one based on the compression of the discontinuous nature of political time on which Daniel Bensaïd was so insistent in his Leninist emphasis on a time 'of the right moment and the singular conjuncture, in which necessity and contingency, act and process, history and event become tied to each other'.[11]

89.
The sequence running from 1 October to 3 October (when everything was brought to a standstill by a Catalonia-wide stoppage) only increased the tempo at which the situation that arose on 20 September developed. It was just after this that the Catalan government should have announced a clear assertion of sovereignty. However, the sudden slamming-on of the brakes following the momentum of 1 and 3 October gave the state time to regroup from its relative disarray and, above all, it allowed the economic establishment to deploy a public and private strategy of fear. The anti-climax of 10 October definitively heightened this dynamic, causing the movement to lose its capacity for initiative at the decisive moment. A strategy of suspension or a suspension of strategy? The suspension policy led to an illusory suspension of strategic time and, with it, a suspension of strategy as such. In other words, the Procés's unexpected and fleeting

Leninist moment evaporated beneath the gutless, routine logic of a Procés bereft of any immediate outcome.

90.
After five years of this evasive Procés, the independence movement collided head-on with the state. 20 September and 1 October, and the much-feared implementation of an unprecedented battery of repressive measures in the event of independence being proclaimed, showed up the strategic weakness of the false hypothesis of 'disconnection'. The hypothesis collapsed, but its failure did not give rise to a new, solid strategic perspective based on a combination of mass mobilisation and civil disobedience, institutional disobedience and the search for strategic alliances in the rest of Spain to complement the unilateral path. It did not move on from regular, episodic mass mobilisations once a year to the possibility of sustained mobilisation and disobedience, nor from a unilateral road within an exclusively Catalan conceptual frame of reference to a search for support in the rest of Spain and the insertion of its independence project, without watering it down, into an overall project of breaking with the '78 regime. Neither of these strategic shifts has been developed to its full potential nor explicitly theorised.

91.
The collapse of the movement's strategy came at the same time as its political defeat. This defeat (which was, of course, not necessarily permanent) was never accepted or analysed and so bore no strategic lessons. Denying a defeat is, in effect, equivalent to denying the possibility of a strategic relaunch. There is no future without a balance sheet, without realistic acceptance of the situation, without a careful appraisal of the balance of forces and of the route one has followed. Even though potentially fertile in lessons, if self-deceit and/or short-term tactical manoeuvring prevail, any defeat may simply lead to the codification of previous strategic limitations.

It becomes the repetition as farce of what has been done before, or a hasty overhaul of those actions in the search for non-existent shortcuts. These three dead ends can be seen, to varying degrees, in the politics of the independence movement's different actors. The spectre of the (non-)lessons of October cast a long strategic shadow over the future.

92.
Once the referendum had been held, there then appeared a double challenge that was in large measure contradictory: firstly, the need to regain the initiative and not get stuck in resisting repression without a clear and hope-inspiring assertion of sovereignty; secondly, the need to appeal to the whole bloc that made 1 and 3 October possible and, as far as possible, to the Comuns' social base to try to push its leadership towards support for breaking with the regime. An act of sovereignty was required to fulfil the mandate given by 1 October. But it was strategically essential and democratically necessary to carry it out in such a way as not to break up the alliance with those sectors that had taken part in the referendum but did not support independence. Was this a problem of squaring the circle? The success of 1 and 3 October was due to a social and political space that extended beyond the independence movement and included others who were in favour of a break with the existing constitutional set-up. In party terms, this meant primarily the former leadership of Podem (Podemos in Catalonia) and a minority current in the Comuns, and in social terms it meant a broad layer of social movement and alternative trade union activists. In some ways, the Catalan government's dithering expressed, in a hesitant way, this concern.

93.
Unfortunately, however, ever since 2012 the independence movement has never had a serious policy aimed at seeking alliances with those non-independence forces who were in

favour of breaking with the regime coming out of the post-Franco Transition and enshrined in the 1978 constitution. The traditional blindness of the ANC on this question has been notorious. To improvise such alliances in the midst of a political crisis would have been very difficult. The strategic horizon potentially shared by the bloc developed around 1 October was one of a Catalan Republic and the opening of a Catalan constituent process which, although mostly interpreted in pro-independence terms, does not rule out the possibility of an eventual (con)federation. This should also have been the strategic axis after 1 October. In fact, these aims should have been the clearly stated framework prior to 1 October in order to weld together a political and social bloc capable of tackling this attack on the state with some guarantee of success.

Irresponsible responsibility

94.
Political crises are moments when possibilities open up (the downside being that risks also increase), although the winners of any political clash with hindsight tend to make a positivist reading of what has happened. The possibilities are certainly finite, not limitless, but every crisis presents distinct, alternative futures. Whether we take one path or another depends on the strategic ability of each of the actors competing within a given relationship of forces. Good decisions cannot make up for objective weaknesses, although they do enable us to take more advantage of opportunities and limit the adversary's ability to act. Political crises should not be subject to voluntarist interpretations, but we should be aware that they are decisive moments in which strategy and decision-making capacity take on their full meaning.

95.
The referendum took place and indignation at the repression propelled the day of mobilisation two days later. The Catalan

government then adopted a dithering policy, as it had not foreseen this situation. It did not know how to deal with the escalating confrontation which it had been obvious would happen if, in one way or another, it proclaimed the Catalan Republic. Nor did it have a strategy of alliances with the sectors that were not pro-independence but in favour of breaking with the '78 regime and had mobilised on the 1st and the 3rd. Following the badly handled 'suspension' of the declaration of independence on the 10th and a failed attempt on the 26th to call elections if the Spanish government withdrew its threat to apply article 155 of the constitution (which allows it to take measures to compel an autonomous community to meet its obligations or to protect the general interests of Spain), Puigdemont's executive was forced to promulgate the Catalan Republic on the 27th. But it had no plan at all for what to do next to turn this proclamation into something that was more than symbolic, nor for how to deal with the repressive backlash by the state. On the contrary, the proclamation was issued knowing full well that there would be no attempt to make it effective. It is hard not to think of Saint-Just's famous warning in his report to the National Convention on 3 March 1794: 'Those who make revolutions half way only dig their own graves.'

96.
Handling time and space is fundamental for any political or social movement. After 3 October the Catalan government and the ANC managed both variables extremely badly. They allowed the initial momentum to pass and engaged in secretive political manoeuvres that were poorly explained and disconcerted and disoriented quite a few of their supporters. In the end they proclaimed the Republic when things had considerably cooled down. And then they avoided doing anything at the institutional level that might have conveyed a real willingness to move towards that Republic. Above all, they avoided street mobilisations or the occupation of symbolic

and strategic spaces. From the 27 October there emerged an absolute vacuum of leadership and a total lack of direction. Puigdemont's executive projected an image of complete resignation and lack of will – a strategic manual of what not to do. The history of popular movements is full of similar situations in which moderate political and social leaders are incapable of coherently conducting the movement they lead. They back down at decisive moments, confound their own supporters and, at the end of the day, encourage reaction in the name of prudence. We can call this the policy of irresponsible responsibility.

97.
What then was possible? And what was the most intelligent option? After 3 October there was no going back. Wavering at the decisive moments after having crossed a certain threshold only serves to hasten defeat and face it strategically unarmed. This is what eventually happened with the symbolic declaration of independence. It does not seem that going off at a tangent by calling an election would have held out great prospects either: it is unlikely that it would have halted the steamroller of repression (although it might have slowed it down) and, in the event of a pro-independence victory, it would have again raised the question of whether to stop or go forward. It seemed like a way of putting off the problems or playing for time without knowing where to go.

98.
It was therefore necessary to go forward, but fully aware of the two decisive variables in the situation: a) a legitimacy that was only relative, as it rested on having won a majority of less than 50% in an irregular referendum; b) the existence of a bloc generated between 1 and 3 October that was broader than the independence movement, held together primarily by its opposition to the authoritarianism of the state, and still able to grow in this direction. The task was to push

this forward and deepen the political crisis. That is what was needed to take advantage of the situation. It required an act of democratic sovereignty that was not exclusively (or irreversibly) pro-independence, and a correct management of time and space.

99.
What was to be done, then? Proclaim the Catalan Republic, call for it to be provisionally recognised internationally and announce that as soon as it was recognised temporarily, its first task would be to hold a new referendum under international supervision. The terms of this new referendum should be open to negotiation, including the possibility of its not necessarily offering a binary choice (independence Yes or No) in the event of there being other real proposals formulated by the Spanish government or the European Union. In other words, there would be an act of sovereignty allowing a democratic decision to be taken by the people of Catalonia in satisfactory conditions; an act of sovereignty based on the 1 October vote without regarding the result as being of itself binding and definitive. A formula of this kind would have been acceptable to the independence movement's social base, would have remained faithful to the (false) promises made prior to 1 October, would have also spoken to the non-pro-independence sectors that had mobilised between 20 September and 3 October, and would have increased the pressure on the leadership of *Catalunya en Comú*. The democratic credentials of the proposal would have been impeccable to those abroad, rendering the European states' cynical inaction more difficult, and its content would not have been perceived as unequivocally secessionist by the democratic section of Spanish public opinion.

100.
How and when should this have been done? The high point of the crisis was reached on 3 October. Anything holding

back the dynamic of 1 and 3 October was only going to enable the state to recover the initiative. So, a decision had to be taken immediately; a decision that would have necessitated prolonging the Catalonia-wide stoppage for a few days more and keeping going the occupation of public spaces. Could this really have led to a break-up of the Spanish state? Was an effective defence of the provisional Catalan Republic conceivable? Both these questions can reasonably be answered in the negative. The point was to try to take the crisis as far as it would go and force a more favourable outcome, thereby weakening the state's position. Such an option logically implied accepting its inherent risks in terms of heightened repression and the possibility of an even more unfavourable conclusion.

101.
None of this was ever on the table. We should not reflect on this as a real possibility, but as a discussion on strategy with a view to revealing unexplored paths and drawing the political lessons of October. Neither the Catalan government nor the leadership of the movement were prepared to push all the way a crisis situation – which they never intended to provoke; nor were those who did argue for or want the break, and were willing to bear the cost of attempting it, in favour of reconceptualising the movement in a broader, democratic-republican sense, beyond the strictly pro-independence slogan. The impotent form the movement's strategic dilemma took on was expressed as a choice between either recklessly trying to turn back while in full stride, or continuing to press forward without questioning the limited legitimacy of the results or the internal social and class composition of the pro-independence bloc. The first option led to defeat in the midst of general disarray. The second encouraged voluntarism without examining the fundamental problems of the movement and its project.

102.

Faced with the indecision of Puigdemont's executive following the suspension of the independence declaration on 10 October, the ANC and the part of the movement in favour of going all the way mostly adopted the discourse of 'reactivating' the declaration, as though this were a simple political-administrative act and as though political decisions could be simply unfrozen; as though mistakes at decisive moments were reversible; as though strategic time could be conducted chronologically backwards. The disconnection fallacy has habitually been accompanied by making a fetish of the declaration of independence, attributing to it a force in itself quite unconnected with how it was proclaimed, the social context or the political conjuncture, a notion refuted by the actual proclamation of the Republic by the Catalan parliament on 27 October. In fact, any rectification of the mistakes committed after 3 October had to be based on generating a new scenario of mass mobilisation that would bolster the legitimacy of 1 October and maintain the unity of the informal bloc generated following the events of 20 September.

103.

The proclamation of the Republic without any strategic plan whatsoever to make it effective represented, to some extent, the culmination of the official policy of the Procés, that is to say the policy of permanently playing for time and systematically avoiding the real confrontation. The road to October, following the commitment to hold a referendum made in September 2016, was the result of a change in direction imposed by the dead end reached by the Procés's own roadmap. The 1 October referendum ended up bringing about a confrontation with the state that de facto contradicted the very essence of the Procés, but which emerged out of it and was managed by it, albeit under the partially outflanking pressure of those outside the Procés. It was a non-Procés moment within the Procés that ushered in a non-Procés phase administered by the Procés and culminated in a non-Procés event – the proclamation of the Republic – in Procés fashion, i.e., symbolically and vacuously.

104.

Comparing the revolutions of the past with contemporary revolutions in *The Eighteenth Brumaire of Louis Bonaparte*,[12] Marx wrote 'There the phrase went beyond the content – here the content goes beyond the phrase.' The phrase going beyond the content, rhetoric far above the real capacity of events to produce a rupture, does not seem a bad description of the essence of the Procés and its current phase. Content going beyond the phrase, a real capacity to produce a rupture in excess of the rhetoric, is also a good description of the fleeting period between 20 September and 1 October whose potential was smothered by the deficiencies of the Procés which had always conditioned this moment of opening and facilitated its false closure.

105.

The limitations shown by the Catalan government at the moment of truth are to be sought in its nature, class composition and political culture. Convergència, the PDeCAT's forerunner, was a neoliberal party forced to take the independence road because it had no alternative. Many of its cadres became independence supporters while others, like Puigdemont, always had been. But it is a party of order with a conservative social base, not very fond of ruptures and sudden changes, pragmatic and gradualist by nature, linked to the world of business and vulnerable to its pressure (although its big business connections have suffered as a result of its pro-independence turn), and distrustful of popular mobilisation. The ERC, on the other hand, perfectly embodies a synthesis between genuine pro-independence convictions and a political culture not used to struggle. It is gradualist with a progressive middle-class base which, apart from certain sectors linked to teaching, has been largely absent from the major social mobilisations of the recent past on matters other than independence. It lacks punch. It was in these decisive weeks that all the limitations in terms of strategy, project and social base of the forces running the Catalan government and in general supporting the independence movement (with the exception of the CUP, which represents a minority within it) were present in concentrated form. True, these deficiencies had been quite visible from the beginning, but they had not yet undergone a decisive, strategic stress test.

106.
The events of September and October revealed the Catalan government's ambiguity towards popular mobilisation. The extremely poor way it managed the expectations of the movement's supporters between 3 and 27 October simply reflects a conception of politics steeped in institutional manoeuvres and lacking any culture of organising a mass movement. Beyond the government, from 20 September on, the strategic impasse of the ANC (and of the mass-membership cultural association Òmnium, although it played a secondary role and, in many ways, had a bolder policy) was clearly shown up. Ever since it began in 2012, the Procés involved an unprecedented mass movement under the leadership of the ANC. However, its top-down, controlled conception of the movement was more favourable to a culture of representation and delegation than self-organisation.

107.
The partially outflanking dynamic of 20 September and 1–3 October (we should stress 'partially' so as not to exaggerate) was essential for the government and the ANC (and Òmnium), but it also caused them apprehension and fear of losing control of the situation. In the face of the leadership vacuum left by the Catalan government following

the 27 September 2015 election, there appeared a second limitation of the ANC: its subordination to the major pro-independence parties and its inability to take on a leading role independently of them. Its policy after 2012 was to pressurise the Catalan government into going forward, but without ever challenging or embarrassing it. It tamely gave in to the then PM Artur Mas's refusal to go ahead with the referendum on 9 November 2014 after it had been banned by the Constitutional Court and accepted the proposal to transform the 27 September 2015 election into a plebiscite and the subsequent unrealistic roadmap of 'disconnection' which, moreover, gradually left the initiative in the government's hands with the ANC increasingly playing the role of second fiddle.

Strategic self-deception

108.
The democratic character of the independence movement and its struggle against the state's authoritarianism stand in stark contrast to the scant attachment to the truth and openness displayed by the movement's leaders. This is the most disturbing aspect of the Procés, whose leadership always spoke two different languages, one when addressing those outside the movement, the other when addressing those inside it. Paradoxically, this is a feature it shares with the so-called 'new politics' (an imprecise term if ever there was one and of little conceptual use) careful planning – Podemos first and foremost – which has also been given to dissociating words and deeds, and to not doing what they say and not saying what they do. The politics of appearance prevails over the politics of truth.

109.
The echoes of Gramsci, for whom truth and revolutionary politics were intertwined, irrevocably fade away. 'Nothing of what interests it should be hidden from the working class, not

even if the truth appears to harm it in the immediate term; this means the working class must be treated in the same way as an adult who is able to reason and discern is treated, not as a minor under guardianship,' he wrote on 17 March 1922 in *L'Ordine Nuovo*.[13] If we change 'the working class' to 'the citizenry' or 'the people' to bring it into line with the sociological and conceptual reality of the Catalan independence movement, the quotation appears as the exact opposite of what the leaders of the main organisations have done.

110.
Proclaiming the Republic on 27 October, with those on the inside knowing full well that this was a rhetorical and symbolic act, was without doubt an inadmissible deception of the independence movement's own rank-and-file. Politics and truth have historically had a difficult relationship, as Hannah Arendt[14] recalled in her well-known essay, where she pointed out that truthfulness is not usually considered a political virtue. It should be specified that this applies to the politics of the state, governments and the conventional electoral arena. It has also been the politics of the Procés (not to mention, of course, of the adversaries of the Procés).

111.
A politics of the subalterns ought to aspire to something else, although historically it has reproduced the same pattern as the politics from above. In a complex movement such as the one for Catalan independence, telling the truth and being open about the limitations and contradictions of the movement's narrative and strategy have been key demands of all those who identify with the politics of the subalterns. But those who have participated most in the movement have often tended not to want to rock the boat too much, at least until the strategic collapse after 1 and 3 October, and to accept the movement's strategic framework too readily. At the same time, the criticisms levelled at it by the left outside

the movement, even when they were correct, were stillborn due to their lack of involvement in it and the inconsistency of their own approach.

112.

Strategic lying is intrinsic and necessary to both the neoliberal project and the reactionary and/or neofascist forces on the rise. But for democratic politics, the politics of the subalterns, to make lying an integral part of its identity is to negate its own values and distort its ends. It undermines its potential for change and, in the long run, its credibility. Although lying is functional to all projects of domination, its generalised use by an emancipatory movement becomes self-defeating. It may be useful for the self-reproduction of its leading elites, but at the cost of emptying it of its content. This is what has happened with the leadership of the Procés and Podemos.

113.

In the penultimate chapter of Kafka's famous novel, *The Trial*, there is a dialogue between the central character, Josef K., and the prison chaplain in which the latter predicts his case will end badly. At one point in their conversation, when the priest tells him the story of a doorkeeper standing guard before the court, K. remarks laconically: 'Depressing thought [...] It makes the lie fundamental to world order.'[15] The lie as fundamental to world order, a cruel realisation as valid in the Czech writer's work as in the world it has been our lot to live in. It's another reason why we need to remember that democratic politics must act as a dam against deceit and represent a strategy of truth – a strategy of truth that implies not hiding the truth about the strategy.

114.

Lying has coexisted in the Procés with self-deception, thereby preventing a coherent discussion on strategy and a genuine learning of political lessons from its successes and failures.

They may have both been confusingly mixed together in the same actors and figures, although the former has been more consistently present among the political representatives of the mainstream independence movement, whereas the second has been more characteristic of the social, cultural and journalistic side of the movement. The strategy of self-deception or the strategic self-deception, whether individual or collective, pursued by the independence movement has served to eliminate from the equation the real objective difficulties of putting its plans into practice. It thought it could dodge, temporarily or indefinitely, the real strategic crossroads, replacing these with a linear movement and deliberately limited confrontations.

115.
Self-deception involves an arbitrary selection of information, leaving aside what we do not want to face and highlighting what apparently confirms our own biased view of the world. In this process, we construct social theories that lend coherence to our skewed perspective. 'The greater the social content of a discipline, especially human,' remarks evolutionary biologist Robert Trivers writing about science and the social sciences, 'the greater will be the biases due to self-deception.'[16] This affirmation is equally valid in analysing politics and strategic thought. In the present case it has been the basis of the 'from one law to another' transition strategy.

116.
In some circumstances, Trivers tells us, self-deception has a certain degree of self-promotion and excessive confidence about it, exaggerating one's own positive features and downplaying the negative aspects. This appears, again, in both the independence movement and the 'new politics' as epitomised by Podemos and the Comuns, neither of them much given to self-critical thinking or sober assessments of their own limitations. To a certain extent, some of this is required

to launch into an adventure, but never as a central element in thinking about strategy. On the contrary, self-deception acts as strategic balsam. It creates a false sense of security that actually fosters mistakes insofar as it implies a loss of contact with reality, paves the way to capitulation or simply puts off discussing crucial matters until they suddenly burst onto the scene. Not wanting to tackle them only leads to arriving at these moments of truth disarmed, in the most literal sense of the expression, thereby opening the door to defeat.

Disruptive powers

117.
According to Badiou, a mass popular event involves a 'reopening of history', a 'break in time' and the creation 'not of a new reality, but of a myriad of new possibilities'. These are familiar features of 1 October, which was experienced by its protagonists as a transformation of their relationship to the world, subjectivising 'an intense time'.[17] A 1 October whose power was nevertheless always impaired by its own limitations and contradictions. This included the distance (and, in the case of Convergència and its milieu, direct antagonism) felt by large parts of the mainstream independence movement towards the Indignados and the anti-austerity 'tides'. 1 October becomes, as the only personal and collective point of reference, an event without any moorings within a broader tradition and experience of struggle. Consequently, all the possible lessons cannot be drawn from it. Thus, 1 October had a contradictory power: disruptive, because of its challenge to the Spanish state's constitutional architecture, and disconcerting, because of its intrinsic limitations.

118.
Žižek writes that in a political event 'it's not only things that change: what changes is the very way in which we measure the facts that are changing. In other words, it's a turning point in the entire framework within which facts appear.' In this sense, 1 October put a strain on the whole political

and institutional framework, altering the way in which it and the movement opposing it were seen, and opening up a new vision of what was possible and impossible on both sides of the conflict. Žižek specifies that a popular uprising becomes an event when it brings about 'a commitment of the collective subject to a new universal emancipatory project, and thereby sets in motion the patient work of restructuring society'.[18] It is here that the limits of 1 October can clearly be seen. Its immediate potential, never fully realised, was as the bearer of a political change unconnected to any socio-economic transformation and dependent on representative politics. This curtailed its emancipatory content. There was an imminent internal tension between its democratic and disruptive potential and the weakness of its political proposal and strategic conception, which did not prevent one from being clear about which side one had to be on and what attitude to take to try to resolve this tension satisfactorily.

119.
1 October was a two-sided event. A referendum organised from above and a referendum organised from below intermingled with each other. A disruptive soul and a managerial spirit coexisted in tension. A powerful radicalisation and a timid mobilisation went hand in hand in a complex combination. Procés-ism and trans-Procés-ism appeared simultaneously. Two 1 Octobers in one. However, the untimely thrust did not have enough power to impose itself. The two sides of 1 October were asymmetrical, not so much on account of the event in itself, but because of the political and social context in which it occurred and because of the nature of the forces and organisations in contention. In short, it became an event whose own maximum potential was curtailed by the limits of the way it was managed and by the limits of the 'independence' slogan itself, its social base skewed towards the middle classes and its separation from the legacy of the Indignados movement.

120.

The relationship between politics, economics and society can be clearly seen in the Catalan crisis. Politics operates with relative autonomy and has its own logic in regard to economics and society. It is not a mere reflection of them.[19] But it cannot operate completely separately from them or be turned into a solely discursive construction. It is tied to a material reality in which relations of force are at work. If the autonomy of the political is conceived (or is unconsciously practised) as unconnected to this material reality it leads onto the terrain of empty discourse, worthless promises and fantasy – strategic phantasmagoria – and, consequently, to political impotence and the inability to carry out what is proposed and declaimed. And, in the context of a confrontation with the state, not just a discursive dialectical tussle, the risk is of being crushed by the materiality of the power relations that are concentrated there. Unleashing material forces in a real movement such as happened on 1 October, but then leaving them suspended for the benefit of an immaterial, symbolic political action, opens the way for a political reaction by the state which, far from being satisfied and pacified by its opponents' discursive symbolism, takes advantage of this to suppress them and thereby ward off the spectre of a real counterpower that hesitatingly began to raise its head on 1 October.

121.

The outcome of October and the errors of the independence movement's leadership after 1 October reveal the contrast between the Procés's formal heroism and its real post-heroic dimension. Its strategy for the struggle and its conception of how to achieve independence (disconnection and from one law to another), its leaders' lack of real conviction and the existence of two languages – public and private – during the entire Procés created an artificial, false heroism that was to collapse in the decisive weeks of October. The temporary epic from 20 September to 3 October was unable to overcome the structural post-heroism of the Procés and, fundamentally, the epic from below could not stifle the post-heroism from above. Epic in its words, the political class of the Procés was fatally post-heroic in its deeds in the decisive events at the critical moments.

122.
The crisis of October was an episode of what Gramsci called 'great politics', that is to say 'questions connected with the foundation of new states, with the struggle for the destruction, defence or conservation of particular organic socio-economic structures'. However, it was approached by the independence movement's leadership with a 'small politics' mentality, 'small politics' being concerned with 'the partial and daily questions that arise within an already established structure in the struggles for pre-eminence among the various factions of the same political class'.[20] Going about a 'great political' objective on the basis of a 'small politics' practice has, in fact, been a constituent feature of the Procés.

123.
What occurred had features of a political moment understood, as Rancière put it, as 'when the temporality of consensus is disrupted. It occurs when a force is capable of exposing the imagination of the relevant community and of contrasting it with a different configuration of the relationship of each individual to everyone else.' But by its very nature it failed to follow its logic to the end. For Rancière, a political moment simultaneously expresses the clash between the people and the institutions, the broadening out of what is 'thinkable' and the ability of the forces from below to overflow the limits of the state and representative politics. That is where October's deficiencies appear, which are, in the final analysis, the result of the Procés itself: the limitations of independence pure and simple, and of a movement structured and headed

by the ANC (and Òmnium) until 20 September, under the leadership of the Catalan government. 1 October partially overcame these limitations, reflecting a politics that exists 'through the action of collective subjects who concretely change situations by asserting their creativity and restructuring the world'.[21] But it always remained subordinate to the general framework of the Procés and coexisted with an institutional politics that was its nemesis. Was this, then, a self-curtailed political moment? Or, perhaps, the draft of a political moment?

124.
October is the source of intersecting spectres. The real October intersects with the spectre – desired and feared in equal measure – of the potential October. Only imaginable counterfactually, the potential October poses us the typical question of great occasions: what could have been done, but wasn't, what possibilities existed that were not fulfilled? This implies a strategic discussion, perhaps a lament, on the bad handling of the decisive moments. However, October's complex nature and the immanent limitations of the proposition of independence pure and simple, make it necessary to think about the potential October differently, in a broader sense. In other words, the question must be raised not only of what was allowed to get away after 1 October, but how else the event and the road leading to it might have been constructed. Questioning along these lines leads once again to the founding deficiencies of the Procés and the tragic impossibility of establishing any synergy between the path opened up following the Indignados movement and the route marked out by 11 September 2012. As a source of learning, the potential October must therefore be analysed along two dimensions, concrete and abstract, conjunctural and structural. The first concerns how better advantage might have been taken of the fork in the road that was opened up then. The second involves asking how an even bigger fork with fewer contradictions could have been opened up.

125.
October revealed an insurmountable contradiction in the independence movement: on the one hand, it was the bearer of a demand – the creation of a Catalan state – that is unacceptable to the Spanish state and radically conjures up one of its worst historical nightmares, the break-up of Spain; on the other, it has been an extraordinarily moderate movement in the way it acts and in its conception of political change. The radicality of its demand – the break-up of the Spanish state – and its moderate nature place it in some ways in a strategic position that is hard to get out of. Without intending to make any kind of historical comparison, it is hard not to recognise in the following famous passage from Marx's *The Eighteenth Brumaire* the type of political and strategic powerlessness that were experienced in those decisive days of September and October 2017: 'But the revolutionary threats of the petty bourgeoisie and their democratic representatives are merely attempts to intimidate the opponent. And when they have run into a blind alley, when they have compromised themselves sufficiently to be compelled to carry out their threats, they do this in an ambiguous way, avoiding the means to the end like the plague and clutching at excuses for their failure. The blaring overture which announced the struggle dies away into a subdued grumbling as soon as it is due to begin, the actors cease to take themselves *au sérieux*, and the action totally collapses like a balloon pricked by a needle.'[22]

A coup d'état by the state itself

126.
The king's speech on 3 October had several aims. It was a signal to the EU that Spain would not accept any deviation from the script it had followed until then according to which the Catalan question was a merely internal affair. It kept the PSOE in line – a PSOE, moreover, eager to be kept in line. It conveyed firmness to Spanish public opinion and a sensation of being in control. This blackshirt-like behaviour

by the highest authority of the state, perhaps a true reflection of its deepest nature, signified the definitive institutional legitimation of bourgeoning reactionary Spanish nationalism and anti-Catalan hooliganism.

127.
A coup driven by the state itself is the simplest way to define the battery of measures that Mariano Rajoy's government, with the support of the PSOE and the 'antinationalist' centre-right Ciudadanos (Citizens), announced on Friday, 20 October. They were approved by the senate on 27 October. It was more than just the application of article 155 of the Spanish constitution. What Rajoy announced was the de facto suspension of Catalonia's self-government as a whole using article155 as a legal pretext. The fact that there were no precedents for its implementation, together with the exceptional institutional situation of the moment, enabled the Spanish government to take decisions that were not only authoritarian and anti-democratic, but of doubtful constitutionality. Power violates its own rules under cover of force and the creation of an exceptional situation. It was the 'Schmittian moment' of the Procés, or more precisely of the anti-Procés. It activated the safety mechanisms it had at its disposal to double down and change the rules of the game, using the legitimacy of the old rules and promising to defend them.

128.
In a climate of exception, measures were taken in this way that in themselves subverted the previous order, but in the latter's name and based on its legitimacy, with the aim of manoeuvring to alter the political and social dynamic in Catalonia, and return to a new 'normality' more favourable to the state. This was a frontal assault on democracy in the name of democracy to bring in a new democratic 'normality' in which everything runs along acceptable channels after having put things in order during a period of 'exception'.

All of this, far from being a strange anomaly, is a clear example of the nature of capitalist law and the capitalist state in general (and of the 1978 Spanish political regime in particular). It dismantles at a single stroke all the foolish and fetishist ideas of law, legality and the institutions to which we grow so accustomed in times of routine 'normality'. October 2017 was doubtless a veritable practical crash course on the theory of the state, which forced the movement, whose common sense avoided contemplating a clash with the state in favour of a tranquil disconnection, towards accelerated strategic development, something which it has not yet succeeded in doing.

129.
The authoritarian backlash by the state was both a violation and a reification of the law. It was based on a restrictive interpretation of democracy as the 'rule of law' and, at the same time, it was a violation of the law by political power. Although apparently contradictory, these two processes are complementary. There is no political possibility at all beyond an immovable law that is interpreted in a biased fashion for the benefit of the powers that be. An arbitrary interpretation of the law goes hand in hand with its reification. The law thus determines what is or is not democratic and power determines what is legal. The circle closes into an authoritarian schema that devalues the concepts of both democracy – reduced to legality – and the law, whose foundation is removed from the popular will and limited to a self-serving interpretation of it by a unified state power, without any mechanisms of internal separation of powers or of external control.

130.
This is a unified power, but it is shaped by internal logics and specific sub-interests, and not by a hierarchical chain of command at the service of the executive as has sometimes been simplistically asserted, as though the government gave

orders to the judiciary. It is a de facto unification in the face of the state's enemy, but it exists amid the divergent interests and goals that express the distinct agendas of the different fractions of the leading elite and the various currents and clans of the right, in a conjuncture in which its most reactionary elements have been strengthened.

131.

The result has been the sui generis application of the enemy's criminal law, to use the well-known expression of German jurist Günther Jakobs,[23] referring to the implementation of a battery of exceptional, belligerent measures such as the anti-terrorist legislation after 11 September 2001. The October crisis led to an informal version of the enemy's criminal law, implicit but never formalised, based on an illegal interpretation of the existing laws rather than the production of new, officially passed, emergency legislation. A combative judicial system used to fight the enemy within, in which justice becomes 'the continuation of politics by other means', to paraphrase von Clausewitz's[24] famous aphorism on war and politics. A continuation of politics based on the negation of all politics other than the use of force.

132.

The 'Schmittian' break with the rules of the game implies, of course, an intention to produce a new normality that would make another moment of crisis less likely. It is from this perspective that the more or less explicit demand by Spanish nationalism's hard-line wing for Spain to be transformed into a 'militant democracy' should be seen. The term comes from German jurist and political scientist Karl Löwenstein[25] who, after going into exile in the United States in 1937 and under the impact of the rise of Nazism, pointed out that parliamentary democracies need constitutional mechanisms to defend themselves against those who take advantage of its institutions to subvert them. Although the militant democracy label can be applied to many situations, it implies an institutional arrangement that declares substantial aspects of its own constitutional framework unamendable. Its supporters in Spain have generally cited as an example the Federal Republic of Germany, whose 1949 constitution declared unconstitutional all those parties having as their aim to harm the institutional order and threaten the state's existence.

133.
The balance sheets are clear. It is well known that these constitutional precepts served not only to make it difficult for neo-Nazi forces to exist legally, but also to outlaw the German Communist Party in 1956, pass laws banning left-wingers from working in the civil service and pursue tough repressive anti-terrorist policies in the 1970s. If implemented in Spain, it would mean an intensification of the repressive logic against the independence movement and in some ways the criminalising of its aims and objectives as such. The next step would be the generalisation of this criterion to apply to all enemies of the state as the final, institutionalised culmination of the internal coup carried out during the October crisis which, in the name of defending the state, in fact was intended to accentuate its most authoritarian features. An institutional backlash that sought to compensate for its lost legitimacy with force.

Dilemmas of the left hemisphere

134.
The Catalan October put the Spanish left through a tough test that showed up its programmatic and strategic limitations. The vast majority (with only a few minor exceptions) were caught in a vice between their own uneasiness regarding the Catalan question and a hostile environment that made it very difficult and reckless to distance themselves from the pro-regime 'holy alliance', especially as the creation of this holy alliance had been indirectly facilitated

by the Spanish left's years of programmatic ambiguities. In addition, the left's failure to perform its proper functions also helped to create a political and cultural climate that grew implacably tense when a critical moment and a real crisis of state arrived. The fundamental problem for organisations such as Podemos and Izquierda Unida (United Left) is that in spite of their generic defence of the right to self-determination, they almost always conceive it as linked to a federal outcome and are reluctant to recognise the right to separation as such. In other words, they conceive it as a right the exercise of which is controlled and the result predefined.

135.
Despite arguing on the whole for a democratic position, Izquierda Unida general coordinator Alberto Garzón sometimes tended to equate the two sides of the conflict. Although in one of several interventions into the debate he wrote that 'it is absurd to lump all nationalisms together',[26] in fact his policy failed to distinguish Spanish nationalism's specific contemporary function from that of dominant Catalan nationalism and observed the clash between them as a passive spectator. 'Granting Spanish nationalism and Catalan nationalism the same abstract status, it is not possible to take sides in advance with either of them,' he continued, without pointing out that historically their roles have been different and that today the latter is not expressed by denying anybody's democratic rights. He asserts that he is 'convinced that Spanish nationalism has created thousands of Catalan nationalists. But it is often forgotten that a Spanish people also exists and that Catalan nationalism creates as many Spanish nationalists.' In this, he avoids the fact that, although it is true that anti-independence Spanish nationalist propaganda in a lot of the media has helped to strengthen a reactionary Spanish nationalism, the comparison is asymmetrical. The experience of suffering each is totally different for those who react against them, because of their different natures.

136.
In response to the proposal for independence, Garzón posited a federal solution. A 'federal state that recognises the peoples and nations of Spain and does not pit them against each other, is a beautiful aspiration'. No doubt, but as he formulated it, it had two innate limitations. The first is that it was conceived exclusively as the result of an overall break with the 1978 framework, brought about by a new (and desirable) political majority in Spain as a whole; it had no answer when faced with a situation in which such a majority did not exist and there was massive pressure in Catalonia to exercise the right to self-determination which, in his schema, was limited to a merely theoretical, but not a real, right. The second is that, although his federalism was formally plurinational, it actually appeared more like that of a uninational state, the result of a mere linear self-transformation of the present state and not an alliance of peoples and national political subjects.

137.
In the various debates on the left, Alberto Garzón has shown an accurate and positive understanding of society's plurality and the plurality of the working class. He avoided reducing everything to class and playing down differences within the class, such as those of gender and ethnic group, whether in the disputes among various sectors of the Spanish left on the relation between identity politics and class struggle or on the role of immigration.[27] Successfully steering clear of the workerist and national-corporativist traps, his position, however, fails to strategically integrate national plurality into a complex perspective linking the universal and the particular. In spite of formally internationalist arguments in which he advocated finding 'formulas enabling us to talk of a democratic and social rupture, in which the underdogs of our respective peoples can cooperate', these remained in fact subordinate to conventional Spanish nationalism.

138.
Podemos' position was unquestionably democratic and at times courageous, but it revealed a fundamental strategic incapacity – doubtless extremely hard to avoid – to develop an anti-'78 regime, centre-periphery dialectic. This was an analogous limitation to that of the Catalan independence movement, although coming from the opposite direction. It saw 1 October as simply a 'mobilisation' and not a referendum, on the grounds that it lacked sufficient formal guarantees. However, it ignored the fact that the central government was mainly responsible for this and it seemed to overlook the fact that what happened on 1 October would seriously affect the feasibility, positively or negatively, of bringing about its own proposal for an agreed referendum in the medium term. The limitations of this position were apparent in a joint opinion piece published by Podemos general secretary Pablo Iglesias and Catalunya en Comú coordinator Xavi Domènech in which, in spite of deploying a fairly coherent argument regarding plurinationality and the crisis of sovereignties, they asserted that 'the 1 October mobilisation can be an act to affirm rights and sovereignty in a situation that needs to be unblocked, given the PP's resounding failure and its repressive drive. In this sense – as a political mobilisation – we think it is legitimate and we support its being held. But afterwards, 2 October will arrive and then it will be necessary to continue working for a referendum that must speak to all those affected.'[28]

139.
Instead of denying the 1 October ballot's status as a referendum, it would have been more consistent, given the central government's refusal to authorise a legal consultation, to regard the Catalan executive's proposal as the only possible referendum existing on the horizon and, in spite of its deficiencies, deserving of support, even if it were seen only as a test of strength with a view to obtaining an agreed

ballot in the future. But its status as a mobilisation and not a referendum was decreed in advance, as though it were inevitable and had nothing to do with the policies of those who regarded it in this way. In fact, it would have been more logical, even from the formal programmatic standpoint of Podemos and Catalunya en Comú, to raise the need to work to make it a referendum, while warning that in the end it might turn out to be no more than an 'act of affirmation of sovereignty' due to repression by the state. And to clarify that if things did turn out like that, the act would not have been in vain, as it would be another step up in the political pressure to achieve a referendum accepted by the state. Separating 1 October and the proposal for an agreed referendum in terms of strategy only contributed to the political passivity of those who supported it and the weakening of any real prospect of an agreed solution.

140.
Does this mean the Spanish left cannot criticise the Catalan independence movement's limitations? Of course not. But any criticism, if it is to be sincere and credible, must be accompanied by a prior defence of Catalonia's democratic rights and, above all, a firm rejection of the state's and Spanish nationalism's authoritarianism. Not just its most excessive and abusive manifestations, but analysing its relation to the very nature of the political regime born of the Transition. Taking one's distance from the reactionary nationalism of one's own nation and accepting the legitimacy of the demand for independence (not the same thing as necessarily agreeing with it) is the first, necessary condition for practising genuine internationalist solidarity. And, possibly, a condition for federal or confederal coexistence.

141.
In the face of an absolute closing of the ranks by the bloc comprising PP, PSOE and Ciudadanos, by all the institutions

of state with the King at their head, by the financial powers-that-be and the major media conglomerates, Unidos Podemos sailed against the current, alone defending a democratic position. Although limited and not without contradictions and mistakes (in particular its lukewarm attitude to 1 October), the policy of Podemos (and to a lesser extent Izquierda Unida) was at least a dignified and noteworthy democratic exception. The party's internal dynamics, however, displayed a feature to be taken into account: its middle-level regional and local structures (except for the Catalan leadership) appeared less able to withstand the pressure of the situation and tended to adapt more to the predominant Spanish nationalism than its core leadership with Pablo Iglesias at its head.

142.
How is this dynamic to be interpreted? Rather like the nth example of the failure of Podemos' organisational and political model. An organisational failure because, from the beginning, the combination of top-down centralism and authoritarianism discouraged many of the best cadres, silenced those who voiced criticism and, in local and regional structures, promoted opportunists without any qualities other than their loyalty to the central leadership. A failure of the political model, because its concentration on electoralist tactics and communications policy downgraded programmatic principles and neglected cadre training, except in regard to technical matters or questions of communications. The rank-and-file and middle-ranking cadres received hardly any political education on the national question or its relation to the crisis of the regime, apart from generic declarations on the commitment to a plurinational state, with very little concrete content and without linking this to any historical or theoretical tradition. As the situation became tenser and the 'Catalan crisis' came to a head, many of the party's middle-ranking leaders and rank-and-file members were politically disarmed and had difficulty in following the

line or actively defending it outside the party. The superficiality of the electoral-communicational policy, although pursued doggedly by those at the top, thus ran up against the complexity of real politics.

143.
In and around Podemos and Izquierda Unida, alongside these organisations' official positions, there also existed a strong current of Spanish nationalism, aligned with the forces of the regime by way of a Spanish nationalism dressed up as internationalism. In Podemos this current of opinion existed mostly below the surface, although one of the party's ideologues, Juan Carlos Monedero, constantly flirted with such views. In the world of Izquierda Unida and the Communist Party of Spain (PCE), the PCE's former general secretary, Paco Frutos, was the most notable figure holding such views. His position reflected both an adaptation to Spanish nationalism and the general programmatic decomposition of the communist movement faced with the decline of its political tradition in a world in rapid transformation.

Contradictions, paradoxes and (im)purities

144.
Social mobilisations usually have contradictory consequences and the lessons the masses draw from them are complex. Social mobilisation, as is well known, is generally episodic and it is likely that the vast majority of those who have taken part in pro-independence demonstrations will demobilise in the event of victory and go back to the private sphere of their daily lives. It is also clear that the social bloc behind the process that began in 2012 is heavily skewed towards the middle classes and certain sections of the working class, leaving out large parts of the latter. The independence movement's potential as a process generating an awareness of struggle and collective organisation is

ambivalent due to its peculiar combination of being driven from below and from above, and of being both a social and an institutional movement. And, in general, the national question has an ambiguous function. On the one hand, it is a source of collective identity and demands. On the other, it is a lever pulling in the direction of an inter-class and statist logic that subordinates all other matters, a mechanism for taming the popular movement by integrating it into a national consensus. Social and institutional disobedience to the Spanish state fosters a culture of struggle, but can easily end up in applause for the Mossos d'Esquadra, the Catalan autonomous community's police force.

145.
The Procés has been a challenge to the state, but also an attempt to relegitimise the Catalan ruling elite. Resistance to the Spanish authorities has given rise to an overlegitimation of the Catalan political class which, unlike its European equivalents mired in endless austerity and limitless mediocrity, does possess a narrative (albeit weakened in the present phase) and, perhaps, a project (or at least the appearance of a project, and that is what counts). This is the main strategic problem to be faced by those who advocate changing the economic and social model, something that without a doubt requires a crisis of legitimacy of the traditional political representatives if it is to come about. There will be no important social transformations in Catalonia without this.

146.
During the Indignados movement, the gulf between the people and the political elite was at its widest. But since then, things have turned around. We have gone from the demonstration on 15 June 2011 surrounding the Catalan parliament, to calling for the freedom, or an end to the persecution, of the Catalan politicians suffering repression or exile. Political solidarity with them and the necessary condemnation of state

repression, however, cannot ignore this crucial question. At the same time, the movement's logic means that the incipient loss of confidence in the pro-independence parties because of their muddled strategy is channelled towards strengthening new social leaders and media personalities who repeat all of the movement's foundational inadequacies.

147.
In spite of all these limitations and ambiguities, it is undeniable that a victory or a defeat will have a very different impact on the Catalan society of the future. If the lesson the independence process teaches is 'Yes we can', social participation, commitment and mobilisation will be more highly valued and will have greater weight in the country's political culture. If what remains of the pro-independence adventure is a grim 'No we can't', apathy and cynicism will grow. The independence process can leave a residue of empowerment or a trail of disillusionment. To struggle and win or struggle and lose are two distinct experiences that, whatever one thinks of the independence project, are going to play a part in shaping Catalan society's relationship with collective action and its perception of the future. It is paradoxical, by the way, that this type of consideration is glaringly absent from a political organisation such as Catalunya en Comú that formally upholds the importance of social movements in its strategy for change and has a large selection of leaders who, in their ever more distant former lives, had a strong activist culture and biography.

148.
Those on the left, both in Catalonia and the rest of Spain, who have remained opposed to or aloof from the independence movement since 2012, have done so pointing out, with greater or lesser skill, the process's innumerable contradictions, the most notable of all being the presence at the head of the Catalan government of a neoliberal party,

upholder of a strict policy of social cutbacks after it came to power in 2010, and which had never been in favour of independence. Beyond the specific analysis of the movement that began in 2012, this permanent insistence on its contradictions and imperfections, to the extent of sometimes wildly exaggerating them, reflects an underlying approach to social reality that is far too scholastic, and which is often found in left-wing organisations faced with phenomena that do not fit their schemas. To a greater or lesser extent, contradictions are part and parcel of all social processes. It is the result of the complexity of human societies and how conflicts are expressed within them. A movement does not contain only contradictions and limitations; how it evolves also produces contradictory and limited results. This has to do with the old problem that social theory calls the unintended consequences of social action.

149.
Any strategy for breaking with the existing order and for social change must be able to operate in a context of contradictions and limitations if it is going to try to resolve the former in an emancipatory direction and extend the boundaries of the latter. Pure strategy is precisely that which is able to function in a complex, contradictory and impure world. The aim of pure strategic reason is not to find pure processes and struggles, but to provide direction amid the contradictions and limitations of real struggles. Attempting to find unpolluted processes actually leads to a fossilised strategy, forever waiting for something that never happens. Strategy in its highest state entails accepting the limitations of political and social struggles and, by extension, of one's own strategy.

150.
'Whoever expects a "pure" social revolution will never live to see it. Such a person pays lip-service to revolution without

understanding what revolution is,'[29] wrote Lenin in 1916, polemicising against those in the socialist movement who failed to support the Easter Rising in Ireland earlier that year. In October 2017 we were not seeing a revolution or an insurrection, but the same idea can be usefully applied to that huge convulsion. Faced with the imperfections of a real conflict, there are two choices: to opt for a passive approach and, thereby, involuntarily help to accentuate these deficiencies, or for an active approach seeking to intervene in the reality and modify it in the desired direction. The first choice leads, depending on the particular case, to passive or abstract radicalism, simplistic propagandism or institutional routinism, none of which has anything to do with a serious attempt to change the world.

151.
Rather than seeing it as an awkward, paralysing nuisance, a sort of unending anomaly, it is more fruitful for the left to take the Procés as a strategic stimulus, as a test of its own ability to operate in a paradoxical and contradictory environment, to approach it as a source of lessons, in a situation not of our own choosing, seeking to relate to a complex dynamic with the aim of helping to reduce the space occupied by the right within it. Moreover, a policy of passively waiting ignores another decisive question: such a moment of intensified conflict between the state and the independence movement, such as occurred in October, was also a key opportunity to try to shift the balance of forces within the movement to the left, to help the more militant sectors to play a more prominent role in a situation in which the forces in favour of 'order' within the movement found it more difficult to operate than those seeking to break with the existing order, and to try at the same time to broaden its programmatic and strategic horizons. In other words, it was a critical moment for reshaping the movement and encouraging its internal reorganisation through its conflictual interaction with the 'outside'.

152.

The contradictions and limitations of the pro-independence movement produced, as a result of the condensation of the five years of the process in the 'battle of 1 October', some sudden and striking paradoxes, which could translate into situations either comic or tragic. The days leading up to 1 October were certainly paradoxical. Parties of rebellion calling for order and calm. Leftists trusting in the Catalan police. Right-wing forces calling for institutional disobedience (albeit elegantly dressed up as complying with the new Catalan legality). Alternative and/or libertarian activists wanting to vote. People not in favour of independence voting for it. Left-wingers used to being on the front lines of conflicts occupying a discreet and uncomfortable position in the background. Reactionary governments accusing those wanting to hold a referendum of carrying out a coup. In the world of real activity, when social processes speed up, any strategic thinking that does not want to become fossilised almost before it is born must plunge into a situation replete with contradictions, in which things are not what they appear to be and the consequences of actions are not always clear. The paradox of strategy is that it can often be overtaken by the paradoxes of reality itself. And the paradox of paradoxes of real politics is that they can sometimes stimulate strategic thinking that overcomes the paradoxes that had hitherto disarmed it.

1   Karl Marx, *Capital*, Vol. 1, London, Penguin Books in association with *New Left Review*, 1976, p. 344.
2   The scene can be viewed at: www.youtube.com/watch?v=an8_D73m2rE&spfreload=10. The scene and the conflicts between HAL and the crew are a reflection on human and artificial intelligence, the limits of both and the relationship between humans and machines.
3   Michael Hardt and Antonio Negri, *Empire*, Harvard University Press, 2001.
4   Ferran Requejo, 'Serem prou forts per a aguantar la nostra legalitat sense fer cas de l'altra?', *Vilaweb*, 16 March 2017. Available at: www.vilaweb.cat/noticies/ferran-requejo-serem-prou-forts-per-aguantar-la-nostra-legalitat-sense-fer-cas-de-laltra-entrevista/
5   Marina Subirats, 'Una utopía disponible', *La Maleta*, No. 6, Barcelona, 2014, pp. 10–13.
6   Frederic Jameson, *Archaeologies of the Future: The Desire Called Utopia and Other Science Fictions*, London, Verso Books, 2007.
7   Daniel Bensaïd, *Le pari mélancolique*, Paris, Fayard, p. 291.
8   Leon, Trotsky, *The Lessons of October*. Available at: www.marxists.org/archive/trotsky/1924/lessons/index.htm
9   Daniel Bensaïd, op. cit.
10 There are already several journalistic accounts relating the ins and outs of the Procés and the Catalan government prior to 1 October and their subsequent handling of it. Of the most complete, the following stands out: Oriol March, *Los entresijos del 'Procés'*, Madrid, Los Libros de La Catarata, 2018.
11 Daniel Bensaïd, *Un monde à changer*, Paris, Textuel, 2003, pp.153–154.
12 Karl Marx, *The Eighteenth Brumaire of Louis Bonaparte*. Available at: www.marxists.org/archive/marx/works/download/pdf/18th-Brumaire.pdf.
13 My translation (Translator's note).
14 Hannah Arendt, *Truth and Politics*, available at: idanlandau.files.wordpress.com/2014/12/arendt-truth-and-politics.pd.

15 Frantz Kafka, *The Trial*, London, Penguin Books, 2000, p. 171.
16 Robert Trivers, *The Folly of Fools: The Logic of Deceit and Self-Deception in Human Life*, New York, Basic Books, reprint 2014, pp. 303-304. Trivers formulated these thoughts in studying the relations between biology and the social sciences, and the latter's scant knowledge and use of the former.
17 Alain Badiou, *The Rebirth of History: Times of Riots and Uprisings*, London, Verso, 2012, 142, 69, 109, and 90.
18 Slavoj Žižek, Event: Philosophy in Transit, London, Penguin, 2015.
19 Daniel Bensaïd, op.cit.
20 Antonio Gramsci Q13 §5. My translation [translator's note]. There is no complete English translation of the *Notebooks*. The English critical edition of the *Prison Notebooks*, edited by Joseph A. Buttigieg, has three volumes including *Notebooks 1–8*.
21 Jacques Rancière, *Moments Politiques: Interventions 1977–2009*, New York, Seven Stories Press, 2014.
22 Karl Marx, op. cit.
23 Günther Jakobs, *On the Theory of Enemy Criminal Law*, Henning Rosenau and Sanyun Kim eds., 2010, available at: www.academia.edu/22864807/G%C3%BCnther_Jakobs_On_the_Theory_of_Enemy_Criminal_Law_Zur_Theorie_des_Feindstrafrechts_in_Straftheorie_und_Strafgerechtigkeit_167_82_Henning_Rosenau_and_Sanyun_Kim_eds._2010.
24 Carl von Clausewitz, *On War*, Princeton, Princeton University Press, 1989 (edited and translated by Michael Howard and Peter Paret).
25 Karl Löwenstein, 'Militant Democracy and Fundamental Rights', *The American Political Science Review*, 1937, Vol. 31, No. 3, pp. 417-432, and Vol. 31, No. 4, pp. 638-658.
26 Alberto Garzón, 'La abstracta independencia de Cataluña: respuesta a Pau Llonch', *Público.es*, 16 July 2017. Available at:

blogs.publico.es/otrasmiradas/9579/la-abstracta-independencia-de-cataluna-respuesta-a-pau-llonch/. All the quotations from Garzón at this point and the following three have been taken from this article, which was a rejoinder to a previous article by Pau Llonch: 'Una brizna de concreta realidad (carta a Alberto Garzón)', *Público.es*, 14 July 2017. Available at: blogs.publico.es/otrasmiradas/9534/una-brizna-de-concreta-realidad-carta-a-alberto-garzon/. My own contribution to the debate between them can be seen at: Josep Maria Antentas, '1 de octubre: terciando en el debate Llonch-Garzón', *Publico.es*, 18 July 2017. Available at: blogs.publico.es/tiempo-roto/2017/07/18/1-de-octubre-terciando-en-el-debate-llonch-garzon/.

27   A large part of the first debate was generated by the book: Daniel Bernabé, *La trampa de la diversidad*, Madrid, Ed. Akal, 2018. The IU general secretary wrote a critical review of it in: Alberto Garzón 'Crítica de la crítica a la diversidad', *El diario.es*, 24 June 2018. Available at: www.eldiario.es/tribunaabierta/Critica-critica-diversidad_6_785731424.html. The origin of the controversy over immigration is in the article mentioned above: Héctor Illueca, Manuel Monereo and Julio Anguita, op. cit. Garzón distanced himself from the position of these three authors in several subsequent statements.

28   Pablo Iglesias and Xavier Domènech, 'Catalunya, un sol poble', *El Periódico de Catalunya*, 16 July 2017. Available at: www.elperiodico.com/es/opinion/20170716/pablo-iglesias-xavier-domenech-catalunya-un-sol-poble-6171617.

29   V.I. Lenin, 'The Discussion on Self-Determination Summed Up'. Available at: www.marxists.org/archive/lenin/works/1916/jul/x01.htm.

3
'A Single People?'

Divorces and marriages

153.
The history of Catalonia has been marked by a complicated combination of the national question and the social question, between class and nation. The two have often gone their own ways, but have never been completely separate. This has posed a big challenge for the left, which it hasn't always dealt with successfully. The 'national question' has been an uncomfortable one for the workers' movement at several moments in its history, and for later analysts as well. Similarly, in reverse, the reality of a workers' movement with its own dynamic beyond Catalanism has clouded a certain image of Catalonia that nationalists were keen to canonise. Today there are many flawed, political readings of Catalan history, which try to interpret this in the light of the current independence movement, or less frequently, in terms of opposition to independence. A fight over the past to give legitimacy to the present, and back a vision of the future.

154.
The contradictions of the past are simplified through those of the present, in a double operation: what has gone before is seen through today's spectacles, and the past is used to justify the present. Partial and selective memory leads to a skewed interpretation of current realities, while the latter reinforces a certain reading of 'national' history which largely ignores class contradictions. Seeing history from the perspective of the Procés results in two problems: interpreting past political

Catalanism in terms of an independence movement, when it was mostly regionalist or federalist (with the exception of the 'separatist' positions developed in the 1920s and 1930s, especially around the Estat Català, and after 1968 by the Partit Socialista d'Alliberament Nacional), and analysing the workers' movement in terms of its relations with Catalanism, as if it were the latter which set the framework of the future, to which the former had to adjust.

155.
However, it is not possible to judge the history of the popular classes in Catalonia only in terms of their links with Catalanism, as if this were the only socio-political yardstick of Catalan history for interpreting the social and political position of all the other actors. Nor would it be correct to do the opposite, and regard the national question as a permanent anomaly that distorts the natural development of the workers' movement, as something that divides the imagined, natural unity of the class, or as a perverse, cross-class impulse that upsets the pure class consciousness of the workers. It is better to approach Catalan history from a broader perspective, in terms of a series of complicated divorces and marriages between Catalanism and the workers' movement, which have involved big strategic choices and struggles for the leadership of the country.[1] These have shaped projects which cannot be understood separately, even when they have been opposed to each other. It is the history of a relationship that has been fraught but prolific, of dangerous liaisons and strategic combinations that run deep in Catalan society and politics.

156.
Published in 2014, *La formació d'una identitat (The Shaping of an Identity)*, by Josep Fontana[2] has been one of the most popular histories of Catalonia written in the period of the Procés. Fontana was an important historian and Marxist thinker in Catalonia and in Spain more generally.[3] His

work succeeds in combining a long view with an ability to synthesise, which allows him to give a general interpretation of Catalan history without neglecting the details. His starting point, however, is the historical development of what he regards as Catalonia's specificity, which sometimes borders on exceptionalism. This tilts his book towards a Catalan history excessively focused on the national question. He tends to over-emphasise the elements that point to a continuous historical identity, spanning the medieval, modern and contemporary periods, and to pay less attention than he should to those socio-political features of the popular classes that least fit in with Catalanism.

Spectres of the 'Emperor of the Paralelo'

157.
Catalanism was diverse from the start. A conservative, traditionalist soul coexisted alongside a more progressive one, linked to federal republicanism. From 1870 to 1890, the latter was predominant. In response, a conservative national sentiment developed and prevailed in the 1890s, led by traditionalist intellectuals who converged with a Catalan bourgeoisie that found itself frustrated and excluded by the centralist regime of the Restoration. This led to a divorce between Catalanism and republicanism. The latter, for the most part, came to see the former as expressing right-wing positions on economic, social and cultural questions. Yet the republican movement always retained a Catalanist streak within it.[4] Weak and fragmented, Catalan republicanism began to lose touch with a workers' movement that, after the end of the First Republic, had begun to follow a path of its own, separate from the republicanism of the petit bourgeoisie, even if many points of contact remained.[5]

158.
Alejandro Lerroux was active in republican circles from his arrival in Madrid in 1886. He first made his name when he

defended in his paper, *El Progreso (set up in 1897)*, *the anarchists persecuted in the Montjuic trial*.⁶ With this he gave a libertarian and radical tone to the republican message, and reached an audience of workers that went beyond the traditional petty-bourgeois support base. He developed a good relationship with the anarchists, including a friendship and collaboration with Ferrer i Guardia in Barcelona. He was a popular speaker, with great charisma, and after being elected a member of parliament for Barcelona in 1901 he became the moral leader of republicans in Catalonia and the movement's main moderniser. After the Republican Union was set up in 1903, he set about building a real mass, urban party, based on the proactive, street politics he had tried out in his 1901 election campaign. This led to a solid movement with roots throughout the territory, based on a network of Houses of the People, which, although still cross-class institutions, were anchored in the Catalan working class. Lerroux's ideology was a programmatically weak mixture of workerism (filling the vacuum left by traditional republicanism and a minority Socialist Party), anti-clericalism and anti-nationalism.⁷

159.
In the years from 1903 to 1905, Lerroux's opposition to Catalanism was essentially a left-wing critique of the conservative nationalism of the Lliga Regionalista. It attacked the latter's lack of links with the workers, and built successfully on the anti-Llague sentiment of traditional republicanism, at a time when left-wing political Catalanism barely existed. During this phase, Lerroux combined his critique of conservative nationalism with formal support for Catalan autonomy, and professions of Spanish patriotism (when he was speaking in Madrid). In the years that followed, from 1906 to 1908, Lerroux came into conflict with the new coalition between republicans and Catalanists, the Catalan Solidarity, which won the general elections in April 1907, as national sentiment gained ground throughout Catalan society. In the process,

Lerroux's opposition to nationalism slipped into outright Spanish patriotism, defending the integrity of the Spanish state against the 'separatist' threat.

160.
The Radical Republican Party was founded at the beginning of 1908, and reached its high point between 1909 and 1910, winning the Barcelona local elections in 1909, and the legislative elections in 1910. But in the early years of the second decade Lerroux's republicans would lose their decisive influence among the Catalan working class, mainly to the anarchists, but also with growing competition from a pro-nationalist, left-wing republicanism, which for the first time now had popular support and political connections. The party soon became involved in corruption scandals related to its local government work in Barcelona, which would stain its reputation, and in a complicated attempt to soften its verbal radicalism, as a way of developing more cross-class support and increasing its presence in Spanish politics beyond Barcelona. It became more and more a prop for the Liberal government in Spain, based on the middle class and increasingly alien to the world of the workers of Barcelona. It had begun its unstoppable journey from the Emperador del paralelo of earlier years to the right, a journey which concluded in its alliance with the Spanish Confederation of the Autonomous Right (CEDA) during the II Republic. End of the journey.

161.
Lerroux's project set the class struggle against the national question, pushing Catalan workers to oppose Catalan national demands; it sought to separate them rather than add them, as Andreu Nin, among many others, would later point out.[8] But it did not base its success on dividing workers according to where they came from, as many mistakenly alleged at the time and since. In fact, most of the working class in those days

was of Catalan origin, although some did come from Spain. So, its working-class support was not based on 'non-Catalan' immigrants. Its social roots were among Catalan-speaking, Catalan workers, who associated the national question with backward, conservative positions. It muddled class and nation in contradictory ways. In spite of its workerism, it didn't define the social question in terms of class, and it didn't have clear, socialist aims. Its programme was confused, and the movement was mainly characterised by demagogy, caudillismo, careerism and an opportunistic manipulation of popular protests (for example, it supported, after the fact, the uprising of the 'Tragic Week', or Semana Trágica, in which its supporters had played a major role but where the party itself had a been timid at best). For all these reasons, its historic role was negative. Which should not prevent us from recognising its real achievements in organising and mobilising, both essential tasks of any project for emancipation.

162.

The Lerroux movement is often seen as an anomaly in the history of the Catalan people. But in fact it is a fundamental part of the history of Catalonia and its oppressed classes. Few spectres have had such a permanent presence in their history. But the pale spectre of the Lerroux movement as it really existed has been overshadowed by the double spectre of it as anathema to dismiss the enemies of Catalanism, and as the threat of a division among the people on national grounds. As a result, the strategic lessons that should have been drawn from the rise of Lerroux between 1901 and 1910 have not always been presented clearly. The imaginary movement, reduced to artificially imported anti-nationalism, has prevented a thorough understanding of the real Lerroux movement.

163.

A proper balance sheet of Lerroux's impact reveals, firstly, the limitations of a conservative Catalanism, with no social dimension, and of a middle-class, Catalan republicanism that was excessively subordinate to the former. Second, it shows the ultimate impossibility of building a majority political block in Catalonia, oriented towards the left, from outside of nationalism. Third, it reminds us that political opposition to Catalanism ultimately serves the state. Fourth, workerism without a class project for social change leads nowhere. Fifth, caudillismo, demagogy and a lack of scruples are contrary to any aim of emancipation. Sixth, it pointed to the weaknesses of an apolitical libertarianism, which by neglecting the political representation of the workers opened the door to opportunist attempts to manipulate the workers' movement. And seventh, it showed the importance for every movement for social emancipation to build a real counter-power, its own counter-institutional network (cultural associations, or casales, cooperatives, and so on). This is a key element to understand the rise of Lerroux and his movement, and even more the eventual leading role that anarchism would come to play in the Catalan working class, through an impressive experience of self-organisation, in the workplaces and neighbourhoods. If we understand them well, these are all lessons, both positive and negative ones, that remain relevant for us today.

Worker and popular dilemmas

164.
Anarchism was traditionally far removed from the politics of Catalanism. Nevertheless, the first anarchist collectives between 1870 and 1880 had a distinct Catalanness, even if they did not argue for nationalism or develop specific positions on this.[9] Towards 1890 an anarcho-communism developed that was cosmopolitan and resistant to the national question, just as Catalanism came to be dominated by its most conservative currents. For its part, the anarchist National Labour Confederation (CNT), created in 1910, generally distanced itself from the national question. The divorce between

anarchism and Catalanism was exemplified by the opposition of the CNT (with the exception of Salvador Seguí) to the campaign for Catalan autonomy launched in 1918, in an international context that favoured the development of national demands.¹⁰

165.
Under the dictatorship of Primo de Rivera, the CNT maintained its traditional line in relation to Catalanism and the national question. It did collaborate with Catalan nationalists and Macià within the Free Alliance's Action Committee, in the first half of 1925, to bring down the dictatorship. But it does not seem appropriate to call this a nationalist or pro-independence turn by the CNT, as the independence movement has sometimes done.¹¹ Such fleeting alliances should not conceal the weak links between CNT supporters and Catalanism, nor, more generally, the complexities of Catalan society on this question.

166.
Among left-wing, Catalanist republicans at the beginning of the 20th century, there were a number of proposals and controversies over how to link the national and social questions and how to relate to the workers' movement. These expressed their growing concern to overcome their own limitations, and those of the non-nationalist socialists of the PSOE, and develop a successful project in opposition to both conservative Catalanism, and Lerroux's republicans. Most notable were those of Gabriel Alomar – originally from Mallorca but settled in Barcelona – to work out a synthesis of Catalanism with socialism, albeit socialism with a liberal, moderate bent. His theses, put forward mainly in his 1910 lectures, '*Negacions i afirmacions del catalanisme*' and '*Catalanisme socialista*', claimed that Catalanism could only triumph if it linked up with the workers' movement and went beyond its existing centre of gravity in the petit bourgeoisie and

among professionals. After a first phase of Catalanism dominated by the conservative bourgeoisie, and a second by petit-bourgeois republicans, it was necessary to move into a third phase of fusion between Catalanism and the workers' movement, in order to develop a genuine mass movement.[12]

167.
The Spanish and Catalan socialist movement did develop a policy on the national question, albeit with internal disagreements. The PSOE shared the complexities, contradictions and controversies of international social democracy on the national question. Initially, it opposed the Catalan national movement. Then it shifted its position, in a contradictory way, largely due to the influence of new Catalan leaders coming from the failed Republican Nationalist Federal Union (UFNR). This had been created in 1910 as a broad alliance between republicans, federalists and Catalanists, but it lacked a political structure or culture, as was the wont with republican personalities, who had little grasp of modern, mass politics. The 1914 polemic between a youthful Andreu Nin and Antonio Fabra Ribas, in the pages of *La Justicia Social*, on the Catalan national movement, with the former in favour and the latter against, represented something of a foundational act in the internal debates of the socialist movement.[13]

168.
In 1918, the PSOE supported the campaign for Catalan autonomy, although it always remained timid on the national question and did not explicitly include the right to self-determination in its programme, which was part of its political weakness in Catalonia. This led to repeated tension among its Catalan supporters. The main result of this was the split of 1923 that produced the Catalan Socialist Unity (USC, or Unió Socialista de Catalunya), bringing together former members of the PSOE, groups coming from the pro-nationalist,

liberal socialism and people from the world of culture who were looking for an explicitly reformist option.¹⁴ Only after October 1934 would the PSOE adopt clearer support for the nationalities and their autonomous status. And even then, the national question would remain a source of tension that would continue to affect the party in the future, including in its post-Franco phase, and showed the strategic difficulty of combining class and nation.¹⁵

169.
In the 1930s, during the II Republic, there were frequent disputes and divorces, alongside periodic, pragmatic alliances, between a revolutionary workers' movement, which was mainly anarchist and organised around the CNT, and the left-wing, nationalist republicans who were represented by the Esquerra Republicana de Catalunya, or Republican Left of Catalonia (ERC). The CNT never developed any systematic theory on the national question, and never integrated this into its strategic perspective. While the ERC had its roots in the rabassaire or share-cropping peasantry, the urban petit bourgeoisie and tradespeople, and some small groups of employees and office workers.

170.
The electoral dominance of the ERC in this period went hand in hand with a social divide in Catalan society. Urban growth produced new working-class suburbs which encouraged greater spatial and horizontal segregation and more inward-looking neighbourhoods with new forms of solidarity.¹⁶ This meant a real, physical separation between the liberal and popular nationalist project of the ERC, and much of the Catalan workers' movement, especially that organised around the CNT. In addition to the programmatic differences over the Catalan question, there was a political divorce and the disenchantment of the workers' movement with the Republic and the policies of the ERC, in particular its repressive aspect.¹⁷

Only the treintista faction of the libertarian movement, led by figures like Juan Peiró, and which in 1933 joined the Workers' Alliance promoted by Joaquin Maurín's Bloc Obrer y Camperol, or Workers and Peasant Block (BOC), included the right to self-determination as part of their revolutionary strategy; they saw the proclamation of a Catalan Republic as a step towards revolution in the whole of Spain.[18]

171.
The communist currents, both those tied to Moscow and the unorthodox ones, were divided and had little audience until 1934; yet they made the right to self-determination a central part of their programme, albeit in a rather unoriginal way. In the case of the former, the Communist Party of Spain (PCE) evolved, after the 6th Congress of the Third International, in 1935, towards a policy of 'nationalisation' in which the self-determination of peoples and the colonial question would lose importance. In parallel, its equivalent in Catalonia, the United Socialist Party of Catalonia, or Partit Socialista Unificat de Catalunya (PSUC), was founded in 1936 with a programme that defended the Catalan Republic within the Union of Iberian Socialist Republics. After the Civil War, under the leadership of Joan Comorera, it put forward a confederal, 'national line'. This led to a confrontation with the PCE and the expulsion of Comorera in 1949. However, it was among anti-Stalinist Marxists, including especially Joaquim Maurín and Andreu Nin, that the most interesting theory of the time was developed on the relationship between the national question and socialist revolution, and the dialectic between centre and periphery in Spanish politics.

172.
At the head of the BOC, which was set up in March 1931, Joaquim Maurín argued for a working-class, peasant and nationalist programme, whose approach to the national question, while still framed with references to Lenin, was influenced by federal

republicanism and Catalanism. It proposed dismembering Spain as a condition for then forming an Iberian confederation, and pointed out how the integrated, unitary model of the Second Republic had prevented a true break with the old monarchic state. The national question was incorporated into a strategic perspective of 'socialist-democratic revolution', developed in his 'Towards the Second Revolution', or *Hacia la segunda revolución (1935),* as the strategic task of the working class.[19] So, after a first phase led by the conservative bourgeoisie embodied in the League, or Lliga, and a second led by the petit-bourgeois of the ERC, after October 1934, he proposed a third phase of the Catalan national movement, led by the workers' movement, in which the historic choice was 'socialism or fascism'.[20]

173.
As founder of the small Communist Left, or Izquierda Comunista (IC), Andreu Nin had a more pragmatic view of the national question, in line with the tradition of Lenin, as a means to advance the social revolution. He thought the workers' government could not neglect the national movement and leave nationalist demands exclusively to the bourgeoisie, although it only needed to support the progressive aspects of those demands. As one of the tasks of the democratic revolution, he supported the right to self-determination, and thought this included the option of separation, although he did not himself call for independence. Any internationalist perspective must recognise such a right, he argued, and to oppose the national liberation movements of stateless nations, in the name of internationalism, would be to play into the hands of the bourgeoisie of the dominant nation.[21]

174.
After their clear differences in 1931, when Nin regarded Maurín's positions as separatist and influenced by petit-bourgeois nationalism,[22] the two drew closer together after the creation of the

Workers' Alliances by the BOC. From 1933–34, the latter paid less attention to the radicalisation of certain strands of Catalanism, and more to the unity of the workers' government, and a balance sheet of the events of October 1934. This allowed the creation of the POUM, in September 1935, as a fusion of the BOC and the IC. Its position on the national question was a compromise, and as such was open to interpretation. It combined Maurín's view with a more pragmatic one, one that was less pro-independence and more autonomous of Catalan nationalism. The right to self-determination, including separation, was promoted as a way of guaranteeing closer unity among workers and as the basis for a future Confederation.

175.

The Catalonia of the future will be very different from the one that Nin and Maurín knew in the 1930s, in terms of social structure, class composition and the convergences and divergences between the workers' government and Catalanism. Maurín developed the more original thinking, in which Marxism touched on federalism and Catalan nationalism, with greater political concessions to the latter. Nin retained more strategic independence from nationalism, and limited himself to applying Lenin's approach to the reality of Catalonia. Neither's ideas can be applied mechanically to today's situation, without becoming static formulae. They need to be put in context if we are to understand them properly. But their reflections on strategy remain a historical inspiration, all the richer for having never really been applied.

176.

The end of the Civil War and the consolidation of the Franco dictatorship opened a new chapter in the history of Catalanism and the workers' government. It was precisely in the context of the anti-Franco resistance of the 1960s that class and nation could combine in a more durable fashion, even though by this time a majority of the Catalan industrial working class was made up of migrants from other parts of the Spanish state. The two came together to confront a dictatorship that was an enemy of both Catalanism and the working class. This convergence was led by the workers' movement, which defended Catalan national rights as its own, supporting in general a federal, plurinational position. The connection between the national and social questions took on a strategic and political importance never seen before. That does not necessarily mean that the identification of migrant workers with Catalanism ran very deep; but it was politically effective. 'Un sol poble', or 'a single people', was the best expression of this.

Alliances for 'a single people'

177.
'This task – this battle, I would call it – falls to all of us who, as citizens of this country of ours, want to live in democracy and freedom. [...] We should all demand that the Catalan language be taught to everyone, because in Catalonia no one should feel discriminated for reasons of language. Because every one of us, Catalans by descent and new Catalans, make up a single people [un sol poble]'.[23] These words by the historian and activist, Josep Benet, were delivered on 24 March 1968, in Badalona, alongside the philosopher Manuel Sacristán and the writer Joaquim Molas, as part of a tribute on the centenary of the linguist and father of modern Catalan grammar, Pompeu Fabra (1868–1948). Benet thereby coined the decisive slogan of *un sol poble*, which summed up what would become the dominant view within the anti-Franco movement in Catalonia, of the relation between the national question and the social question. Since then, the slogan of 'a single people' has become central to the political imagination of Catalanism, repeatedly reappearing at decisive moments, including in October 2017.

178.
Benet's 'single people' aimed to secure social cohesion and avoid divisions over origins and national identity between workers and other popular classes. His biographer, Jordi Amat, recalls that Benet was ideologically 'a nationalist committed to the popular classes',[24] for whom 'a single people' was a proposal for coexistence from the point of view of Catalanism. The impact of Catalonia's great floods on 25 September 1962 was a key moment in the development of his thought, and the particular moment when he first pronounced those words was marked by the controversy that followed the publication of the book Catalanism and Bourgeois Revolution, by Solé Tura. Benet's thinking sought unity among Catalans. That meant first ending the division between winners and losers after the Civil War. Then it meant uniting locals (including those who had migrated in earlier times) with the new immigrants who had arrived during Franco's time.[25] This twin unification shows the cross-class, nationalist logic of his thought. That is seen as an obvious strength by his very intelligent, and very moderate, biographer. In fact, however, it is at the root of his strategic limitations, limitations that in the end he shared with the PSUC and most of the workers' movement.

179.
In both Benet's use of the slogan *un sol poble*, and that of the Catalan United Socialist Party (PSUC), there were therefore contradictions, and a darker side. The desire for social cohesion that it expressed was mainly intended to avoid a split identity among the working classes and the people. But like all strategies involving a situation of national oppression, and like all appeals to 'the people', it could also take on a cross-class meaning and be understood in terms of class collaboration. It was certainly this slogan that became the banner of anti-Franco reformism, and which marked the historic National Day demonstration of 1977. But the political limitations of

the workers' movement should not lead us to minimise the strategic importance of avoiding a split over origins within Catalan society and its popular sectors. The concrete development of the 'single people' slogan should not overshadow its positive aspects, nor lead us to forget its other potential variants, which were not developed.

180.

'A single people' could also have been used to lead towards a radical break, as a way of bringing together those below in opposition to those above, as the banner for a strategy of uniting the workers in a struggle against Franco based on the workers' government. It was in this space between the 'single people' as it really existed, and the 'single people' as it might have existed, that the strategic debates of the time unfolded. These were dominated by reformist ideas. But that does not diminish the strategic importance of combining national and social demands. 'A single people' is not in itself the problem; only its consensual, cross-class, reformist interpretation. The strategic aim of avoiding a split between Catalanism and the workers' movement, as it existed during the Republic, was correct. Not so the reformist, step-by-step approach to this adopted both by Benet's social nationalism and by the PSUC, with its policy of national reconciliation and later of Eurocommunism. The spectre of a reformist 'single people' should not be allowed to cloud the glimmer of light offered by its revolutionary version.

181.

The debate on the national and social questions was shaped by the scale of migration after the civil war, especially from the 1950s onwards. People came to Catalonia from many different parts of the Spanish state, bringing with them a mix of local and regional identities.[26] The weight of these regional differences necessarily produced a pluralist identity, beyond the shared experience of being migrants and

Castilian speakers. Bit by bit, they became the majority of the Catalan working class, which underwent profound internal changes. By the end of the Franco era, most of the workers in and around the city of Barcelona were of migrant origin. They coexisted alongside smaller industrial enclaves where the workers were mostly Catalan in origin and more closely linked to Catalanism. These indigenous workers were more spread out geographically than the migrants, who were concentrated in the urban centres and industrial belts that were decisive in the struggle against Franco.[27] That is why the debate on immigration was so important, with obvious strategic ramifications.

182.
The policy of integration advocated by the left, and of synthesis between the national and the social, rested on an objective reality in which social integration was already developing in everyday life.[28] That is to say it was a deliberate political choice, that was neither inevitable nor mechanical, and was therefore strategically astute. But it was also based on a social reality that made it possible, and which left little room for opposition to Catalanism on the left, at a time when Spanish nationalism was associated with Franco. Nor was there space for anti-migrant racism, as the arrival of new workers coincided with rapid economic growth, when the class dimension was fundamental to the definition of collective identities.

183.
During the 1960s, with the growth of a workers' government opposed to Franco, following the miners' strikes in Asturias in 1962, and of the student movement after 1964, Catalanism took progressively a more social turn. The historical context forced conservative nationalists to shift towards the left, adopting social concerns that had been missing in the past.[29] Benet's journey from Christian democrat to fellow

traveller of the PSUC in the closing days of the Franco era illustrate well this move. But in spite of this movement towards social concerns, the Catalanism promoted by sectors of the middle class or even the bourgeoisie could never compete with the leadership of a left inspired by Marxism. It is in this context that we have to see Pujol's attempt to present himself as a social democrat, or as part of the centre left. In reality, his was always a conservative nationalism, set against progressive Catalanism and seeking to counter the influence of Marxism.[30]

184.
In this historical context, with the political and cultural hegemony of the workers' movement in the opposition to Franco, the nationalist bourgeoisie in Catalonia ended up adopting a definition of Catalan identity largely inspired by the former, and which was very different to the image of traditional, conservative nationalism. Pujol's famous phrase, that 'a Catalan is anyone who lives and works in Catalonia', was in this sense a formulation clearly influenced by the workers' government, and which reflected the adaptation of traditional nationalism to a social and demographic context that was very different to that of Catalonia before the war. Conservative positions were clearly on the back foot, in the face of the rise of ideas more or less inspired by Marxism.[31]

Transitions and dislocations

185.
The first elections to the Generalitat or regional government of Catalonia, in 1980, gave victory to the moderate, conservative nationalist, Jordi Pujol. He was the most prominent figure of the nationalist bourgeoisie that opposed Franco. He had active support from business and the media, in a concerted fear campaign over a possible victory of the communists of the Unified Socialist Party of Catalonia (PSUC), or their participation in a coalition government

with the Catalan Socialist Party (PSC). During the Transition, Pujol managed to become the political representative of the Catalan middle class, with a moderate nationalist proposal combined with immaculate anti-Franco and democratic credentials. He followed a dual strategy. Publicly, he cultivated the image of a firm and intransigent opponent of Franco, but with reasonable, moderate proposals. In private he sought to negotiate with those around Franco who wanted to open up the system.[32] He succeeded in making himself the guarantor of a peaceful, gradual, political change. This appealed to a moderate sector of Catalan society, whose opposition to Franco had been passive and expectant, and had never supported a radical break.[33] Later, once in power, the growth of neoliberal consumerism and individualism fed naturally into Pujol's project.

186.
Pujol's victory, in an election campaign marked by a climate of hysterical anti-communism and direct interference by the bosses, brought to a peaceful close of the Transition in Catalonia which the state had managed to channel three years earlier through its Operation Taradellas. That involved the restoration of the political institutions that had existed in Catalonia before the Civil War, including the Generalitat and the legitimate president in exile, Josep Taradellas, a progressive liberal who was decidedly anti-communist and authoritarian. Although this implied, paradoxically, de facto recognition for the republican legality prior to Franco, the restoration of Taradellas at the head of a regional government that was largely symbolic and without real powers, recognising the legitimacy of the monarchy and the denial of the right to self-determination, was a manoeuvre to neutralise the left and steer towards reform rather than rupture. Pujol initially mistrusted Operation Taradellas, fearing he might be eclipsed by the president in exile. But in fact, it helped to consolidate the movement around Pujol, at the expense of

the left. As Juliana has pointed out, the return of the president in exile implied the 'return of the nation'. It allowed a whole section of Catalan society, which was expectant but passive, 'to reconnect with Catalanism without having to go through the left'.[34]

187.
The rise of Pujol began a long phase of conservative hegemony in the Catalanist movement, and brought to an end the period of the 60s and 70s, when the workers' government was its backbone. Throughout his long time in office (1980–2003) Pujol combined a pragmatic, gradualist approach to the transfer of powers from the Spanish government with a style that was nationalist and conservative, even romantic. His administration concentrated on developing Catalan social identity through three means: linguistic immersion in the schools, which made sure students knew both Catalan and Castilian; the creation of a media system – TV and radio – in Catalan; and also, the promotion of a network of Catalanist and nationalist, cultural and social associations, which he wasn"t always able to control as much as he would have liked.

188.
The destruction of the workers' government after the Transition led to a shift in the concept of 'a single people'. Originally it had a double significance, social and national, expressing the desire to integrate immigrants from the rest of the Spanish state into the Catalan nation, within a framework of social integration. But once the Transition was complete, the link between the national and the social was broken through a dual process. The rise of Pujol in 1980, with an identity-based view of the nation and flavoured with economic neoliberalism, gravitated towards the middle class, while it gave second place to the working class, which had been the basis of opposition to Franco.

189.
With Pujol and his supporters in power from 1980, 'a single people' lost any sense of an intersection between class and nation. It became a simple assertion of a people without a state, a people skewed towards the Catalan-speaking middle class, in which the working class, especially that part of it coming directly or indirectly from Spanish migrants, came to play a secondary role, and was gradually written out of the national narrative and its media image. Pujol's election as regional president meant the Catalan identity was 'institutionalized' through the Generalitat and the Convergence and Union alliance, or CiU.[35] The synthesis between nation and class was also undermined by the collapse of the workers' movement, itself the result of neoliberal restructuring and the movement's own process of institutionalisation and bureaucratisation.

190.
The key to the separation of class from nation was the defeat of the workers' government during the Transition. A devilish combination between the left's institutionalisation and self-destruction, and neoliberal restructuring, changed completely the terms of the equation. Class identity itself was undermined, consigning the remnants of the workers' government to the periphery of Catalan politics, as the political, social and cultural driving force of society shifted towards the middle classes and a defeated and demoralised working class, in the throes of deep internal change, came to play a secondary role. Weakened from below, with its social base in tatters, and absorbed into the state from above, the historic workers' government ceased to embody a project of social change and a dynamic linkage between the identities of class and nation. Structurally, part of the Catalan working class was pushed aside, both socially and in terms of the prevailing national narrative; it came to feel increasingly disaffected with the Catalan institutions, albeit in a passive way.

191.
There is a view on the left, a minority one among Catalan organisations but more widely held among Spanish ones, that it was the workers' government's support for nationalism that helped to undermine its support within the working class. But in reality it was not the nationalism of the workers' organisations that lost them support in the Pujol era, but their institutionalisation and their adoption of social-liberal positions. With a movement that was weakened from below on the one hand, and on the other a conservative and neoliberal nationalist project, working people of Spanish migrant origin took second place; they were no longer active subjects, and their only link to both Catalan and Spanish institutions, and to political participation in general, was as voting fodder for the PSOE-PSC.

192.
The alternative was not to replace a 'Eurocommunist', Catalanist workers' government with radical, anti-nationalist workers' government (like the CNT in the 1930s), but rather with a radical, Catalanist one. Anti-capitalist and anti-neoliberal radicalism, seeking mobilisation in the streets rather than working through institutions, and with a commitment to Catalan national rights in a framework of freely adopted Catalan identity, were the roads that could have been taken, but were not, to revitalize the idea of 'a single people' and free it from its initial limitations.

Tensions and articulations

193.
In Catalonia from the 1980s, there coexisted two counterposed projects for national identity, one driven by the Catalan government, the other by the Spanish state itself. However, counterposed did not mean antagonistic or incompatible, only different and in a permanent state of complementarity with tension. The two worked in parallel but often

overlapped, sometimes harmoniously and sometimes in conflict. They were two counterposed projects, in the context of a society in which broad social sectors have experienced a dual national identity, with only mild antagonism.

194.
The consolidation of Pujol's movement relied on a narrative of historic resistance to national oppression and the rebuilding of what Franco had destroyed. Democratic Spain did not have a founding myth of anti-fascism like other European countries, because of the nature of the process of Transition. But opposition to Franco did play a decisive part in developing the official national narrative of Catalonia, in which not only the workers' government but also part of the bourgeoisie had anti-Franco credentials, even if there was no substantial and specific break with Franco's system.

195.
The Spanish nation-building process lost momentum in the institutions of Catalonia as the regional government developed its own institutional architecture, as powers were transferred and what became known as the 'Catalan media space'[36] was consolidated, with TV3 and Radio Catalonia taking the lead. For this reason, writers like Molina and Quiroga stress the importance of the private sphere as the main support for Spanish national identity in Catalonia, and as a counterweight to the Catalan nationalist project promoted by the Generalitat. However, both of them qualify their analysis by recognising that the Catalan public and semi-public spheres were not without Spanish national symbols, in a way that was relatively compatible with the Catalan identity. Sport, music and TV all reinforced an identification with the Spanish nation, although these informal expressions of identity 'lacked a narrative that was powerful enough to question that of Catalan nationalism'.[37]

196.
Their thesis is quite carefully considered, but it does tend to present the informal, private sphere as a bastion of resistance for a Spanish identity under threat from the growing Catalan nation-building process. It underplays the strength of the Spanish national project in the public and semi-public spheres in Catalonia, although it does recognise how this has been promoted through the state media. In fact, the power of the Spanish state media is fundamental for understanding the influence of the project to secure Spanish identity in Catalonia. It has been this system of state or public media that has done much more than the private sphere to support the Spanish national project in Catalonia. These writers' claim that Catalonia is a 'territory in which *de facto two states operate with counterposed national programmes, and since 2012, with opposing projects for the future*',[38] gives an artificial sense of symmetry. The Generalitat is in fact a sub-state entity, subordinate to the central state, as the events of October 2017 made very clear. In Catalonia, the central state has had an 'absent presence' and a 'present non-absence'.

197.
The evident hegemony of pro-independence positions in the Catalan media has led some critics[39] to talk about a 'spiral of silence'. They claim that opposing opinions are rendered invisible, using the well-known concept introduced by Noelle-Neumann to refer to situations where alternative opinions are self-censored by those who hold them, out of fear.[40] Apart from the fact that opinions that are not favourable to independence also appear in the Catalan media, albeit less frequently, this argument does not offer an accurate description of the Catalan situation, which is characterised by a dual media system, one Catalan and the other Spanish. The pro-independence movement, and earlier Catalan nationalism, have been dominant in the Catalan media space (which includes print media that do not favour

independence and have traditionally been in Castilian), but not in Catalonia as such, where the media scene in shared with Spanish media, which are massively opposed to pro-independence positions, and often privilege the most virulent expressions of such opposition.

198.
Although this split-media landscape, with two poles bearing different national, and largely linguistic, narratives, worked without too much conflict in practice, it does reflect the dysfunctional nature of the autonomous state, which had real plurality but could not achieve really plurinational institutions. A genuinely plurinational state would not be based on two parallel media networks and the coexistence of two distinct national narratives. Rather it would be anchored in a hybrid narrative and a mix of languages, where the state's own institutions and media would promote this plurinational and multilingual message. It would not delegate half of the work to the Catalan administration, in a division of labour that the conservative Catalan nationalists took advantage of to justify themselves and present themselves as the incarnation of Catalan identity.

199.
The lack of a pro-Spanish narrative as a coherent alternative to the nationalist narrative in Catalonia since the 1980s should not be seen so much as the result of a specific weakness resulting from the control of Catalan institutions by Pujol and his nationalists; rather it should be seen as the result of its own weakness *per se*, and of its inability to develop any credible and integrating vision of Spain, beyond its association with European modernity. The latter always resulted in a weak shared identity and narrative, which collapsed completely with the crisis and could not resist the neoconservative turn promoted by Aznar, failing in its attempt to overcome the fiasco of the truncated attempt to build a Spanish nation.

200.
In no way can you talk about the existence in Catalonia of two closed national communities, one of native Catalans and another of Spanish migrant origin. On the contrary, cultural and social mixing were very important from the 1960s onwards. These happened in the context of a social model with a shared cultural and national basis, accompanied by social and geographical mobility linked to employment in the public sector, wider access to higher levels of education and mass consumption. The success of the policy of linguistic immersion from the 1980s, which guaranteed education in Catalan, was the cornerstone of this. It produced a bilingual society in which everyone spoke and understood both Catalan and Castilian, even if some had the former as their native and main language, and others the latter.

201.
However, real and potential tensions clearly remained between the two national identities; there were different levels of identification with the Catalan or Spanish nationality, of consumption of the corresponding Catalan or Castilian-language media, and of symbolic and emotional connection with the Catalan or Spanish institutions. In this context, the development of a pro-independence movement divorced from any project for social change ended up leading to a social and political polarisation that was fed by the Spanish state institutions and media. The clearest expression of this came with the elections on 21 December 2017, whose results seriously undermined the concept of 'a single people', both sociologically and in terms of political strategy.

202.
In the imperfect intersection of class and nation, between class division and national identity, Catalonia has seen the emergence of a sort of double nation, of two nations split but overlapping diagonally. Both divisions can disappear or

deepen, depending on how they are seen and combined. To some extent, the institutions, cultural policies and media of the Spanish state and the regional government have favoured the creation of 'imagined communities', to use Benedict Anderson's famous phrase.[41] These are alternatives but not incompatible. They are partly included within each other and connected by a complex relation of complementarity and competition; overlapping imagined communities that are not mutually exclusive but in a state of tension; or indeed, one plural imagined community in which Catalonia and Spain cut across each other in an asymmetric way that varies from situation to situation. Either way, dual national identities have been the norm for most Catalans, even after the rise of the independence movement, and this reveals a society that combines difference and integration.

The legacy and spectre of Pujol

203.
The politics of Pujol, as Amat recalls very well, combined a 'a regionalist strategy in Spain to acquire more powers, which were then used to promote a nationalist political culture in Catalonia'.[42] The Spanish government's reluctance to transfer powers and the CiU's nationalist portayal of itself as a victim fed off each other. Pujol was able to turn the CiU into a permanent protagonist of this 'low-intensity conflict'.[43] It was a conflict with a large measure of theatrics, which allowed the CiU to appear as the indispensable key to Catalan politics and the embodiment of the Generalitat and the nation itself. Pujol's policy was always based on ambiguity and a double discourse, which he adapted according to the context and his audience. He almost always sounded more radical when he was speaking in public in Catalonia, and more moderate in his private negotiations in Madrid. The old Catalan nationalist idea of reforming Spain was ever present in Pujol's positions, but it was more tempered, in part because the modernisation

of Spain had already happened. One of his main characteristics was to seek to exert influence over Spanish policy, without ever taking part in a Spanish government, which would have undermined his strategy of playing the nationalist victim in Catalonia.

204.

The movement around Pujol was an essential prop for the state that emerged in 1978. Proof of this could be seen in the Banca Catalana scandal. It was a classic case of corrupt banking, in which the bank's directors got rich as they led the financial institution into bankruptcy, with taxpayers then having to pick up the tab. The government of Felipe Gonzalez, through the Attorney General, prevented the case from reaching the Supreme Court, blocked the investigation by the prosecutors, Carlos Jimenez Villarejo and Jose Maria Mena, and got the Barcelona Regional Court to close the case. It was a perfect portrait of how the system worked: on the one hand, the symbiosis between a justice system still in the mould of the Franco era, the political system and the financial elite; on the other, how the pro-autonomy nationalism of Pujol served the 1978 Spanish state, how it could be used by the central government in exchange for services rendered and to come, while presenting any attack on itself as an attack on Catalonia.[44]

205.

The Pujol project of Catalan nation-building was generally shared by the majority of Catalan political parties, even if they didn't share the specific nationalist justification used by Pujol, nor his conception of the nation. In other words, pro-Catalan sentiment had become accepted across Catalan society, but not so nationalism as a way of viewing the world. This was never the perspective of the workers' movement, which shared even less Pujol's view of what a nation was in general, and what the Catalan nation was in particular.

This is what caused the left's endless irritation with what it saw as Pujol's outdated cultural policies.

206.
Pujol combined an open, inclusive concept of the nation, using the slogan, 'Catalans are those who live and work in Catalonia', inspired by the practice of the workers' government, with a restricted vision of Catalan identity and hostility to any ideology that wasn't nationalist. This Catalan identity was deeply imbued with traditionalism and a romantic idea of the nation. The latter aspect increased during his time in government, after the workers' government and the left's narrative of emancipation had been rooted out. In a minority under Franco, Pujol's nationalism, based on culture and identity, became hegemonic after 1980. His policy combined 'metaphysics and opportunism', in the words of Jaume Lorés.[45] In other words, it used strong nationalist rhetoric alongside pragmatic deal-making with the state. It played deliberately the card of anti-Marxism in the first phase of the Transition, until this became unnecessary, after the PSC-PSOE abandoned any pretence of leftism, and the PSUC went into crisis. With the rise of Pujol, the pushing aside of the workers' government and the hegemony of the PSC on the left, the idea of the 'people of Catalonia', with the working class at its core, which had been dominant in the opposition against Franco, now evaporated, along with the political capacity of the workers' movement itself.

207.
From the moment Jordi Pujol came to power, the national question became the centrepiece of Catalan politics. It was his Convergence and Union coalition that set the agenda, while other political currents had to adapt to its terms and its definitions, playing on its terrain. This was based on a certain disregard or exclusion in relation to Catalan society, as the workers' government decomposed, the working class

fragmented, and individualism gained ground. The identification between Pujol = CiU = Catalonia succeeded in asserting its hegemony and assimilating the whole with the part. The CiU divided politics between 'us' and 'them', where 'us' was defined in terms of national identity and merged the Convergence with Catalonia itself. At its zenith, the CiU became the 'party of the nation',[46] capable of identifying itself with Catalonia, embodying an 'us' that appeared as an expression of the whole and representing the collective interests of the nation to the rest of the world.

208.
The end of the Franco era, the rise of Pujol and the decay of the workers' government partly split the Catalanist consensus within the anti-Franco movement. Not over nationalism itself, but over its political expression. Pujol's nationalism and left-wing Catalanism developed different projects, although they continued to rest on a shared foundation (the defence of Catalan self-government and language immersion) which was the central pillar of Catalan politics. At the same time, a new, activist nationalism was emerging, for example the activism around the Crida a la Solidaritat (Call for Solidarity) in 1981. This was the first social expression of an incipient independence movement.[47] But it was largely disconnected from the workers' government, which was in retreat as its social base suffered from an economic crisis that hit Catalonia particularly hard. In time, part of the left and the workers' government, while not actually breaking with the Catalanist consensus, began to feel uncomfortable with some of its basic premises. It was the creation of the Babel Forum in 1996, and later of Ciudadanos in 2006, by forces coming for the most part out of the PSC, some of them close to the PSOE, that marked the first serious break with the Catalanist consensus by some on the centre-left.

209.
Official Catalanism in Catalonia represented, according to Guillem Martinez,[48] a particular version of the Culture of Transition. 'Catalanism', like 'democracy' in the Spanish state, was the fetish word, unquestionable yet defined very narrowly in its practical sense. It is worth pointing out, however, that criticism of Pujol's particular version of Catalan nationalism should be made from within the sphere of Catalanism; it should avoid sliding into a falsely leftist rhetoric that ends up serving Spanish nationalism and the foundations of the 1978 Spanish state. What looks like an anti-Catalanist radicalism can easily come to legitimate the founding asymmetry in terms of national identities of the state that came out of the Transition, and forget the primarily defensive nature of Catalanism, in effect reducing it to its most traditionalist and conservative version.

210.
Pujol's long time in government from 1980 to 2003 allowed him to rewrite his own history and his role in the history of Catalonia, presenting himself as the guarantor of every democratic, political achievement made. The reality, however, is that Pujol and his movement played a secondary role in the anti-Franco movement, which was dominated by the workers' government. It didn't have a prominent part in the united mobilisation that characterised the last phase of the opposition to Franco, which was led by the Assembly of Catalonia set up in 1971. And in the first general elections in 1977 its results fell well short of Pujol's own expectations. Nor was the CiU the originator of the failed attempt to reform the Autonomy Statute, undertaken in 2003 as part of an alternative project of the Catalan left in competition with Pujol's project. Indeed, the pro-independence Procés has been the first big project for rupture or transition that the right-wing convergence has led, albeit precariously; and even that wasn't begun by the right.

211.

Within the anti-Franco movement, Pujol defined himself as a nationalist but not so much as an heir of the historical Catalanism. Pujol's anti-Franco nationalism rejected the legacy of Francesc Cambó's Regionalist League, which had collaborated with Franco, but also sought to minimise that of progressive Catalanism in the 1930s, especially that connected to the workers' movement. In its early days, it described its doctrine as 'personalist nationalism', which conceived of the nation in terms of 'wanting to be' *(voler ser)*, of 'wanting a way of being' *(voler tenir una forma de ser)*.[49] This was a specific reconstruction of syncretic, conservative nationalism, with a variable geometry of doctrine that combined elements of social Catholicism, conservatism, liberalism and pro-Europeanism, without adopting any precise ideological or historical affiliation. Later, after it came to power in 1980, Pujol's movement sought to wipe out the anti-Franco legacy of the nationalist workers' government led by the PSUC. This was only achieved later, especially from the 1990s onwards, as it consolidated itself in power and the Franco period receded into the past. As always happens, the winners write, or rewrite, history to suit themselves, using their control of the present to manipulate the past.

212.

A minor anecdote from October 2004, at the presentation of the memoirs of the writer Raimon Gil, who was a key figure in the anti-Franco Catholic nationalism of the 1950s, illustrates this rewriting of history. One of the speakers at the event stated unequivocally that 'Catalan universities were run by extreme Marxist teachers, like Manuel Sacristan and Pierre Vilar, who for several generations allowed our historic memory to be distorted and prevented Catalan youth from seeing and judging their past correctly'. This was a gross falsification. As Fernandez Buey points out,[50] it glosses over the obvious fact that not only were Catalan universities not run by Marxists, but in fact many left-wing academics were repressed, including Sacristan himself, who was expelled from the university in 1965 for political reasons (after earlier, in the fifties, being moved from the faculty to the Archbishopric of Barcelona).

213.
This incident, which happened just after the end of the Pujol era, reflected a changing tendency in the historical relationship between conservative nationalism and the intellectual milieu. The CiU had understood the importance of the world of culture to cement its hegemony, and promoted a decidedly traditionalist cultural policy based on a system of patronage. However, in its first period in power it did not see it as a priority to consolidate an intellectual milieu of its own that could dispute the hegemony of the PSC. Pujol's movement, and Pujol himself, were stubbornly anti-intellectual, a legacy they seemed to have inherited from Gali.[51] They saw the world of universities and intellectuals already lost to the centre-left. Pujol paid little attention to the development of doctrine. He had poor relations with intellectuals and while in power he didn't see it as strategic to win them over. The only important exception was the work of the Acta Foundation, created in 1987 by the politician, historian and cultural activist, Max Cahner (Councillor for Culture during Pujol's first period from 1980 to 1984). This aimed to create a space for young, nationalist intellectuals who wanted to modernise conservative Catalan nationalism, shed its traditionalist elements and successfully compete with the urban, cosmopolitan Catalanism of Maragall.[52]

214.
In the 1980s, the centre-left linked to the PSC controlled the university and the intellectual milieu, where Pujol's movement was weak and the Marxist left was in retreat. This began to change in the 1990s and into the 2000s. A new group

of neoliberal, nationalist intellectuals came to the fore, mixed with a new generation of politicians from Pujol's CDC, often under the auspices of organisations like the Trias Fargas Foundation (created in 1995) or the Catalunya Oberta Foundation (launched in 2001 by Lluis Prenafeta, a key Pujol supporter and the historic representative of the movement's liberal wing).[53] They sought to adapt to the Catalan context the neoliberal worldview that seemed unquestionable on the international stage in the first half of the 1990s. These were the days of what Ignacio Ramonet dubbed *la pensée unique*,[54] and this monolithic ideology of neoliberalism remained in good form through the second half of the nineties and into the new millennium, although it had begun to be questioned by the anti-globalisation movement and the first failures of globalisation.

215.
If Pujol's movement, while in government, neglected work on the intellectual front, once in opposition the battle of ideas (conducted in close collaboration with the Catalan nationalist media machine) became much more decisive.[55] Liberal nationalism was forced to go on the offensive. Institutions like the CatDem Foundation, started in 2007 under the leadership of Agusti Colminas, became key in this new phase; it had the aim of supporting Mas's refoundation of Catalanism and attracting independent and centre-left figures. Thus, a cultural and media apparatus emerged, which would reach its zenith with the beginning of the pro-independence Procés in 2012. This saw the conservative nationalist intelligentsia, now converted to support for independence, acquire cultural hegemony, albeit in a context after 2008 where neoliberal ideas were in crisis and facing widespread opposition from 'common sense'. This meant that the (neo)liberal, pro-independence movement had permanently to confront the spectre of 15-M and the anti-austerity protests, and the intellectual rebirth of critical ideas inspired by Marxism.

216.
Works like *Els Assassins de Franco (2005)* by Francesc-Marc Alvaro (who a couple of years earlier had published Ara si que toca, a detailed account of the end of the Pujol era),[56] were good examples of the thought and aims of this new strand of conservative nationalist intellectuals on the offensive. Several among them came to prominence, as young academics and journalists giving voice to a newly radicalised conservative support for independence. The most important would be Jordi Graupera. In the essay mentioned above, Alvaro launched a frontal attack on the whole anti-Franco, left-wing elite and its role in the change of regime and afterwards. Although his criticism was correct in the way it questioned the Transition, the part played by the left and the subsequent evolution of many former leftists, he really used those failures as a pretext to discredit the left as a whole, without distinction, from a liberal-conservative, anti-communist position in the best tradition of cold war warriors.

217.
In time the roles seemed to be reversed and it was the centre left, once the linchpin of the world of culture and the intelligentsia, that seemed to lose its voice, unable to come up with a convincing response to either the 15-M or the crisis of the state model. At the same time, following the earthquake of the Indignados movement in 2011, the 'outsider' left enjoyed an important new political and cultural visibility. Unfortunately, however, it fell short in the face of the growing pro-independence process and was unable to develop a convincing, updated strategy for 'a single people'. Either it found itself alone within the movement for independence and lost contact with those outside it, or it remained a passive observer outside the Procés and was left behind by the polarisation generated during the October days.

218.
Pujol and his project for building a nation from 1980 onwards have a contradictory relationship with the emergence of the

pro-independence movement. The latter would not have happened without the former, which laid the foundations of a Catalan political and cultural nation-building that was key to the launching of a mass independence movement, at a moment when a Spanish nationalist offensive combined with economic crisis. The strength of this process to build a Catalan national identity explains why, years later, it became the social and historical backdrop for the independence movement. But its weakness also shows how the independence movement was born from frustration and a feeling of political, social and existential anxiety about the future. In other words, the independence movement exists because it was preceded by the strong development of a Catalan nation-building process but also because this was structurally weak in the face of a state that never accepted plurinationality in a consistent and positive way. The independence movement is thus simultaneously an expression of strength and of weakness. The Convergence governments produced a cultural and political context that favoured their nationalist project. But in the end, it left them behind, as a result of that contradictory combination between their comparative success in consolidating Catalan social identity and the failure of the Spanish state to become a truly plurinational state.

219.
From Pujol to the Procés, the CDC took a long journey towards support for independence. Beginning at the end of the 1990s, the turn became sharper in the 2000s, especially after the party went into opposition in 2003 and had to reinforce its political agenda in order to compete with the ERC. Its support for independence remained gradualist and pragmatic. In fact, it was more a programmatic change in the party's theory and strategic focus than in its political culture (as was clear in its 2006 pact with Zapatero for a minimal statutory text). In November 2007, Artur Mas launched his proposal for the 'Gran Casa' (Big Home) of Catalanism, aimed at positioning the CDC at

the centre of a renewal that was intended to reach beyond the party itself. The key to Mas's case was Catalonia's right to decide, as a lever to achieve 'full nationhood'. These ideas were made official at the party's 2008 congress, whose platform did not include the expressions 'independence' or 'own state'.

220.

Following the ruling by the Constitutional Court on 28 June 2010, the CDC moved into the new, post-autonomism phase with the proposal for a fiscal pact. This was the centrepiece of its campaign for the elections that autumn, the cornerstone of exercising the right to decide, and the first step in a 'national transition' whose final destination remained uncertain. Under pressure because of the policy of public spending cuts, the 15-M revolt and the Mareas (Tides, the social protests against cuts) that followed, the CDC turned further towards a pro-independence position; it needed a narrative that would give meaning to its policies and provide a perspective beyond merely managing neoliberal austerity. Its Reus Congress in March 2012 approved the aim of 'our own state', but without yet mentioning independence as an objective. But this was the target already adopted by most of the party's supporters. This evolution was completed with the 11-S demonstration later that year, when Mas, without using the word independence, embraced the call for a referendum on self-determination in the next parliament. To this end, he appealed for an 'exceptional majority' in the polls, which he brought forward to 25 November 2012.

Language wars

221.

It was at a state school in Santa Coloma de Gramenet, and the year was 1982. The school was called Rosello-Porcel, and that is where the plan for 'linguistic immersion' in the state education system was hatched. It was implemented the following academic year, 1983–4, in 19 schools of the mainly

Castilian-speaking municipality, on the outskirts of Barcelona. The initiative came from a group of parents and teachers, who wanted teaching to be done in Catalan, while guaranteeing the teaching of Castilian as well. They wanted children to be competent in both languages. It was this combination of citizen initiative and support from the town hall, which was run by the PSUC, that led the Catalan regional government to roll out the immersion programme in this municipality.

222.
Contrary to what is sometimes now said by people with a faulty memory of history, linguistic immersion was not something imposed by conservative Catalan nationalists. It was a strategic commitment shared by the workers' government, a strong trade union and social movement around education, and by parents of migrant origin who wanted their children to speak Catalan in order to avoid them being treated as second-class citizens. In fact, in the parliamentary debates between 1980 and 1983 which led to the passing of the Law on Linguistic Normalisation in 1983, the initial proposal of the CIU was to make Catalan the language of education, but it left the door open for exceptions at some schools, which could have led to a de facto dual linguistic system. It was the position of the left-wing parties, the PSUC and the PSC, which in the end prevailed, with the aim of avoiding any possible social or linguistic segregation in schools.[57]

223.
Linguistic immersion was, therefore, the result of a desire for equality and an anti-segregationist culture, in which the debate over language always had a social and class backdrop. This made it possible to avoid the segregation of pupils according to language, and therefore a linguistic duality defined largely in terms of class and urban space. It was a key mechanism for social integration. Overall, it has been regarded as a model by international bodies like the European Commission's High

Level Group on Multilingualism, set up in 2005, which called it an example to be followed in other countries with similar language situations.

224.
Three decades after the beginning of linguistic immersion and the so-called policy of 'normalisation', the evolution of Catalan usage had been contradictory. Schooling in Catalan, which became a full teaching language in the 1990s, made for widespread knowledge of the language; the Catalan-language media created a symbolic universe in Catalan; its use by the institutions turned it into a language with prestige. But its use as the everyday language of society lagged behind. Undoubtedly the biggest achievement was to avoid the crystallisation of two separate linguistic communities, while ensuring a good knowledge of both languages.

225.
At the same time, contrary to the usual propaganda of the Spanish right, all official reports show that the level of students' competence in the Castilian language in Catalonia is on a par with the average across the Spanish state, and above that in some monolingual autonomous regions. Another indication comes from the results of university entrance exams in Catalonia. Marks in Castilian have been systematically higher than in Catalan for more than a decade and a half.[58] Immersion has not at all been a means of eliminating Castilian in Catalonia, as its detractors have tried to make out.[59] Rather it has been a way of preventing segregation and consolidating real bilingualism.

226.
The nature of the Spanish state consolidated this bilingual reality, but in separate, institutional and media compartments. It reinforced two different linguistic-institutional ecologies: the institutions of the Generalitat and the public and private media in Catalan, on the one hand, and on the

other, the institutions of the Spanish state and the public and private media in Castilian, located mainly in the context of the Spanish state, but in some cases also located in Catalonia. But what was decisive was that these two compartments operated within a society that was bilingual and linguistically integrated, not split into two communities. If there had been a state of a genuinely plurinational character, the linguistic division between the spheres of the Catalan regional government and the Spanish administration could have been more intertwined, more mixed. It is this fixed, institutional duality that has been the decisive problem. But its original sin is the lack of plurinationality in the character of the state. This generates a defensive, pro-Catalan reaction within the regional institutions of Catalonia, using nationalist arguments as justification.

227.
From the start, the Spanish nationalists in Catalonia always had linguistic immersion in their sights. One of their first steps was the Manifesto of the 2300 in 1981, which was a somewhat isolated initiative. It met with opposition from the entire Castilian-speaking Catalan intelligentsia, and was outstripped by the impact of the pro-Catalan language activity of the recently created Crida per la Solidaritat. In the 1990s, there was a second chapter in the 'language war'.[60] It started, symbolically, with the front page of the ABC newspaper on 12 September 1993, under the headline, 'Just like Franco, but in reverse: the persecution of Castilian in Catalonia'. It mobilised a small number of organisations that were ideologically diverse but had considerable influence in the media. It came to a partial stop in 1996, when the PP needed an agreement with Pujol's CiU to form a government, and in exchange sacrificed its leader in Catalonia, Vidal-Quadras, who had been one of the promoters of the language war. Nonetheless, the PP did position itself outside the consensus on language, and opposed the Law on Linguistic Normalisation adopted in 1998. This first split did not hinder the process of linguistic

normalisation, but it did normalise opposition to it. It meant the normalisation of the struggle against normalisation.

228.
The real impact of the language war on Catalan society was rather limited. It was more important as a propaganda tool for the Spanish right to bolster its anti-Catalan message outside Catalonia than having a real effect on Catalan politics. However, it did mark a turning point, after which propaganda on the language question became a recurrent theme of the Spanish political and media landscape. As such, it began a period of institutional attacks by the state to destabilise the Catalan linguistic model, and it gave rise to a social and political bloc in Catalonia which, albeit a minority, would make the fight over language one of its main battlegrounds. Its next step would be, as we mentioned earlier, the creation of the Babel Forum in 1996, which this time was located more clearly in the cultural world of the centre-left.

229.
In the early days after Franco, much of the Spanish left intelligentsia supported the restoration of the Catalan language. But as time went on its sympathy for Catalanism, and especially its language policy, dissipated. If the Law on Linguistic Normalisation, in 1983, was widely supported outside Catalonia, by 1998, when the Catalan government put forward a new Law on Language Policy, the situation was different. The distance from the Franco era, the consolidation of Spanish nationalism, even of an open kind, the fact that the workers' government was no longer the leading force for change, and the perception that Catalan was no longer a persecuted language, but rather the language defended by the conservative Catalan government, all contributed to this change of attitude. The confusion of Pujol with Catalonia, so carefully constructed by the CiU to turn him into the embodiment of the nation, had its effects outside Catalonia too.

230.

Inside Catalonia as well, the change in the status of Catalan, from a language banned by Franco to one promoted by the Generalitat, led to a change in how people saw the language debate. Pujol's cultural nationalism and its traditionalist approach aided this change, accentuated by the disappearance of social and political leadership from the working class, and its widespread depoliticisation. Some sectors within Catalonia began to see Catalan as a language of the establishment. Divisions and doubts over language multiplied.

231.

Linguistic immersion at school has been widely accepted by the Catalan left. However, there has been some controversy, more intellectual than really political, among some on the left, about other aspects of linguistic normalisation. These include the use of language in the media, in the institutions, in cultural policy and the political life of the left itself. In a context where the Catalan language had been consolidated, but under the control of Pujol's conservative nationalism, some progressive nationalists warned of the negative consequences of its language policy, in so far as it could alienate and cause disaffection among part of the population. This was the argument, for example, in 2002, of Manolo Vasquez Montalban, for whom 'the Generalitat's cultural policy made the mistake of assuming that it only needed to worry about the linguistic normalisation of Catalan, without taking a position on Castilian. This gave the impression that the language policy aimed to convert Catalan into the main language.'[61]

232.

The paradox is that, in spite of giving the impression it wanted to turn Catalan into the main language, the reality on the ground was different. The linguistic policy in defence of Catalan was essential to avoid its disintegration, in a context where the central state did not promote multilingualism at all. That is separate from the fact that support for Catalan and immersion at school went hand in hand, for the CiU, with a rather romantic, nationalist discourse that made the language question one of the key themes of a permanent nationalist campaign to benefit itself. Pujol's movement had a very limited and traditional idea of culture, and of Catalan culture in particular. Its narrow definition of Catalan identity never could or wanted to understand Catalan culture in a plural and pluri-lingual way, mistakenly leaving in a limbo those expressions of Catalan culture expressed in Castilian. The contradiction, therefore, is that the language policy of the regional government did not make Catalan dominant, but it did give that impression, by presenting itself as part of a nationalist cultural policy with a restricted notion of Catalan identity, in a situation where there was no alternative narrative to challenge this conservative nationalism from the left.

233.
With the alliance between class and nation undone, the left marginalised and the nationalist right in the ascendant, the conversion of the region's institutions and media to the Catalan language helped to distance and alienate relatively (it is important to emphasise the 'relative' here) part of the Catalan population, of Castilian-speaking origin, from the Catalan institutions. The basic problem behind these negative effects of imposing the Catalan language were not a result of the policy of linguistic normalisation itself, but rather of the partial rupture in the dynamic relationship between class and nation, and in the alliance between the social and the national that had been embodied in the anti-Franco slogan of 'a single people'.

234.
Among the Catalan left, there tend to be two counterposed and mistaken attitudes towards this. The first is to ignore

the issue and avoid the problems it entails. The second is to misinterpret it by confusing causes and consequences, and as a result to question the use of the Catalan language in the Catalan media and institutions, proposing for example that they should become bilingual. This ignores the fact that at the Spanish state level the institutions and media are not bilingual, and in fact this state only promotes the Castilian language. As a result, that would be a death sentence for Catalan, which would be left with no strong institutional support at all.

235.
This second attitude often goes along with a defence of Castilian as the language for political propaganda and activism, arguing that this is a remedy that can reconnect with those sectors of the population that had been lost. But 'using Castilian' systematically (as opposed to using it in certain circumstances) doesn't solve the underlying problem, and just creates another, which is making it impossible to consolidate Catalan at all. Such consolidation has long been understood within a bilingual, Catalan and Castilian, framework, and since the 1990s a plurilingual one. The problem has not been that the message is in Catalan, but the lack of credibility of the messenger (that is the workers' movement and the traditional organisations of the left, now a caricature of what they once were), and of the ways those messages are communicated, by a left that is inward-looking and absorbed by the structures of representative politics. False shortcuts at the level of communication cannot compensate for strategic weaknesses.

236.
Language has not played a central part in the Procés that began in 2012, in contrast to the early post-Transition period. Only after the October crisis, when right-wing, Spanish nationalists began to talk of the need to use Article

155 to undermine the Catalan educational and media system, did the language question recover its earlier importance. In general, whether for tactical reasons or out of conviction, much of the pro-Independence movement has taken on board the idea of a bilingual Catalonia, with Castilian as a joint official language in any future independent state.[62] But that attitude has always existed alongside another, more nationalist one, which tends to see Catalan as the only national language, and Castilian as an anomaly, the result of historical imposition. That was the more or less explicit view of those who, in March 2016, signed the manifesto, *For a true process of linguistic normalisation in an independent Catalonia*, launched by the Koiné group (meaning 'common language' in classical Greek).[63] That was a gross tactical mistake, which only gave succour to anti-Catalanist sentiment. The underlying problem with such an approach was that it seemed to privilege Catalonia as a metaphysical entity over and above the people who actually lived there, and to fetishise the idea of its true historical origins, which were interrupted by a later, 'anomalous' evolution. Castilian, according to this view, is permanently reduced to a foreign body, and not a reality that is also part of Catalonia's history.

237.
The current language debate takes place in a Catalonia that, since the beginning of this millennium, has been much more than bilingual, with about 300 languages being spoken. The most important of these, after Catalan and Castilian, are Arabic, Romanian and Amazigh or Berber,[64] without counting the growing use of English as a foreign language. Successive regional governments have adopted measures to ensure that the role of Catalan in the educational system is not undermined and that Castilian becomes, by default, the only common language in schools. These have included the school adaptation workshops (in the final period of the Pujol administration) and the 'Plan for Language and

Social Cohesion' or the 'Plan to Update the Programme of Linguistic Immersion', during the Tripartite governments of Maragall and Montilla.

238.
Linguistic pluralism has been accepted by Catalan nationalists as already part of the structure, and as such is no longer up for discussion. It has been seen as a change in the context, which means the challenge is to develop a social model where everyone can speak and understand Catalan and Castilian, while many will also use their own, different languages. Nonetheless, nobody has drawn the concrete political and institutional conclusions from this; learning and using other native languages (as distinct from English) tends to be seen as something that belongs to the private or community sphere, and not as something that the educational system should guarantee, in a more than symbolic way. Bit by bit, however, these other languages are in practice becoming part of the educational landscape.[65] This remains an outstanding challenge for any strategic thinking that seeks to combine the defence of Catalan with an inclusive kind of Catalanness, with social pluralism and an intransigently multilingual activism in opposition to any kind of *monolingual anthropology*.

Emergence of the orange people

239.
The 21-D victory of the Ciudadanos party, when it won 1,109,732 votes (25.37 per cent) in the Catalan elections of December 2017, was achieved largely by mopping up the right-wing, Spanish nationalist vote at the expense of the PP. It also benefited from a higher turnout, and captured many of those popular and working-class voters who would previously have abstained. It was favoured by tactical voting against Independence, which adopted the mantle of Spanish identity and won good results in both the upmarket neighbourhoods and the workers' districts

of the big cities. It was both a defensive and reactive vote based on identity, and a vote for order based on fear. The rise of Ciudadanos expresses two underlying dynamics. It is a devilish combination between an exclusionary logic of national identity and the political and cultural destruction of the working class. Yet to a considerable extent its vote was probably temporary, or at least limited to regional elections. It would probably not be repeated at municipal or general elections.

240.
The success of the orange party[66] was based on a mixture, firstly, of a discourse in favour of democratic regeneration and neoliberal modernisation, which attracts both the better-off classes and the most conservative sectors of the working class, which embrace an individualist mentality of meritocracy, and secondly, an appeal to a Spanish, anti-independence identity which historically had been built on the basis of marshalling origins and language (Castilian-speaking Catalans of Spanish origin) to shape both the individual and the collective political identity. Ciudadanos is, broadly, a Macron-style project of mainstream, neoliberal modernisation, which can present itself as outside the traditional political class. The appeal to identity that underpins its electoral support and the development of its policies is similar to the logic of the far right in Europe (but in this case it is not an assertion of national identity in opposition to foreigners, but of the dominant Spanish national identity in opposition to Catalan identity, which is seen as inferior and subordinate to the former).

241.
The electoral victory of Ciudadanos was based on its ability to make visible those who felt ignored, and an appeal to those who felt left out of the Catalan national narrative, and especially the pro-independence one. The feeling of exclusion under the earlier, pro-autonomy version of Catalan nationalism

exploded as rebellion under the pro-independence version, which was seen as a threat. The demonstrations against the Procés were not non-Catalan, but the expression of another Catalonia that didn't feel included by the pro-independence movement and subordinated its Catalan identity to its Spanish one. Ciudadanos did not deny Catalan national identity, but treated it as secondary to Spanish identity. Its assertion of Catalan identity was a paradoxical one. On the one hand it spoke to the feeling of exclusion and marginalisation among its potential audience, saying that they too were Catalans, yet it also saw Catalonia and this Catalan identity as subordinate to the Spanish nation. In other words, Ciudadanos offered a different national narrative, which combined the demand for full respect for Catalan identity with its subordination to Spanish identity.

242.

We need to grasp both aspects of this position, to avoid confusing it with either a crude rejection of Catalan identity or a sincere defence of another possible Catalan identity. The policy of Ciudadanos is not to deny Catalan identity but to offer a version of Catalan identity that is dependent on Spanish identity. This is a dual but asymmetric identity, where the Spanish identity undermines the persistence of the Catalan identity and renders it merely complementary. Its language policy is a good illustration of this. In the name of defending bilingualism, it conceals a policy that, in the medium term, would condemn Catalan to a secondary status and to crisis, accentuating its far less favourable position compared with Castilian.

243.

One of the attractions of Ciudadanos in Catalonia is its position as a (false) outsider, separate from the Catalan establishment, and embodying a reality that is distinct from Catalonia's official public sphere. But when we analyse this, we should remember that something similar has happened with Cuidadanos throughout the Spanish state, where Rivera's party has managed to project itself as something apart from the political system and the traditional elites. The difference is that in Catalonia, Ciudadanos can also use the national question and language to strengthen its anti-establishment profile. But this factor alone does not explain its success. In any case, once again the solution cannot lie, neither for tactical reasons nor as a matter of principle, in trying to compete with Ciudadanos on its own terrain. We need to (re)build a political movement for change that can organise the subaltern classes beyond their relationship with the media and with elections.

Cracks in 'a single people'

244.
The current independence movement has taken up again the idea of 'a single people', but with a different meaning and stripped of its original class dimension. So says the historian, Marc Andreu,[67] an expert on the anti-Franco workers' government and the historical evolution of working-class neighbourhoods. However, he fails to lay responsibility for this decoupling of the social and the national at the door of the left and its increasingly bureaucratic and social-liberal character. The slogan thus becomes empty rhetoric, an attempt by the independence movement to present itself as the embodiment of 'all' the people, but without developing an effective strategy to achieve that. That is, it is more a communicational slogan than a strategy. It is this contemporary split between the nationalist project and the social question that has broken the idea of a single people in half, preparing the ground for a fracture over identity and giving a boost to Ciudadanos. For there to be a single people in the sense that there is a minimum consensus in society about social and cultural norms and a collective identity, there must also be a single people in terms of equality and social justice. That has been completely

eliminated in the current economic crisis, something the independence movement has never faced up to. And this is the Achilles' heel of its basic strategy.

245.
In this sense, the strategy of the independence movement has been weaker than that of the workers' government in the 1960s and 70s. The latter knew how to combine the social and the national levels, while the independence movement has rolled out its proposals on the assumption that these are sufficient in themselves, and that the social question can be ignored. Initiatives like Sumate, which tried to win support for independence among Castilian-speaking Catalans, or the promise made by Oriol Junqueras, the Chairperson of the ERC,[68] that Castilian would remain a joint official language in any independent state, have not been enough to bridge a certain sociological gap. And, despite the good intentions behind them, they are a sorry caricature of a serious policy to win grassroots support in the post-working-class suburbs and other more Castilian-speaking communities. That would inevitably mean questioning the premise of independence pure and simple, or 'first independence, then the rest'.

246.
Now a shadow of its former self in terms of implantation and political capacity, and having lost its central role in history, the workers' government was also unable to do what it had done fifty years ago. The same goes for the new forces that emerged from the 15-M Indignados movement, which saw the independence movement as an annoying anomaly that interfered with its strategic vision, and not as a challenge that required it to adjust that vision. The spectre of past alliances hangs over the inconsistencies and omissions of the present. The spectre of a previous 'single people' hovers above its current, twofold caricature, whether that

be the propaganda version of the independence movement, or the open opposition to this expressed by the heirs of the historical workers' movement, who in the process are paralysed by another spectre, as they grossly idealise and romanticise their own past.

247.
The lack of attention to working-class neighbourhoods by the independence movement is part of a long tradition of such neglect. It began with the institutionalisation of the workers' government after the Transition and its turn to social-liberalism, and Pujol's conservative nationalism based on the middle class and the less urban areas of Catalonia. That was followed by the cosmopolitan, social-liberal Catalanism of Maragall which tried to win the support of middle-class, former Convergence supporters, against a background of the exclusion of working-class communities after decades of neoliberalism. This synthesis of Catalanism and social-liberalism held little interest for most of the working class in the post-industrial suburbs, who watched passively and from a distance the whole process of reform to the autonomy statute. On the other hand, the new left that emerged from the 15-M, Podemos and Comunes based a large part of its success on winning back support in working-class neighbourhoods. However, it did this in a superficial, electoralist and media-driven way, which did not sink deep roots and could do little to reverse the historical tendencies of social, cultural and political disintegration. As a result, it was very vulnerable to changes in the situation. In fact, this was a kind of positivist-progressive electoralism, which worked well as long as it was swimming with the current unleashed by the 15-M explosion. But it proved unable to develop in an adverse situation where it did not control the agenda or the terms of the debate.

248.

In 1845 the British conservative politician, Benjamin Disraeli, published his novel, *Sybil, or The Two Nations*, about the miserable conditions of the English working class.[69] Since then, the idea of 'two nations' has been used repeatedly to refer to the social divide. John Dos Passos would make another classic reference to it in *The Big Money*, the third volume of his U.S.A. trilogy. There, referring to the inequalities of wealth and power between the rich and the poor, he said 'we are two nations'.[70] It is useful to repeat this in the current debate in Catalonia, because it points to the close link needed between the social and national questions in order to think about the meaning of 'a single people' in a way that is emancipatory and strategically useful. The very idea of 'a single people' needs to be updated in relation to the social changes in Catalonia: the fragmentation of society, the cultural changes, the eruption of feminism since the 1970s, the growth of individualism, and especially the impact of new migration from outside the Spanish state. 'A single people that is plural'? 'A people of peoples'? In any case, it implies a desire to find shared points of reference in the framework of cultural plurality and diversity, and of the struggle against a matrix of specific oppressions. Working in this direction means going beyond the strategic limits of the independence movement and the passive approach of those on the left who point out those limitations, but have no plan for overcoming their own and intervening in the real process.

249.

'A single people' with no class dimension becomes empty rhetoric, an attempt to be 'everything', but with no way of developing a concrete strategy to achieve it. It doesn't come out of any real struggle or organisation or proposal to link politically different mobilisations and social sectors. It is not an attempt to consolidate a dynamic coming out of experiences that are diverse, but which have enough common ground to make that possible. It is based solely on the idea of linear growth in the number of people supporting independence, and the impossibility of any alternative proposal emerging. It does not confront the limitations of its own project. In other words, 'a single people', as used by the 'mainstream' independence movement, comes closer to self-deception than to *strategic imagination*.[71]

250.
The slogan of 'a single people' has also been used by those around Catalunya en Comú to justify their policy of seeking to build a broad majority in favour of the right to decide, but opposed to 1 October and the pro-independence road map. 'A Single People' was precisely the title of an article by Pablo Iglesias and Xavier Domenech,[72] then secretary general of Podemos and national coordinator of Catalunya en Comú respectively, in which they recalled the complex and plural nature of 'a single people' as a political subject bringing together a political and social majority. Although their combination of the social and national dimensions within 'a single people' brought them back to the original formulation of the slogan, their proposals were so abstract and lacking in any credible road map, and so passive in relation to the independence movement, that they lost any strategic value. It seemed more as if they were using this stale formula to justify their lack of policy, as a kind of *anti-strategic* policy or a strategy of no policy.

251.
The paradox of the twin limits in the contemporary use of 'a single people' is that the independence movement, and Catalan nationalism in general, often forgets that the left and the workers' government played a decisive part in blocking any hint of a split along identity lines in Catalan society. Partly, this denial of the historical role of the workers' movement is

a result of its own current weakness and its lukewarm attitude to independence. The remains of what was the workers' movement, and the organisations that to some degree are part of its legacy, do lay claim to its historical achievements, but in the form of a frozen memory, completely disconnected from their current political practice. That practice is characterised by a timid approach to both the national and the social questions, and by an absence of any real attempt to organise workers and the popular classes for anything more than elections, of any real intervention in society beyond the media and the institutions, and of any new ideas about class and nation. The independence movement in general, and the pro-independence left in particular, has oscillated between giving up on the post working-class Catalonia of (direct or indirect) Spanish origin as a lost cause, and simply denying the problem. Meanwhile the non-independence left has confined itself to pointing out the problem, even exaggerating it, and using it to justify inaction or, at most, to celebrate its own 'glorious' past.

252.
The decisive question is how to define the notion of a 'people'. The challenge is to make it not just about identity, but to give it a definition as a political subject aiming at emancipation, one that is directly associated with an understanding of its internal plurality and the plurality of oppressions and dominations that affect it. This means not just making a list of undifferentiated woes, nor dissolving the people into an amorphous mass where both class and nation evaporate, but forging strategic links. In fact, the challenge is to define the 'people' in terms of a combination between class, nation, gender and ethnicity; as a synthesis between different situations of subalternity and oppression and resistance to exploitation, not as separate entities that combine from the outside, but as realities that see themselves as connected from the inside. In this sense 'a single people' is the expression of

a plural articulation of the subaltern. We are not very far here from the classic formulation, 'the people united will never be defeated', or the 'tous ensemble' of the French strikes in 1995. This is a people that needs to define itself strategically in terms of a class politics and of the subaltern whose stuttering starting point was the Indignant explosion against austerity in 2011. It is also a people that needs to find a complex combination with the demand for independence embodied in the 'people of the Procés', who themselves face the challenge of avoiding any nativist split in Catalan politics, between the locals (with their twin identity as Catalan and Spanish) and the new intercontinental migrants, and of expressing the full plurality of these oppressed conditions. What is needed is a synthesis of syntheses, a combination of combinations.

253.
'A single people' in its classic version aimed to combine class and nation in a situation where there was a workers' movement and class politics, but organised around a subject and an identity that was masculine and essentially industrial, and a nation whose main challenge was to bring together native Catalans with those 'other Catalans' coming from domestic migration within the Spanish state. Now the class is being reshaped, as a political subject and a collective identity that is more diverse and mainly located in the service sector, that is both masculine and feminine and ethnically more mixed. At the same time, the nation is no longer just a combination of two realities (those of Catalan origin and those coming from Spanish migration), but a more varied combination of origins, languages and ethnicities. Finally, class and nation now share their leading role in the struggle with other situations and identities, which demands a more complex conception of both, and stronger links between the struggle against exploitation and all other forms of oppression.

254.
Appeals to the people have abounded in Catalan politics. They have included appeals to an undifferentiated people, centred on the middle class and defined exclusively in terms of its national identity (the mainstream independence movement); to a people conceived in terms of class and from below, but too homogeneously in terms of nationality and identity (CUP); to the populist conception of an amorphous people, mobilised for electoralist purposes but without any internal, strategic links (Podem-Podemos); or through a representative-electoral appeal based on ideas of citizenship and identity and an appeal to common interests (Barcelona and Catalunya en Comú). But the weaknesses in these different conceptions of the people reduce this, for different reasons, to a strategic spectre: a spectral people that reflects a spectral strategy – no doubt in different degrees, with some merit in the approaches of the CUP and the Comunes.

Images of the nation

255.
The 1980s and 90s were marked by a collision between the culturally decrepit nationalism of Pujol, which had broken free from the ideological influence of a workers' movement in decline and reaffirmed its more traditional nationalist colours, and the liberal-progressive cosmopolitanism of Maragall. The latter sought to reach out from Barcelona to the world and saw Catalonia as a small, closed place, although in the end it had to embrace a more conventional nationalism in order to engage with Catalan politics. This combat, or semblance of combat, between nation and the universal republic, between a traditional Catalonia and one that was open to the world, reflected well the spirit of the times and the vacuum left by the left after the Transition.

256.
In second half of the final decade of the last century, under the leadership of Josep Lluís Carod-Rovira, then secretary general of the ERC, the moderate left, pro-independence current of

nationalism underwent an important theoretical renewal, stressing a pluricultural, integral conception of the nation, based on citizen rights. It was, to borrow a phrase from Josep Ramoneda, a kind of 'secularisation' of pro-independence nationalism,[73] positing itself as an alternative kind of nationalism, one that was open, modern and social-democratic, in contrast to the federal cosmopolitanism of Maragall and the closed, backward-looking nationalism of Pujol.

257.
It was, however, an alternative that was trapped in its own nationalist cosmovision, as became clear during the 15-M protests in 2011. Carod-Rovira himself, upset by the lack of interest in self-determination exhibited by the Indignados, wrote a sinister article defining those occupying the squares as 'Spaniards' and urging them to go and protest 'in their country'. Obviously, this contradicted any inclusive vision of the nation and sought to discredit the massive rebellion against financial power by using arguments that served the interests of the right-wing Convergencia in power.[74] In fact, his words reflected the discomfort of Catalan nationalism and the pro-Independence movement, both of the right and the left, at a movement that galvanised social discontent along lines that had nothing to do with the national question and which operated at the level of the Spanish state.

258.
More recently, Carod-Rovira has proposed moving beyond the debate over identity, towards one about sovereignty: 'Those in favour of Independence should be promoting a vision of the country and of society which is not nationalist or essentialist or ethnic, not based on where citizens came from, but on sovereignty and the development of the future'. The nation, he goes on, should be understood 'not as something mythical, supernatural or unchangeable, but as a shared space of interests, points of reference and, yes, of emotions. Sweden, to take one example, is not only the

homeland of the Swedish language and culture, but also of welfare, equality of opportunities and civil rights.' This implies a Catalan national identity that is open, inclusive and in development: 'Catalan national identity, the current collective identity, is an open, dynamic project-identity, under permanent construction. I am talking about a Catalan society with very diverse origins, of a single people that includes the existence of shared and simultaneous identities'.[75] This series of statements sums up the virtues of this renewal in Catalan nationalist thinking which left behind Pujol's romanticism in favour of a civic, citizen nationalism, but also its inherent limits. These are the result of projecting the nation as the main framework for thinking about the world and politics, creating an 'imagined community' of 'shared interests' which obscure social and class contradictions and favour a progressive, social-democratic mentality.

259.
Catalan concern over identity roams between the uncertainties caused by globalisation and the certainty of the Spanish state's inability, especially after its neoconservative retreat, to assume its pluricultural character. The pro-independence project presupposes a 'state-building' which rests on a 'nation-building' that is strong enough to have launched the former, but weak enough still to feel threatened. The achievement of a state therefore appears, for the Independence movement, like a guarantee of survival for the nation itself. A nation to which, in reality, very little thought has been given, partly because it was already taken for granted, and partly because the important, recent, demographical, social and cultural changes never found an equivalent expression in terms of politics or struggle, which would have made them impossible to ignore.

260.
The Independence movement of the 21st century has a nationalist support base, but defines its project in terms of more

pragmatic, instrumental arguments. It involves a renewal of the traditional, conservative nationalism of Pujol, but also goes beyond the old, federalist nationalism. It brings together a liberal, pro-independence nationalism (of the pragmatic variety associated with the various clans coming out of the old Convergencia), a centre-left, pro-independence nationalism around the ERC, whose current programmatic and cultural principles continue to draw on the renewal carried out earlier by Carod-Rivera and on ideas developed by some of those coming from the socialist tradition of Maragall, as well as the anti-capitalist, pro-independence position of the CUP, which harbours several different notions of the nation.

261.
There are those who have moved from classical nationalism to support for Independence, because they became convinced that without a state of its own, the future of the nation was very uncertain. That has been the case with Vicenç Villatoro, one of the intellectual leaders of liberal-conservative Catalan nationalism, whose personal journey is characteristic of a whole generation.[76] In the opposite direction, however, there is a certain kind of support for Independence which claims it is not nationalist at all. In reality, most of these 'non-nationalist' independence supporters really are nationalists, even if they have taken on board and trivialised à la Billig[77] the codes of Catalan nationalism. Nevertheless, the fact that they take their distance from 'nationalism' puts the debate on a more fruitful, more political and strategic, terrain, and indicates their desire to keep well clear of any kind of nationalist bigotry.

Spectres of the (im)migrant nation

262.
Given its dual character, as a historical zone of passage, both a corridor and a frontier, and since the 19th century as a pole of economic development, immigration has been a substantial part of the history of Catalonia and its popular classes,

especially in the previous century. The history of migration, and of immigrants, fuses with that of Catalonia. It is impossible to understand the latter without the former. It is impossible to understand the people's struggles and the political conflict without the role of immigrant workers. And it is also impossible to grasp the strategic dilemmas and debates between the workers' movement and Catalanism, from the end of the 19th century to the Civil War around these issues. That includes the continuous use of terms like 'foreigners' as anathema to stigmatise certain movements or blame immigration for certain problems. That was the case, for example, with the policy of the regional government under the ERC during the Republic, which linked unemployment to immigrants and thus divided the workers.[78]

263.
The new immigration from the mid 1990s (1,080,000 people between 2000 and 2008[79]) has led to the most important cultural and social transformation of Catalan society in modern history. These new 'other Catalans' have played a decisive role in the Catalan economy, similar to that of their predecessors between the 1950s and 70s. But they have not played an equivalent socio-political role, nor have they had an equivalent impact on the public sphere. They were able neither to build political and cultural institutions of their own, nor to spearhead a revitalisation of the depleted, 'autochthonous' workers' movement (unlike, for example, what happened with Latinx immigrants into the United States in the 1990s and 2000s).

264.
The limited, but growing, socio-political impact of the new immigration has gone hand in hand with a lack of strategic thinking about Catalan national identity, of the sort carried out earlier by the anti-Franco movement. Doing this would have meant discussing anew the meaning of 'a single people'

and of the formula, *els altres catalans* ('the other Catalans'), coined by Francisco Candel in his book of 1964 (although he had used it before in an article written in 1958 in the magazine, *La Jirafa*).[80] This would need to be reformulated in line with the increased national and linguistic diversity of Catalan society, while relating this to the impact of a reaffirmed national identity, encouraged by the regional government since 1980.

265.
The question of migration is decisive for any movement in Europe. It is a key thermometer, although not the only one, for evaluating the reactionary or emancipatory content of a given social struggle, and an important barometer of the level of understanding of the historical period. A false step here means irreversible slippage. The Catalan Independence movement has not addressed the issue explicitly, but in general it has avoided xenophobia and demonstrated solidarity, with an inclusive vision of the nation. For their part, Catalonia's new immigrants have remained quite distant from the Independence movement. It is likely that most of them with the right to vote have actually opposed independence, out of distrust for a change they had not expected.

266.
The twin route that we outlined earlier (paragraph 46), firstly of extending Catalan identity to include new cultural and linguistic characteristics, and secondly of separating citizenship from nationality, seems to be the internationalist path towards overcoming the strategic impasses of Catalan nationalism and the Independence movement, without falling into a paralysing, cosmopolitan or post-national abstraction, which has no practical answers or capacity to act in the face of a movement like that seen since 2012. It also provides an alternative to the growing xenophobia and nativism which, in Catalonia, overlaps with the block of forces opposed to

independence, led by the PP and Ciudadanos, even though these parties have not made any explicit connection between their opposition to independence and their xenophobic policies.

267.
When the reactionary forces in the Spanish state, and in Catalonia too, make opposition to Catalanism and independence, along with xenophobia, the two main pillars of their politics (the other pillars are traditional sexism and law and order), the need to build democratic and strategic alliances against common adversaries seems obvious. But this clashes with what has been a founding principle of the movement, its support for Independence 'pure and simple', Independence 'and nothing else', and its tendency to distance itself from any other question, effectively silencing it. It also collides with the movement's inability to locate itself within the dialectic between centre and periphery, and to favour a democratic, anti-regime break with the growing, reactionary retreat of Spanish nationalism into authoritarianism.

268.
To break with any kind of xenophobic, nativist perspective, it is not enough to think about a culturally inclusive model of the nation; we need to combine, strategically, class, nation and immigration. In the first place, that means a plural conception (plurinational and pluricultural) of the class itself, pushing away the sinister spectre of a class conceived in terms of national priorities (whether Spanish or Catalan). Secondly, it means reconceptualising the nation in the twin sense described above, broadening the meaning of Catalan identity and disconnecting this from citizenship. Thirdly, it means rebuilding a new, plural subject, a 'subaltern bloc of the 99 per cent', as the vehicle for a project of emancipation that is able to seize political and intellectual leadership of the nation. All this can only be born from a programme of struggle and an experience of shared struggle. That's the

reason for the decisive importance of new experiences of trade unionism and urban activism, where 'native workers' (with the double historical meaning that has in the case of Catalonia) rub shoulders with workers coming from the last two decades of immigration. That is where the liberators of the future are being forged. The Independence movement cannot ignore them.

1   José Luis Oyón and Juanjo Romero (Eds.), *Clase antes que Nación. Trabajadores, movimiento obrero y cuestión nacional en la Barcelona metropolitana (1840–2017)*, Barcelona, El Viejo Topo, 2017; Andrew Dowling, *La reconstrucció nacional de Catalunya*, Barcelona, Ed. Pasado y Presente, 2017.
2   Josep Fontana, *La formació d'una identitat*, Vic, Ed. Eumo, 2014.
3   Several summaries of his work can be found in articles published after his death. For example: Xoaquin Pastorisa, 'Josep Fontana (1931–2018)', Viento Sur, 28 August 2018, available at: www.vientosur.info/spip.php?article14112; Marc Andreu, 'Llegir Josep Fontana és la millor manera de mantenir-lo viu', Crític, 29 August 2018, available at: www.elcritic.cat/blogs/sentitcritic/2018/08/29/llegir-fontana/; and Xavier Domènech, 'Josep Fontana: maestro de maestros', El Diario.es, 28 August 2018, available at: www. eldiario.es/tribunaabierta/Josep-Fontana-maestro-maestros_6_808479174.html.
4   Pere Gabriel (2000), 'Las bases políticas e ideológicas del catalanismo de izquierdas del siglo XX', *Espacio, Tiempo y Forma*, Serie V, Historia Contemporánea, No. 13, pp. 73–103.
5   Josep Fontana, op.cit.
6   The military trial that followed an attack on the Barcelona Corpus procession of 7 June 1896. It involved anarchist activists and was plagued with irregularities.
7   Here and in the following two points, I am guided by and summarize the interpretation of: Joan B. Culla, *El republicanisme lerrouxista a Catalunya (1901–1923)*, Barcelona, Curial Edicions, 1986. See also this work, which is both a biography of Lerroux and a study

of the movement: José Álvarez Junco, *El emperador del paralelo. Lerroux y la demagogia populista*, Madrid, Alianza Editorial, 1990. A more recent contribution to the debate on Lerroux and his movement, which is very much in the same vein as the two previous works cited, is: Xavier Domènech, 'El color de la llibertat. Sobre lerrouxisme i catalanisme (abans i avui)', Crític, 25 April 2015, available at: www.elcritic.cat/blogs/sentitcritic/2015/04/10/el-color-de-la-llibertat-sobre-lerrouxisme-i-catalanisme-abans-i-avui/.

8   Andreu Nin, 'Qué significa Lerroux en la política española?' in Andreu Nin, *La revolución española (1930–1937)*, Barcelona, Ed. El Viejo Topo, 2008 (a collection of articles edited by Pelai Pagès). The text was published originally in the magazine *Comunismo*, No. 30, November-December, 1933.

9   Pere Gabriel, 'Obrers i sindicats el segle XIX, fins els anys de la primera guerra mundial: Catalanisme i catalanitat' in José Luis Oyón and Juanjo Romero (eds), op. cit., pp. 87–116..

10   José Luis Oyón and Juanjo Romero, 'Introducción: trabajadores, movimiento obrero y cuestión nacional en la Barcelona metropolitana, 1840–2017' in José Luis Oyón y Juanjo Romero (eds), op. cit., pp. 9-60. With the development of the Process, a debate re-emerged over the figure of Salvador Seguí, who some have described as pro-independence, referring to his supposed remarks during a speech at the Madrid Athenaeum in October 1919. These remarks were cited from memory by his friend, the writer and trade unionist, Pere Foix, three decades later. (See: Pere Foix, *Apòstols i mercaders. Quaranta anys de lluita social a Catalunya*, Perpinyà, Fundació Sara Llorens de Serra, 1957). Several authors have shown convincingly that this interpretation of Seguí as pro-independence is not valid. See: José Luis Oyón and Juanjo Romero in the text mentioned at the beginning of this note, as well as: Xavier Domènech, Hegemonías, Madrid, Ed. Akal, 2014, pp. 171–72. More generally, Seguí was someone that both Catalan reformist socialism, of the Bloc Obrer i Camperol, and left-wing Catalan nationalism in the 1930s referred to and tried to link to their own positions. See: Isidre Molas, 'Pròleg' in Isidre Molas (ed.), *Salvador Seguí. Escrits*, Barcelona, Edicions 62, 1975, pp. 5–15. I discuss Seguí in more detail in: Josep Maria Antentas, 'Catalonia: the national question and labor's strategic dilemmas', *Labor History*, 2020, Vol. 61, No. 5–6, pp. 621–639.

11   The pro-independence reading of the CNT's position is in: Marc Santasusana, *Quan la CNT cridà independència*, Barcelona, Editorial Base, 2016.

12   Gabriel Alomar, *Negacions i afirmacions del catalanisme, i Catalanisme socialista*, Barcelona, Fundació Rafael Campalans, 1989. For a summary of Alomar's thought, see: Isidre Molas, 'El liberalisme democràtic de Gabriel Alomar', *Recerques: història, economia, cultura*, No. 23, 1990, pp. 91–111. I discuss Alomar in more detail in: Josep Maria Antentas, 'Catalonia: the national question and labor's strategic dilemmas', op.cit.

13   The polemic began with a first article by Nin, 'Socialismo y nacionalismo' on 7 February 1914, which was followed by a response from Fabra i Ribas, and a further reply from Nin, on 28 February, 'Socialismo y nacionalismo. Calma, calma... Con los nacionalistas, no; con el nacionalismo, sí...'

14   Pere Gabriel, op. cit.

15   José Luis Martín Ramos, 'Social y nacional, por ese orden. El ordenamiento de ejes en el marxismo político en los años del antifascismo, 1934-39', in José Luis Oyón and Juanjo Romero (eds), op. cit., pp. 241–258.

16   José Luis Oyón, *La quiebra de la ciudad popular*, Barcelona, Ediciones del Serbal, 2008.

17   Chris Ealham, *La lucha por Barcelona. Clase, cultura y conflicto (1898–1937)*, Madrid, Alianza Editorial, 2005.

18 Albert Balcells, *Marxismo y catalanismo 1930–36*, Barcelona, Ed. Anagrama, 1977..
19 This text was published again in 1966, under the title, *Revolución y contrarrevolución en España*, París, Ed. Ruedo Ibérico, with a new 'Introduction' and some changes to the original text. For a summary of the basic ideas developed there on the national question, see: Jaime Pastor, op. cit., pp. 112–116. A selection of Maurín's writings can be found in: Andy Durgan, (ed), *¿Socialismo o fascismo? Joaquín Maurín y la revolución española 1934–1936*, Zaragoza, Gobierno de Aragón, 2011. The history of the BOC is analysed in: Andy Durgan, *El Bloque Obrero y Campesino (1930–1936)*, Barcelona, Ed. Laertes, 1996.
20 Isidre Molas, op. cit. There is a remarkable similarity between the three phases scheme (bourgeoisie, petit-bourgeoisie and workers' movement) put forward by Alomar, and the later theses of Maurín. This has also been noted recently by Antonio Santamaría, 'El debate Nin/Maurín sobre la cuestión nacional', *El Viejo Topo*, No. 357, 2017, and by Xavier Domènech, 'Para mí, E.P. Thompson es el mejor historiador de todos los tiempos', *La Trivial*, 27 June 2018. Given this similarity, it is also worth understanding the differences between their two schemes. The first is less important, and a consequence of the twenty years that passed between the two. Alomar posed the transition from the phase of the petit-bourgeoisie to that of the workers' movement as a condition for the development of a mass movement that could achieve victory. By Maurín's time, there was already a mass, nationalist movement rooted among the people and the petit-bourgeoisie, organised around the ERC, so he posed the transition to leadership by the workers' movement only as a condition for victory. The second, more important, difference is that Alomar was a liberal and reformist socialist whose strategy was based on a logic of gradual change; while Maurin proposed a strategy of 'socialist-democratic revolution'.
21 The most systematic expression of Nin's theoretical and strategic ideas on the national question is to be found in a work published in 1935: Andreu Nin, *Els moviments d'emancipació nacional*, Barcelona, Editorial Base, 2008. For his political positions and the way they evolved, see also various articles included in: Andreu Nin, op. cit. and Andreu Nin, *L'incendi perdurable. La qüestió nacional a l'Estat espanyol*, Tarragona, Ed. Lo Diable Gros, 2017.
22 Their differences were expressed in a number of talks at the Madrid Athenaeum in June 1931. For his part, Maurín stated: 'We are separatists, but not separatists from Spain, rather separatists from the Spanish state.' He proposed smashing the state to form a 'true Iberian unity'. Two days later, Nin said: 'Maurín's separatism is a Marxist heresy. We Marxists cannot promote a separatist movement. If it exists, we will accept it, but we should not create it.' I take the words of both from: Albert Balcells, op.cit, pp. 50–52.
23 I take the Benet quote from his recent biography by Jordi Amat, *Com una pàtria. Vida de Josep Benet*, Barcelona, Edicions 62, 2017, p. 390. The orginal in Catalan, as relayed by Amat, reads as follows: 'En aquest treball - en aquest combat, diria - ens hi trobem tots els ciutadans d'aquest país nostre que volem viure en democràcia i llibertat. [...] Tots reclamant que l'ensenyament de l'idioma català sigui una realitat per a tothom, perquè a Catalunya ningú es pugui sentir discriminat per raó d'idioma. Perquè uns i altres, catalans de llinatge i nou catalans, formem un sol poble'.
24 Ibid., p. 482.
25 Ibid.
26 Martí Marí, 'De inmigrantes a ciudadanos: la (re)construcción de las identidades nacionales en Catalunya de la dictadura a la democracia 1939–1986', in José Luis Oyón and Juanjo Romero (eds.), op. cit., pp. 285-308.

27 Sebastian Balfour, *La dictadura, los trabajadores y la ciudad*, València, Edicions Alfons el Magnànim, 1994.
28 Martí Marí, op. cit.
29 Jordi Amat, op. cit., p. 244.
30 Jordi Amat, op. cit., p. 308.
31 Marc Andreu, 'Un sol poble?', *Crític*, 15 September, 2017. Available at: www.elcritic.cat/blogs/sentitcritic/2017/10/15/un-sol-poble/.
32 Andrew Dowling, op. cit., 2017, p. 209.
33 Jordi Amat, *El llarg procés*, Barcelona, Ed. Tusquets, 2015.
34 Enric Juliana, 'Un contrato basado en la ambigüedad' (interview with Steven Forti), *Tiempo devorado: revista de historia actual* 2 (3), 2015, pp. 124–131.
35 Andrew Dowling, op. cit., 2017, p. 246.
36 The term was coined by Josep Guifreu. See among others: Josep Guifreu y Maria Corominas (eds.), *Construir l'espai català de comunicació,* Barcelona, Centre d'Investigació de la Comunicació, 1991.
37 Fernando Molina and Alejandro Quiroga, '¿Una fábrica de independentistas? Procesos de nacionalisación en Catalunya', Steven Forti, Arnau González and Enric Ucelay-Da Cal. (eds), *El proceso separatista en Cataluña. Análisis de un pasado reciente (2006–2017)*, Granada, Comares, 2017, p. 68.
38 Fernando Molina and Alejandro Quiroga, op. cit., p. 69.
39 Pau Marí-Klose, 'La batalla por la hegemonía epistémica', *El Periódico*, 4 December 2013. Available at: www.elperiodico.com/es/opinion/20131204/la-batalla-por-la-hegemonia-epistemica-por-pau-mari-klose-2894915
40 Elisabeth Noelle-Neumann, *La espiral del silencio*, Barcelona, Paidós, 2010.
41 Benedict Anderson, *Imagined Communities*, London, Verso, 1983.
42 Jordi Amat, *La conjura de los irresponsables*, Barcelona, Anagrama, 2017.
43 Andreu Dowling, op. cit., 2017, p. 231.
44 For a detailed study of the scandal, see: Pere Ríos, *Banca Catalana: caso abierto*, Barcelona, Península, 2015.
45 Jaume Lorés, *La transició a Catalunya (1977–1984)*, Barcelona, Empúries, 1985, p. 31.
46 This idea is developed in: Paola Lo Cascio, *Nacionalisme i autogovern. Catalunya 1980- 2003*, Catarroja, Afers, 2008.
47 Enric Monné y Lluïsa Selga, *Història de la Crida a la Solidaritat en defensa de la llengua, la cultura i la nació catalanes*, Barcelona, La Campana, 1991.
48 Guillem Martínez, 'Pla, Pujol y el viaje a ninguna parte', *El diario.es*, 16 August 2014. Available in: www.eldiario.es/zonacritica/Pla-Pujol-viaje-parte_6_292280776.html.
49 Jordi Pujol, 'Fer poble, fer Catalunya', *Construir Catalunya*, Barcelona, Pòrtic, 1980, p. 22.
50 Paco Fernández Buey, in a letter published in *El País* on 16 October, responded to such distortions of history by recalling that Marxists like Sacristán had never governed the university and that the secret reading of works like those of Vilar played a decisive role in understanding the history of Catalonia. Paco Fernández Buey, 'Respeto a las personas y a las palabras', *El País*, 16 October 2004. See: Jordi Mir y Víctor Ríos, *Francisco Fernández Buey. Filosofando desde abajo*, Madrid, Los libros de la Catarata, 2014, pp. 100–101.
51 Albert Manent, *Crònica política del Departament de Cultura (1980–1988)*, Barcelona, A contravent, 2010.
52 For a brief summary of the role of Acta, see: Jordi Amat, op. cit., p. 336.
53 Antoni Trobat, 'Intellectuals del sobiranisme liberal: de la Fundació Acta al Procés independentista', *Crític*, 17 September 2017. Available in: www.elcritic.cat/reportatges/intellectuals-del-sobiranisme-liberal-de-la-fundacio-acta-fins-al-proces-independentista-17618.
54 Ignacio Ramonet, 'La pensée unique', *Le Monde Diplomatique*, January 1995, p. 1.

55   Jordi Amat gives a good and precise account of this whole process of intellectual reconstruction in his work cited earlier: *La conjura de los irresponsables*.
56   Francesc Marc-Álvaro, *Els assassins de Franco*, Barcelona, Esfera de los libros, 2005; and Francesc Marc-Álvaro, *Ara sí que toca*, Barcelona, Edicions 62, 2003.
57   Paola Lo Cascio, *Nacionalisme i autogovern. Catalunya 1980–2003*, Catarroja, Editorial Afers, 2008 (see pp. 109–127 for a summary of the whole parliamentary debate on the law).
58   Neus Tomás, 'La inmersión en la escuela, el símbolo de la lucha por la igualdad', *El diario.es*, 16 February 2018, www.eldiario.es/zonacritica/inmersion-escuela-simbolo-lucha-igualdad_6_740935909.html; Plataforma per la Llengua. (2011). 'Arguments de suport al català com a única llengua vehicular de l'escola catalana', *Somescola.cat*, available in: www.somescola.cat/docroot/omnium/pdf/Argumentari-Somescola.pdf
59   Although it is not the specific subject of his book, José Enrique Ruiz-Domènec, in his recent *Informe sobre Catalunya. Una historia de rebel·lia (777–2017)*, Barcelona, Rosa dels Vents, 2018, insists on the 'ideological' character of linguistic immersion and its aim of removing Castilian from education on the pretext of social cohesion, pp. 228 and 233.
60   The expression was coined by Eduard Voltas in *La guerra de la llengua*, Barcelona, Empúries, 1996.
61   Víctor Sampedro, 'Insumisos. Diálogo con Manuel Vázquez Montalbán y Lluís Llach sobre nacionalismo y memoria histórica' in *Ciudadanos de Babel*, Madrid, Punto de Lectura, 2002, pp. 79–133.
62   Oriol Junqueras, 'El castellano y la República catalana', *El Periódico de Catalunya*, 23 May 2017. Available in: www.elperiodico.com/es/politica/20121008/el-castellano-y-la-republica-catalana-articulo-de-oriol-junqueras-2221062.

63   'Per un veritable procés de normalització lingüística a la Catalunya independent', 31 March, 2016. Available in: llenguairepublica.cat/manifest/.
64   Official figures from the Generalitat of Catalonia, in the section 'Patrimoni Lingüistic': cultura.gencat.cat/ca/anypatrimoni/temes/patrimoni-linguistic/. The main source of information on linguistic diversity in Catalonia today is the Grup d'Estudi de Llengües Amenaçades (GELA), set up in 1992 (www.gela.cat/doku.php?id=GELA).
65   The Department of Education of the Catalan government has taken some steps towards a greater presence of non-Catalan and Spanish languages in education.
66   Orange is the color of Ciudadanos (Translator's note).
67   Marc Andreu, op. cit.
68   Oriol Junqueras, op. cit.
69   Benjamin Disraeli, *Sybil, or The Two Nations*, Oxford, OUP, 1998.
70   John Dos Passos, *The Big Money*, New York, The Modern Library, 1937.
71   On the notion of strategic imagination, see: Josep Maria Antentas, 'Imaginación estratégica y partido', *Viento Sur*, 2017, No. 150, pp. 141–150.
72   Pablo Iglesias, and Xavier Domènech, 'Catalunya, un sol poble', *El Periódico de Catalunya*, 16 July, 2017. Available in: www.elperiodico.com/es/opinion/20170716/pablo-iglesias-xavier-domenech-catalunya-un-sol-poble-6171617.
73   Josep Ramoneda, 'Vaig votar la CUP i en un referèndum d'independència votaré que sí' (entrevista)', *Vilaweb*, 4 May, 2016. Available in: www.vilaweb.cat/noticies/josep- ramoneda-vaig-votar-la-cup-i-en-un-referendum-dindependencia-votare-que-si/. The ideas of Carod-Rovira can be read in: *El futur a les mans*, Angle Editorial, *Un país, un futur*, Cossetània edicions, *Valls o 2014*, Ed. l'Arquer, Barcelona, published in 2003, 2005 and 2008 respectively.

74 Josep Lluís Carod-Rovira, 'Indignació espanyola', *Naciódigital*, 16 June, 2011. Available in: www.naciodigital.cat/opinio/1964/indignacio/espanyola.

75 Josep Lluís Carod-Rovira, 'N'hem de ser més', *Crític*, 16 January 2018. Available in: www.elcritic.cat/blogs/sentitcritic/2018/01/16/nhem-de-ser-mes/.

76 Vicenç Villatoro, 'Per a mi, la nació és més important que l'Estat' (interview), *Crític*, 24 August, 2016. Available in: www.elcritic.cat/entrevistes/vicenc-villatoro-per-a-mi-la-nacio-es-mes-important-que-estat-11021.

77 Michael Billig, op. cit.

78 Chris Ealham, op. cit.

79 *La immigració en xifres. Nou cicle migratori*, Secretaria per a la Immigració, 2010.

80 Francesc Candel, *Els altres catalans*, Edicions 62, Barcelona, 2008. See also Jordi Amat, op. cit., 2017.

4
The October Crisis (II)

Strategic collapse and foundational limitations

269.
Discussing the Independence movement from the left (whether or not you use that concept) leads you into two levels of strategy that overlap in a sort of spiral. On the one hand, you have to think about what the whole movement should do to achieve its aims, which are shared in varying degrees. On the other, you need to think about what the Catalan left should do to develop its plans for change and social equality, including both the left within the Independence movement, and the left outside. The second entails two more questions: how the left should operate within the movement and how to develop a dialogue between those inside and those outside. So, there are these twin strategic levels whose unification or separation are themselves the subject of an analytical and political strategy.

270.
Since 2011 and 2012, there have coexisted in Catalan society two big narratives and visions for the future. The first is the perspective coming from the 15-M Indignados movement and its political spinoffs, Podem and Catalunya en Comú. The second is the Independence movement. Both succeeded in mobilising proposals for change that were put forward and perceived as straightforward and painless: a new majority in the Spanish state and the independence of Catalonia, respectively. But both have collapsed, at least for the moment, and

need a second wind to have any strong impact again. They still work as legitimate proposals for specific political and social projects, and as hypotheses in the long term, but not as immediate, viable possibilities.

271.

On the one hand, the possibility of a new governing bloc in the Spanish state, opposed to austerity and in favour of an agreed referendum in Catalonia, has now disappeared off the map. It doesn't look possible, either in its original version (a majority around Unidos Podemos), or the caricatured version adopted by Podemos after 2016 (of a government the PSOE of Sanchez and Unidos Podemos on the basis of a common programme, and not simply support from the outside from the latter for the former, as occurred after the vote of no confidence). In this sense, the key to unblocking the situation, which Comú-Podem's spokespeople in Catalonia referred to during the 21-D election campaign, sounded more like wishful thinking than a real option.

272.

On the other hand, the possibility of peaceful independence – the result of gradual, citizen mobilisation, exercise of the civic right to vote, of gradual transition from one legal framework to another and a step-by-step disconnection from the Spanish state – was abruptly ruled out. Both the strategic perspective (whether that was really one of peaceful independence or rather of using the mobilisations to negotiate a deal with the Spanish state), and the public narrative, of the PDeCAT, ERC and ANC, have fallen apart. In turn, the policy of the CUP, of supporting the process and pushing it as far as it could go, has also been weakened, simply because there is no longer a mainstream pro-independence bloc with a clear road map to push. It can only cling to the short-term justifications of Puigdemont. At the same time, the weaknesses displayed by the official, pro-independence bloc reveal the limitations of the CUP's approach of operating entirely within the Procés, while lacking any strategy towards (the social base of) the non-independence left.

273.
During the long journey that the mainstream pro-independence movement began in 2012, the most unusual moment was the launch of the Lluites Compartides (Shared Struggles) campaign by Òmnium Cultural in October 2016. It was promoted by Jordi Cuixart, the most iconoclastic and interesting voice within the official bloc (ANC, Òmnium, ERC, and Convergencia/PDeCAT/Junts x Catalunya). Perhaps for this reason, he was also an undervalued figure with less strategic weight than he deserved. The campaign sought to recognise the social struggles that, since the Franco regime, had contributed to building Catalonia from below; its aim was to weave together discourses for the future based on the past diversity of collective journeys undertaken by social organisations and movements and their respective social bases. A worthy effort, it partially broke with the discourse of independence pure and simple, and shed light on the diversity of struggles and social conflicts that have taken place in recent years in Catalonia. But it did so without questioning the complex relations between the social and national questions in the country's history, or the contemporary strategic divide between the future indicated by 15-M and that of the Procés, and without considering the lessons that the pro-independence movement should draw from this.

274.
Was it just a defensive battle in the face of repression, a real struggle for a future republic, or a self-satisfied defence of the Procés, of an imaginary republic and of symbolic disobedience? Is there a contradiction between those who want independence and those who defend the right to decide, or do the two converge around a shared demand for change?

Should this battle be exclusively a Catalan one, subordinated to politics at the level of the Spanish state, or a dialectical combination between centre and periphery? Undoubtedly, this is the triple strategic dilemma that arose from the October crisis, which hangs like a spectre over the present and throws a long shadow across the future. The dilemma is as complex as it is unavoidable. But is it as insoluble as it is decisive? A thorough-going, strategic rethink fits badly with the immediate demands of electoral politics and with the desires and illusions of urgent social and political change.

275.
It must be acknowledged that neither the independence movement in its plurality nor the Comunes seem to have taken any path to strategic revision commensurate with the challenges posed. Nonetheless, whether accepted or not, there is a clear challenge for everyone: to avoid the triple danger of locking oneself into an illusory proposal for imaginary change, of entrenching oneself in pure resistance, or of accommodating to the very narrow institutional framework of what is possible. Successfully achieving this triple dodge would open the door to charting a strategy of rupture; one that is both offensive and defensive, short and long term, unilateral and bilateral, national and social, democratising, constituent and anti-austerity. A difficult task? Without a doubt. But in the history of popular movements it is often the case that the arduous is also what is necessary.

276.
The main complexity of Catalan politics is that the 15-M movement and its aftermath, on the one hand, and the pro-independence process, on the other, have shaped divergent expectations for the future, even though there are undoubtedly points of contact. This divergence of perspectives expresses, in a broader sense, the complexity of the relationship between the social and the national questions in Catalan

politics and society. More concretely, it takes the form of a lack of alliance between independence supporters and federalists who defend the right to self-determination, in a situation where the impossibility of exercising this right could provide a common ground for action.

277.
The basic political limitation of the independence movement, as we have seen, was to detach its goal of a state of its own from a clear policy against austerity and for a renewal of democracy. It completely separated its project, in some cases consciously and willingly and in others by involuntary omission, from the legacy, meaning and agenda of what had been the 15-M movement in 2011. But the spectres of the revolt of the Indignados continued to haunt Catalan society and could not simply be ignored or drowned out. The promoters of the pro-independence movement gave priority to keeping the Catalan right on board and avoiding any split with it; as a result, from the beginning they lacked any serious analysis of Catalonia's social structure, of the sectors that any project for social change would need to involve, and of how to address the social base of the non-independence left. The skewed version of history that the pro-independence movement has adopted, in which the national aspect obscures all other social contradictions and class occupies a secondary place, has prevented it from drawing the appropriate lessons from the past of the popular movements, including their successes and failures.

278.
Both movements, the 15-M and the independence movement, have galvanised and represented different parts of the 'people' of Catalonia. The 'people of the squares' of 2011 are not the same as the 'people of the Procés', the people of the pro-independence process, although there are important overlaps that should not be overlooked. To do so would imply an

overly Manichean reading of reality. In Catalonia, part of the middle class and the underemployed youth turned towards the 15-M and the political groups that came out of it (Podem, Catalunya en Comú). Another part ended up opting for independence (in its different variants). And, of course, another has been swinging back and forth between the two, providing a fragile bridge between these split futures embodied by the independence movement and the Indignant rebellion and its legacy. But the 15-M, besides its contingent of precarious student youth and the primordial role of the middle classes hit by the crisis, also had a 'neighbourhood dimension', a popular and working-class component at a time when the workers' movement as such was in a state of decomposition. Although essential to forming a majority for change, its (at least partial) outsider status with respect to the independence movement has revealed a fundamental strategic and sociological weakness, which was expressed in all its force on 21 December. A strategic re-articulation of 'a single people' therefore requires the convergence of these split perspectives expressed by the 15-M and the Procés.

279.
A Catalan republic compatible with a final destination of either independence or confederalism, a Catalan constituent process and an immediate citizens' recovery plan – these three elements could have been the basis for trying to resolve the series of contradictions that arose from the split in future perspectives between the 15-M and the independence process. Just as serious as not being able to resolve them has been the surprisingly scant strategic attention that the main actors in Catalan politics have devoted to them over the last five years. Addressing them would have meant operating both inside and outside the Procés, an undoubtedly complex task that the left would have had to embrace as its own. The inertia inherent in the situation, and a preoccupation with tactics, often take precedence over underlying strategic needs. These

unexplored paths remain as future opportunities mislaid in the present, as battles that were lost without ever being fought.

280.
The opposition between a unilateral path (of building up support for a rupture from within Catalonia) and the option of seeking to build a political majority for change in the Spanish state as a whole, has been one of the great strategic dead ends of Catalan politics (and hence of Spanish politics). In fact, unilateralism and fraternity should be seen as complementary. Without a unilateral movement in favour of independence (and/or simply in favour of a referendum), no Spanish political party would support Catalonia's right to self-determination and an approved referendum. Unidos Podemos supports it in response to the reality in Catalonia. On the other hand, a plan for a unilateral break like that proposed by the pro-independence movement, without taking into account what happens outside Catalonia, is not very audacious; it neglects the fact that a general political crisis in the Spanish state would favour its own success.

281.
Rather than a strategic opposition between two conflicting approaches, the challenge is to find a strategic way out, based on a complex dialectic between the centre and the periphery. This implies somehow linking, without conflating, the pro-independence project and that of a rupture in the system across the whole Spanish state. Seeking alliances and winning support outside Catalonia is, if not the main challenge, one of the greatest challenges facing the Catalan independence movement (and those who, without being pro-independence, support the movement in its democratic challenge to the state). This can only be done in three ways: explicitly linking the proposal for a Catalan republic to a desire to see a sister Spanish republic in the future; not separating the commitment to independence from the

possibility of a future confederation; and, in the short term, linking the demand for independence with the struggle for anti-austerity measures that can arouse the sympathy of the Spanish working classes. These are proposals that have been left out of the strategic agenda of the pro-independence leaders. To a large extent, they imply sidelining the right from the political leadership.

Diverging paths on the left

282.
The alternative left that cannot be assimilated to conventional social-liberalism, i.e., the CUP and Catalunya en Comú-Podem, emerged politically weakened from the October crisis and the 21-D electoral challenge, in a situation of extreme strategic divergence between the two groupings. They lacked any contact with each other. Perhaps even more serious than the rift between them throughout this period was the fact that almost no one seemed to care about it. Such a split was seen as normal and fitted in with their respective routines. This was a symptom of strategic thinking overwhelmed by an intractable reality that, let's face it, did not make things easy.

283.
Contrary to conventional media commentary, election results cannot be the only yardstick for assessing the success or failure of a political party's orientation and aims. These must be weighed in relation to a party's overall political influence, its ability to set the political agenda and shape public debate, the extent to which it does or does not act as a political and cultural reference point for broad sectors of society, and its ability to organise and mobilise around its political initiatives. An over-emphasis on analysing elections is, in this sense, just as superficial as an obsession with elections as a strategy. It is a form of political short-sightedness that prioritises immediacy over the underlying tendencies.

284.
The relationship between electoral success and a party's political orientation is, moreover, a complex one. There may be situations in which a party performs badly, not as a result of a wrong political line, but because it stands up for what is right in a challenging situation. Going against the tide can often be the only dignified and, in retrospect, courageous thing to do. But it can be costly in the short term. The opposite is also true: accommodating to the pressures of the moment may in certain circumstances save the situation, but at the price of paving the way for a far-reaching political defeat later on. Parliamentary reformism is a true master at this. Nonetheless, the complexity of this relationship between political orientation, aims and electoral results should not be an excuse for retreating into a mentality of self-justification and isolated resistance when things go wrong. Understanding that there is no straightforward link between election results and political orientation is essential to avoid sliding into either mere self-satisfied resistance or a mindless obsession with results.

285.
Within the independence movement, the CUP, of course, has represented a proposal that goes far beyond pure and simple independence. It has defended a programme that not only links the national and social questions and confronts the shortcomings of the official independence movement, but also put forward an openly anti-capitalist and revolutionary option. It also marked a counter-tendency to the growing institutionalisation of most of the 'forces of change' that emerged in 2014 and 2015, with Podemos at the forefront. However, it has operated too much from within the framework of the Procés, without being able to connect the anti-capitalist character of its programme to a strategic proposal that, while remaining within the framework of the Procés that began in 2012, could also move outside

and help to redefine some of the pillars of the mainstream pro-independence common sense. The CUP's anti-capitalist programme interacted with that of the mainstream pro-independence parties mainly within the institutions of parliamentary activity, in an increasingly turbulent and unstable manner, not in the movement itself, where it was unable to advance proposals that would challenge them to go beyond the limits of independence pure and simple. It was always faithful to its anti-capitalist ideas. It did not renounce them and defended them publicly, but it did not have a policy aimed at the ANC and the movement as a whole to try to make them take on some kind of social content.

286.
The CUP made two important concrete errors, which in part fed back into each other. The first was not having a policy of unity towards that part of the left that was not pro-independence but was in favour of the right to decide. This had three decisive moments: when the constituent Procés emerged in April 2013, when Podemos made a breakthrough in the European elections of 25 May 2014, and when Guanyem (later renamed Barcelona en Comú) was formed in June of the same year. Had they done so, the map of the Catalan left might have been different. But their vision was too much focused on themselves, and they tended to see the building of 'popular unity' as only their own linear growth and not the result of a policy of convergences. In other words, they confused the concept of 'popular unity' with their own slogan, 'Unitat Popular'. The second mistake was to endorse the sequence '9-N + plebiscitary elections + disengagement' in eighteen months, which essentially served to prolong artificially the leading role of PDeCAT in Catalan politics and to take a detour to nowhere for three years. Placed in a difficult position after the 27-S elections of 2015, the CUP overcame as best it could its internal difficulties, which were the result of a mistaken political line. However, it did so with a genuine

display of participation and internal democracy, which was in stark contrast to the authoritarian plebiscites à la Podemos.

287.
In short, it was too caught up in its role as an honest guarantor that the independence process would go all the way to the end, whilst failing to adopt an offensive policy of discussion and challenge towards the left and its social base, which remained distant from the independence movement. Despite this, in the end it played a decisive role in redirecting the unrealistic, post 27-s roadmap towards the referendum as a democratic catalyst. In the phase following the 21-D elections, it became the embodiment of a sincere and combative voluntarism which, however, never questioned the fundamental limitations of the pro-independence movement as expressed at the ballot box, nor those of the CUP's own policy throughout the Procés. This makes it more inclined to confront the capitulation of the mainstream pro-independence movement than to pose the need to reformulate it strategically.

288.
For its part, Catalunya en Comú played a passive waiting game. It pointed out many real problems with the official pro-independence proposal, including the hollowness of the idea of 'independence' as a panacea, the difficulty of turning the pro-independence project into reality, the polarisation between the different identities that it could generate, and the silencing of other issues and conflicts under the sheer weight of the national debate. But its lack of real involvement in the process prevented it from intervening on these problems. Its policy represents the antithesis of any kind of strategic foresight, a kind of paradox of passivity, whereby the contradictions and negative aspects of a situation, which justify a passive policy, only increase as a consequence of the latter.

289.
Acting as an inert bystander in a simmering conflict is not really a viable option. Standing still with no real practical policy in the face of an open conflict does not prevent the world from continuing to turn, it only makes it easier for it to turn in the least desirable direction. 'You are involved,' Pascal reminds us in his *Pensées*,[1] a statement that is also valid at the political and strategic level. Not intervening is in the end another way of doing so. Not turning up for the meeting is a way of being there by omission. Calls for responsibility, while you passively stand and watch, end up turning into irresponsibility through inaction. This infernal spiral of passivity has an aspect of self-fulfilling prophecy; in a way it reflects a kind of strategic nostalgia for a non-existent reality in which neither the independence process nor the national question exists.

290.
The formal position of Comunes posed three interlinked problems. The first was the refusal to give any binding character to the referendum in advance, reducing it to a mere 'mobilisation' in the absence of such guarantees and of any consensus on its convening. This ignored the fact that this lack of a proper institutional framework for 1-O was exclusively due to the refusal of the PP government, supported by all the structures of the Spanish state, to accept the holding of a referendum and, more generally, to the refusal of most of the organisations opposed to independence to consider any discussion of a referendum as legitimate. It also overlooks the fact that 'absolute guarantees', as the third deputy mayor of Barcelona, Jaume Asens, correctly pointed out, hardly ever exist in an election and did not exist, for example, in the referendum on the Constitution in 1978.[2] Moreover, as Albert Noguera pointed out, guarantees 'are not neutral, technical instruments, they are ideological instruments that are in dispute and operate within democratic and social contradictions'.[3] This is

not to deny the importance of guarantees for 1-O, but only to avoid seeing them in a fatalistic and predefined way. They were part of the political struggle to achieve the referendum, and their final nature could only be judged after the event. In fact, this over-emphasis on guarantees contrasts with the reality of the great social and political struggles of the past, which have not usually had much affinity with a priori legal assurances. The background of many of the leaders of Catalunya en Comú in social movements, and their attachment to the 15-M as their founding narrative, sit rather uncomfortably with this passive formalism.

291.
The second problem was to detach what happened on Day 1 from the political situation that would exist on Day 2. Thus, not only did they unilaterally downgrade 1 October to a simple 'mobilisation', but they also failed to appreciate that the results would determine the chances of achieving the declared objective of Catalunya en Comú, a referendum agreed with the Spanish state and backed by guarantees. By arbitrarily watering down the significance of 1-O, the Comunes were also undermining their own formal objective for Day 2. In fact, any attempt to achieve a binding referendum agreed with the Spanish state after 1-O had to understand that this would only be possible if they went all out on 1-O and created a crisis that would weaken the Spanish government. It is obvious that if 1-O were presented as just an unimportant 'mobilisation', reluctantly engaged in, and conceived in a 'light' way so as not to pose too great a challenge to Rajoy's government, then the conditions would not be good for a 'genuine' referendum later on.

292.
The third problem, and the most serious in practical terms, was the lack of any call for active participation on 1 October, which was only partially compensated for by the attitude of

individual leaders who went to vote. This put the Comunes in a very passive position in relation to the October vote, supporting a process that was dragging them along, but without committing themselves to its success. It seemed they had given up in advance on any desire to give a lead. After setting the tone for Catalan politics with their two electoral victories in the general elections of 20 December 2015 and 26 June 2016, and challenging the independence movement's roadmap with their proposal to build a state-wide political majority in favour of the referendum, the Comunes ended up paralysed and on the defensive once the Catalan government set course, more out of necessity than conviction, for a unilateral referendum. Far from strategic foresight, their policy was rather one of passive subordination to the institutions.

293.
In the midst of this passive, lukewarm and demobilising position of the party, some central leaders of the Comunes, who were aligned with the official positions, adopted a slightly more active and empathetic personal stance towards the referendum. This was the case of the first deputy mayor of Barcelona, Gerardo Pisarello, who in an article on 5 September defended mobilising and going out to vote, albeit in the framework of an argument that was full of debatable assertions and was generally very institutionalist in tone. Pisarello said that 'a failure of 1-O would be more than the failure of a government's roadmap. It would be a decisive blow to the possibility of fully exercising the right to decide. And it would also be a blow to the republican, democratic initiatives to challenge the constitutional regime of 1978.' He also indicated that 'a Yes vote would even make sense from the point of view of those who disagree with the government's road map. First, as a form of rebellion against centralism and authoritarianism. And, secondly, because it would also be a way of advancing towards the fundamental proposition of the majority of the "comuns", which is rooted in a tradition

that stretches from Pi y Margall to Joaquín Maurín and Lluís Companys: that of a plurinational agreement, respectful and between equals, which calls into question the oligarchic and elitist project of "conllevancia" (putting up with each other) that has been imposed in recent years, and which opens the way to a new, free and republican form of solidarity and coexistence between the different peoples and nations of the peninsula.'[4] An undoubtedly interesting approach, but one that had no practical consequences at all, apart from giving a thin and self-interested veneer of radicalism to Catalunya en Comú's very hesitant and tactical approach, which Pisarello himself actively endorsed.

The potential of the purple people

294.
Catalunya en Comú, whose predecessor was the electoral coalition En Comú Podem that won the general elections of 20 December 2015 and 26 June 2016 in Catalonia, was founded with the dual aim of exporting the Barcelona en Comú model to Catalonia as a whole and overcoming the limitations that Podem had displayed as a political project in Catalonia. The latter had a precarious existence in 2014 and 2015, culminating in its inclusion as a junior partner in the failed electoral coalition Catalunya Sí que es Pot, alongside Iniciativa per Catalunya (ICV) and Esquerra Unida i Alternativa (EUIA). Podem Catalunya was born of the momentum from Podemos' general expansion in the European elections campaign and its subsequent consequences, but it always had a weak structure, a notable lack of cadres, and was never able to consolidate itself as an actor capable of a serious intervention in Catalan politics.

295.
Podem has been one of the great overlooked parties in Catalan politics, a fact that, in reality, has been indicative of the general strategic fragility of the left and the inconsistencies in

its model of the 'people'. The irruption of Podem into Catalan politics was viewed with scepticism and suspicion by many activist groups. This distrust was similar to that which much of the Spanish left felt towards the creation of Podemos (due to its electoralist aspect, its pronounced personalism, and the quickly confirmed opportunism of its leaders), but it was compounded by a specific factor: doubts about its national project. Many saw it as an imported Spanish phenomenon, as something alien to Catalonia. A perception which, however, only revealed the limitations of the vision of Catalonia held by a large part of the left. Not so much from a conceptual point of view, but rather as a result of its everyday social roots and its biased strategic environment.

296.
Podem was born without giving any thought to how to position itself in Catalonia and how to relate to the independence process that began in 2012 and the Catalan national question in general. It was never able to develop a specific strategy for Catalonia beyond simply replicating Podemos' general framework, and it had a very restricted notion of its own role in Catalan politics. It limited itself to trying to garner votes for Pablo Iglesias' candidacy in the general elections, which was Podemos' overarching goal after its breakthrough in the European elections of 25 May 2014. It always felt much more comfortable with Spanish politics than with Catalan politics, and had difficulties in knowing how to relate the two.

297.
The mismatch between the Spanish national-popular project that the state-wide leadership of Podemos was trying to develop and Catalan reality weakened Podem's potential in Catalonia, while its lack of a relationship with political nationalism ruled it out of any possibility of exerting leadership. In a way, what pushed Podemos towards the 'centre of the stage' in the Spanish state as a whole pushed it partially

to the margins in Catalonia. Podem always defended the idea of a referendum for Catalonia, but it did not develop a position of its own on the Catalan national question and, in organisational terms and in its general conception of politics, it was even a step behind the old and failed model of the 'Catalan federation of the PSOE', that is, a junior Catalan branch of a state-wide party.

298.
But the limitations of Podem should not prevent us from seeing the other side of the coin: the purple party[5] was able to galvanise the support of a popular, 'other Catalonia', outside of the independence movement, with which the traditional left had already lost many of its links. This gave Podem a decisive strategic value, which unfortunately almost no one perceived. It was the first time that a left-wing political party (even though it did not use that concept to define itself) was able to (re)connect with the (post) working-class Catalonia of the suburbs, whose leading political and social role had steadily eroded since the end of the Transition and the consolidation of neoliberalism. The initial experiences of self-organisation in Podem's circles and its plebeian potential were spectacular; so was the way this was completely ignored by a large part of the Catalan left (whether pro-independence or not), and rejected by the mainstream independence movement, which always saw Podem as a threat to its monopoly on the narrative of change. This encapsulates many of the strategic limitations of Catalonia's alternative currents. Little thought has been given to this, but the eclipse of the Podem experience represents one of the greatest unspoken, strategic defeats of the Catalan left in recent history. The fact that it has hardly been noticed only makes it worse.

299.
The nature of Podem, with its considerable power to attract both voters and activists from the 'other', (post) working-class

Catalonia, and its lack of any reflection on the national question given its subordination to the central leadership of Podemos, was also a potential source of strategic and political failings, which in turn reflected quite disparate sociological realities. This opened up the spectre of the development of an extra-Catalanist left, that could develop into outright opposition to Catalanism. And that opened the door to another, even more sinister spectre, that of a political fracture between the popular classes and the Catalan left because of its position on the national question (which goes far beyond its relationship with the pro-independence process). In short, this was a scenario that was, in spite of all the differences, analogous to that which has existed in the Basque Country since the end of Franco's regime: a nightmare spectre that would have permanently guaranteed the absolute impossibility of articulating a new popular and left-wing hegemonic bloc. It meant ghettoising a Podem that had become a powerful political and cultural outlier, but lacked the capacity to provide the backbone of an alternative majority; the corollary of which was to push the pro-independence left into being forever a minority within the Procés.

300.

The spectre of a purple 'Lerrouxism' (conventionally understood in a crude and inaccurate manner as imported anti-Catalan nationalism) once again hovered over Catalan politics. If the bulk of the independence movement, and a significant part of the left, devoted themselves to demonising the newcomer as if it were an apparition to be exorcised, just a passing anomaly, in reality its existence posed a strategic challenge that almost no one wanted to take on as their own: the need to harness the strength of the purple people with the political tradition of Catalanism and the constituent powers deriving from the process in favour of independence. It is true that this was a challenge that had seemed to coincide superficially with the strategic concerns of the Comunes in their initial phase; however, their response to it would end up being a frightful caricature.

301.
It was under the spectral shadow of this bleak future that Anticapitalistes made the most serious attempt of the contemporary Catalan left to update the strategic vision of 'a single people', stripping it of its original reformist allegiances in the anti-Franco movement, and bringing it into interplay with the proposals of heterodox Marxism in the 1930s regarding the links between the national question and the social revolution. Ultimately unsuccessful, this attempt at an update, without fetishising the past or making propaganda for the present, nonetheless remains one of the most ambitious and intellectually fertile of all the projects that unfolded in Catalonia's recent turbulent history. One of its peculiarities was that Anticapitalistes became one of the very few organisations on the Catalan left which, without being nationalist or making independence a defining feature of its programmatic identity, was present at all the major moments of the Procés, defending the 'yes-yes' vote on 9 November 2014 and supporting 1 October with a 'yes' vote. The corollary of that is that it also became one of the few non-nationalist and non-independence organisations that did not find itself in a paralysed, paralysing or half-hearted position during this period.

302.
There were four cornerstones of this anti-capitalist and internationalist attempt to rearticulate 'a single people', which first bore fruit in 2012–14 before the emergence of Podem/Podemos, but which reached its full significance after the emergence of the purple wave. First, it sought a convergence between pro-independence and non-independence supporters around the prospect of a constituent process specifically for Catalonia, where the final destination, in terms of independence or federation, would not be determined in advance. Secondly, and

related to the above, it proposed forms of synthesis between independence and federalism under the mantle of classical internationalism and a rediscussion of historical Catalan federalism, which defended a Catalan republic without a predetermined end in terms of independence or federation, or the defence of independence as a possible path towards a subsequent confederation. Thirdly, it put forward a dialectic between centre and periphery as a way of breaking with the system of 1978 while avoiding Manichean oppositions between unilateralism and fraternity or between change only from Catalonia vs. change from the centre. Fourthly, it aimed to build, on the basis of the above programmatic premises, a pluralist Catalan political subject, with one foot inside and the other outside the Procés, and with a vocation for winning the majority, as a result of convergence between different organisations and collectives and the massive incorporation into party politics of previously unorganised people.

303.
It was symptomatic that Podem only seemed to arouse general interest in Catalonia as a political force following the public confrontation in 2017 between its then secretary general, Albano Dante Fachín, and the leadership of Catalunya en Comú and Podemos, which ended with him leaving the party as he was about to be thrown out by the central spanish leadership of the party. Largely improvised and unexpected, the struggle of Podem's secretary general with Iglesias and the leadership of the Comunes was marked by his constant zigzags and by three structural contradictions. The first was the use within Podem of the same methods that Iglesias used against it, the culminating moment of which was the dismissal of members of Anticapitalistes from the party's leadership. The second was to confuse the legitimate defence of Podem's interests in the face of the brush-offs it received from the leadership of the Comunes with a battle over the party's apparatus and self-affirmation and with the

glorification of the Podemos model (created at Vistalelgre I and reworked at Vistalegre II) whose democratic shortcomings were self-evident. Finally, there was the failure to prepare the party, and its core of middle cadres, for a policy of real commitment to 1 October beyond its media support from above. As a synthesis of these contradictions, Dante Fachín, without embracing independence as a cause of his own, ended up drifting into the independence milieu, which became the target of his discourse and proposals. That was certainly a legitimate choice, but strategically less interesting than trying to act as a bridge between the pro-independence world and the purple galaxy of the Comunes, and to rethink the historical meaning of 'a single people'.

Eurocommons?

304.
Overcoming Podem's structural limitations, both in terms of its organisation and its mission, and moving on to develop a national Catalan party was, therefore, the challenge that underlay the creation of Catalunya en Comú. Unfortunately, things turned out differently, and inter-party negotiations among its founding members took the place of in-depth strategic debate on the main issues, including the Catalan national question. Although conceived with a strategic view to a new political subject that would be Catalan and pluralist, it ended up as a pale shade of this. Its founding congress approved a series of generalities that did not amount to any kind of serious reflection on the national question, nor any serious strategic evaluation of the pro-independence process. By distancing themselves from the latter, the Comunes adopted a consistently passive tactic, keeping a low profile for as long as possible, while waiting for the independence movement to collapse and/or be defeated. In this way, they abandoned any kind of active policy that would seek to strengthen the constituent potential of the independence movement and link the aspirations it embodied with those

of the 15-M movement. The Comunes embraced the idea of reviving a popular Catalanism, but based on the fantasy that they could do this while completely ignoring the independence movement and not by interacting critically with it. The spectres of the Catalanism in the past limited their ability to develop a politics of the present.

305.
Catalunya en Comú's position on the independence referendum of 1 October 2017, cannot be separated from its political future as a whole and from the party's general profile. Its line on 1-O was somewhat autonomous from its positions on economic policy, for example, or its views on the role of the 'street' and the institutions in a strategy for change. But this autonomy was relative. The nature and contours of the Catalunya en Comú project were fundamentally at stake on 1 October. Out of its timid and calculating approach to 1-O emerged not only a Catalunya en Comú with a very low Catalanist profile, but also a Catalunya en Comú that was neither very disobedient nor much in favour of a political rupture. The ambiguities over 1-O expressed in the first instance ambivalences about the national question, but also about the party's impulse to reconstitute the political and social system. This is the decisive fact.

306.
The hesitations of the Comunes in the face of the pro-independence challenge depicted an organisation that was more concerned with conventional governability and the stabilisation of institutions, without the slightest interest in 1-O becoming a factor in the triggering of a decisive political and institutional crisis, within which it would have to operate in order to push for transformational solutions. Its zigzags suggested a political party that would rather close down the institutional crisis from above with a positive, but limited, transformation of the traditional party system in favour of a new one in which

the post-neoliberal left would have greater weight than it had before. It is difficult not to see in this 1-O episode a key moment in the emerging mutation of the Comunes into a 'Eurocommons'. In the shadow of October, its leadership team would have to decide whether to place itself once and for all in the historical and strategic continuity that reached back from the Moncloa Pact (1977) through the tripartite government (2003–10), or whether to put itself firmly on the side of the transformational challenge of the 15-M. It was a crystal-clear dilemma that admitted any number of tactical nuances, but could not tolerate any strategic ambiguity whatsoever.

307.
Catalunya en Comú used the weaknesses of the independence movement to further deepen its own weaknesses. Faced with the strategic weakness of the independence movement as a project for rupture, in the double sense of the difficulties of making it happen and its limitations in terms of emancipatory content, the Comunes refused to put forward any other path towards rupture, but rather sought to chase away any spectre of rupture at all. The contradictions of the independence leaders who found themselves, in spite of themselves, at the forefront of the October crisis were taken advantage of, not to explore other ways of deepening the crisis in a social and transformational direction, but to try to return to normality. The proposal for a new tripartite government between the Comunes, the ERC and the PSC, without any serious programmatic and strategic debate on its objectives, was the concrete formula adopted to represent this perspective. It meant not only closing down all the potential of the October crisis, but also stifling the hopes opened up by the 15-M in 2011.

308.
It is tempting to compare Catalunya en Comú's hesitations with those of one of its founding partners, ICV (Initiative for

Catalonia Greens), in 2014. At that time, ICV adopted a policy of passive indecision which was very similar to that of the Comunes in 2017. In the former case, however, the hesitation was not about whether or not to support the referendum initially planned (which was the result of a broad consensus agreed in Parliament) but, firstly, about how to vote in it. ICV did not reveal its position until the last minute. Secondly, ICV then hesitated over how to react to the 'participatory process' that Mas proposed as an alternative to the referendum once that was banned by the Constitutional Court. To begin with, ICV categorically rejected the ban, only to end up supporting it in a low-key way. In other words, the dilemmas of ICV then and of Catalunya en Comú later reflect the same discomfort with the pro-independence movement and the same inability to think strategically about how to relate it to the new agenda that emerged from 15-M and the Mareas against austerity. When comparing the role of both organisations in 2014 and today, we are inclined to recall Marx's well-known phrase in the 18th Brumaire when he writes that 'Hegel remarks somewhere that all great, world-historical facts and personages occur, as it were, twice. He has forgotten to add: the first time as tragedy, the second as farce.'[6] However, bearing in mind, firstly, that ICV was then a minor party in electoral decline, while Catalunya en Comú later became one of the most important Catalan parties, and secondly, that Mas's government backed down at the drop of a hat while Puigdemont's went much further, it may be that the reality reversed Marx's assertion. If ICV's attitude in 2014 was a farce, that of Catalunya en Comú in 2017 was the tragedy.

Legitimism

309.
Contrary to all expectations, the struggle between the ERC and Puigdemont on 21 December 2017 ended in victory for the latter. The limitations of Junqueras and Rovira's party were, once again, clearly exposed. Lacking 'punch' is the most

vivid description of the lacklustre politics of the official pro-independence movement. This was politics understood as a constant lament for lost opportunities and a refusal to exploit the possibilities of a specific situation to the maximum. It was a politics that had caution as its strategic bedrock. Puigdemont's comeback can be explained by the legitimacy of the presidential figure in exile. In this sense, there was a part of the undecided vote that went to the 'President', who had the skill to build an electoral machine that was partly detached from PDECAT and to adopt a rhetoric that was relatively epic in comparison with that of the ERC (although also lukewarm in absolute terms). He adopted the studied tone of an unspeakable 'maverick', able to argue that what was at stake was not so much his personal candidacy as the legitimacy of the very institution he embodied and of the referendum of 1 October. Puigdemont thus merged his own image with that of the presidency and that of the Catalan people themselves, or at least of those who supported independence. The Procés that began in 2012 has suffered from hyper-presidentialism, with a permanent invocation of presidential leadership, first of Mas and then of Puigdemont, always seen as the key to the whole strategic architecture. This was decisive on 21-D. However, the independence movement has been a peculiar sort of hyper-presidentialism, more linked to the institution than to the person, which is why Puigdemont had to force the situation so much in order not to remain in the background after the election.

310.
The success of the Puigdemont operation is another example of the proven instinct of the Catalan right for self-preservation. Despite obtaining its worst results in history, it resists losing its hegemony over the Catalan nationalist camp for good, using the institutional and social bonds it has forged over decades in power to give it an advantage over its competitors in the pro-independence camp. Such survival skills go hand in hand with structural weakness for a right whose

neoliberal model prevents it from consolidating a firm social base. It can only be partially galvanised by the possibility of creating its own state, but at the cost of a confrontation with the Spanish state that is becoming increasingly difficult to manage.

311.
Conservative Catalan nationalism came to power in November 2010 with an ultra-liberal project of a 'government of the best', which quickly went into sharp decline in both popularity and legitimacy. The independence process that began in 2012 provided it with a narrative to cling to, an epic that it lacked and a *raison d'être* that it had lost. But this was always accompanied by two interrelated and insurmountable contradictions: the contrast between the strategic rhetoric of an easy, painless independence and the real difficulties of the task, and the tension between the real aim of the movement (independence) and that of the Catalan government (to use the independence movement to renegotiate the relationship between Spain and Catalonia). Both contradictions were inherent in the project, and together with the economic crisis and the anti-establishment legacy of 15-M they prevented the Catalan right from consolidating the social base of its new project and crystallising a new social bloc. Therein lay its weakness.

312.
The Catalan right, under the leadership first of Mas (2012–15) and then of Puigdemont (from 2015), has enjoyed political hegemony over the independence process, in the sense that it has always managed to subordinate the movement to its party interests and to pass off its own interests as those of the whole movement. But its hegemony has been unstable, running parallel to a sharp electoral decline and a paradoxical political divorce from the Catalan *haute bourgeoisie*, which traditionally supported it but did not embrace the

pro-independence agenda, despite continuing to agree on the economic programme. The story of the Convergencia (re-founded since 2016 as PDeCAT) has been more like an unstable hegemony under reconstruction, based on a permanent dodge to mitigate its erosion, rather than the consolidation of a new hegemony. The prolonged electoral decline from 2012 forced it to re-found the party in 2016 and then repeatedly seek some kind of electoral pact (Junts pel Sí in 2015 and Junts per Catalunya in 2017) to avoid being tested directly at the ballot box, thus developing a peculiar hegemony by proxy. Convergencia has not been able to consolidate a reconstructed hegemony since its own crisis, while no other political force has been able to effectively veto its plans or pose a decisive challenge to its leadership. Instability and resilience are both features of Convergencia's leading role.

313.
All hegemonies bring together different temporalities: political, electoral, economic and cultural, which intersect in an uneven way. They neither fade nor strengthen at the same speed, nor simultaneously. To understand hegemony is to understand the 'discordance of times', to borrow an expression of Daniel Bensaïd,[7] of every social structure and of the very nature of political conflict. The Procés broke out after the serious crisis of hegemony experienced by the Convergencia (and the PSC), and more generally by neoliberalism, as a result of the 15-M. The Convergencia saw this as an opportunity to revive itself and acquire a new source of legitimacy. At the same time, it understood that if it did not try to ride the still relatively tame tiger of independence, it would be overpowered by it and its crisis of hegemony could become irreversible. To maintain its hegemony, it had to take on the explicitly pro-independence project, which was not its own, while defining it in terms compatible with its own political culture and economic model, and with the aim of

being able to use it as the basis for a political relaunch. This pointed towards a hegemony in the Procés with unstable overtones. It was a political and intellectual hegemony that ran side by side with a permanent electoral decline that only stabilised at very low levels on 21 December 2017, with a difficult process of refoundation to leave behind the burden of corruption and with the piloting of a Procés that, despite the contrast between rhetoric and deeds, prevented institutional normalisation.

314.
As a hegemonic force, the Convergencia managed to subordinate the rest of the pro-independence groups, integrating them in a subordinate way into its strategy. The strength of the Convergencia's hegemony in the Procés has been based on its ability to set the terms of debate on independence on a strictly national basis, empty of any discussion of the economic or social model, and to achieve this subordinate integration of the main political and social actors, with the partial but real exception of the CUP. It managed to achieve this, firstly, through its grip on the key instrument, the presidency of the Generalitat, and, secondly, through its decisive influence in the Catalan media and its capacity to shape public opinion and the dominant narrative. The latter, however, was compatible with a loss of moral credibility, a decisive facet of any hegemony, due to the accumulated weight of past corruption scandals, the decline of the figure of Pujol, his aggressive neoliberal policies and his past support for autonomy rather than independence. The building-up of the figure of Artur Mas, to make him transcend his own party and its political baggage, was the path chosen to compensate for this moral and cultural crisis of the world of the Convergencia. However, this crisis has only really begun to be overcome with the increasingly autonomous role of Carles Puigdemont, the epic of the October Days, the effect of leadership in exile and the launching of Crida

per la República (National Call for the Republic), which, in reality, aims to re-found the sphere of the Catalan nationalist right on cultural and political premises that must be partially different from those of its recent history, precisely in order to maintain the central role it has played in Catalan politics since the Transition.

315.
For five years, the Convergencia had been losing support to the ERC, which was traditionally regarded as more credible in terms of independence, on the one hand, and less associated with the old regime of neoliberalism and corruption, on the other. A change occurred in the first aspect after 21 December, due to the ERC's hesitations in the electoral campaign, the reformulation of the debate in terms of presidential legitimacy and institutional continuity, and the increase in Puigdemont's relative autonomy. But Junts per Catalunya's project in reality had a significant component of tactical and strategic improvisation, of pressing on regardless, which accelerated that already exhibited with the pro-independence turn in 2012. It was one somersault after another, as the ex-Convergent right continued to move between an unfinished refoundation and its own strategic Ponzi scheme.

316.
The electoral success of Junts per Catalunya does not mean that it had finally succeeded in re-founding itself after the failed launch of PDeCAT in July 2016. But it was in a better position to do so, and this is what it intended to do with the Crida per la República, which, for the umpteenth time, would try to play the game of passing off its own interests as those of the independence movement as a whole. It intended to bury the first, failed refoundation of the Convergencia (its transformation into PDeCAT) in favour of a second, within which there was a lingering tension between those who would opt for a gradual return to the path of institutional

normality (no doubt accepting that this would mean losing the political majority within nationalism for a while), and those who, led by Puigdemont, would defend maintaining rhetorically a state of exception, which they needed to sustain the central role of the 'President' in exile, and to be able to implement their attempt at a political re-foundation.

Diverging mirrors

317.
Following on from a self-inflicted defeat at a time when it had reached its peak on 1 October and 3 October, on 21 December the independence movement managed to keep its bewildered social base mobilised, obtaining its highest number of votes ever. It was similar to that of the 'Yes' vote on 1-O (2,044,038), and slightly higher than that of the 27-s elections in 2015 (1,966,508; 47.8 per cent) and the 'Yes-Yes' vote in the non-binding citizens' consultation of 9 November 2014 (1,897,274), although the electoral roll was different then and comparisons are not exact. The strength of the independence movement lies in its consistency and endurance, but its weakness has been its prolonged structural stagnation since 2014. Of course, this does not detract from the fact that it won more votes than the rival bloc and the stability of its social base.

318.
Despite the government's mishandling of 1 October and the anti-climax of the declaration of the Republic on 27 October, the 'pro-independence people' remained massively loyal to their main political and social organisations. In the face of the state's onslaught, they kept up the electoral pressure and did not channel their frustration through a punishment vote in favour of the CUP. The crackdown by the state encouraged independence supporters to close ranks, albeit certainly with less enthusiasm than in the preceding period and with less naivety. This reflects, at a deeper level, one of the essential characteristics of the movement that emerged five years earlier. With the

exception of the decisive days from 20 September to 3 October, it was marked by an institutional logic of representative democracy, particularly after the elections of 27 September 2015. It lacked disruptive capacity and was strictly disciplined by the ANC (and Òmnium).

319.
The independence movement won the 21-D elections, but without a clear roadmap, or even a semblance of one. It was victory without a plan, and, let us not forget, victory in defeat – electoral victory after having lost politically in October because it lacked any initiative. Administering 21-D proved to be complex, now that the official public narrative of easy independence and a peaceful separation had been disproved. The movement that emerged in 2012 had never been so massive or so consistent. It has obtained the highest number of supporters in its history after suffering a serious and self-inflicted political defeat on 27-O and after managing very badly the 1-O. But its founding strategy was finished.

320.
The policy of 'independence first and then everything else', of separating the national question from the social question, of restricting the right to decide and democracy to the national issue, is now an empty formula which has been responsible for the movement's 'collateral damage' and its unintended consequences, whether or not they were foreseen by its promoters. It does not serve to create a broader majority in society, nor to forge a project that guarantees economic and social change. It has given rise to a polarisation based on identity, which is certainly more political and electoral than social, and which has given Ciudadanos a boost in the working-class neighbourhoods. But it has done so against a backdrop of social devastation caused by neoliberalism, the implementation of which counted to a large extent on the complicity of the left and the workers' movement. This is

a decisive question when it comes to apportioning responsibility and seeing the underlying historical reasons for the rise of the orange party.

321.
The independence movement faces a fork in the road in the immediate future. Either it clings to an exhausted strategic paradigm that crashed head-on into the Spanish state, or it re-founds itself in order to keep the flame of rupture burning. In other words: will it opt for strategic immobility, spiced up with a paradoxical combination of its unrealistic founding delusions and a new post-O-27 defeatism and sense of victimhood, or will there be a general re-foundation and reformulation? Strategic immobility will lead to political agony, even if this was disguised in the months after 21-D by a defensive, anti-repressive logic and by Puigdemont's claim to legitimacy, which was as powerful symbolically as it was hollow strategically. The trials of the political prisoners would apparently give a new momentum to the pro-independence movement. But this was likely to be just a way of postponing the debates and the reconsideration of failed assumptions.

322.
This symbolic claim to legitimacy was used as an instrument to consolidate the leadership of the right within the independence movement, and prevented the substantive debate that was sorely needed after 21-D. It led to the election of a new 'President', Quim Torra, whose traditionalist, nationalist views amount to a reaffirmation (or even a deepening) of the most problematic and flawed founding premises of the Procés. Torra's nationalism includes a conception of Catalonia and of the 'Catalan people' that is even a step backwards with respect to that which, in the midst of an anti-Franco movement dominated by the workers' government, had been in the end adopted by Pujol.[8] In fact, his conception of the nation is closer to the most conservative and rigid variant

of Catalan nationalism from the beginning of the 20th century. The hardline nationalist ideology of the new 'President' has not had any concrete consequences for his governmental actions, and it is unlikely that it will. But his election sent a symbolic message to the outside world that undoubtedly weakened the pro-independence movement.

323.
After the end of the symbolic claim to legitimacy and the appointment of the government headed by Torra, it seemed the independence movement could evolve into a current with a proposal to break with the Spanish state, but disconnected from any road map or short-term aim of bringing this about. In other words, it could dissociate its formal objective from its more prosaic day-to-day activities and become the protagonist of a structural conflict in Catalan and Spanish politics, but without any pretence of pushing that through or reaching a concrete resolution. The proposal and rhetoric of rupture would in fact endorse a self-censored approach to conflict whose symbolic strength would be proportional to its acceptance of the rules of the game.

The reformulation on hold

324.
This transition towards a new phase of the independence movement was taking place in the midst of a fierce dispute over its internal reorganisation. Three sub-battles were intertwined here: first, the struggle between the ERC and Junts x Catalunya/PDECAT; second, the struggle between Junts x Catalunya and PDECAT for the final reshaping of the neoliberal centre-right; and third, the tension that set the ERC, PDECAT and the majority of Junts x Catalunya against a social and intellectual pro-independence milieu, in which figures such as Jordi Graupera and the leadership of the ANC stand out, and which, faced with the paralysis of the pro-independence political elite, began to consider the possibility

of a new political organisation that would partly sidestep the party structures and seek to complete what the 'conventional politicians' failed to deliver in October. Political infighting and the electoral logic paralyse any serious strategic debate and hijack the capacity to think in the long term. Short-term factionalism replaces strategic thinking in the *longue durée*.

325.
The victor on 21 December was an 'independence movement without independence', to use the expression of the conservative commentator Enric Juliana,[9] an independence movement that could not achieve independence, but which formally still had the aim of moving towards it, even though it no longer had a convincing plan to achieve it, even from a propaganda point of view (from a strategic point of view its limits had always been apparent). However, in the new stage of the Torra government, the independence movement seemed obliged to move towards a phase not only of an independence movement without independence, but of an independence movement without the aim of independence, combining republican rhetoric with actions that were more in line with autonomy, based on a misleading use of the slogan 'building the Republic', bereft of any real political content. The question was whether this would be sustainable for long or not; whether it would lead to a mood of disappointment and demoralisation, mixed with an exclusively defensive dynamic of opposition to repression and symbolic actions, or whether it would be able to do this while sustaining a strategy of struggle for a whole new period. This could occur simply through the consolidation of a pro-independence bloc too weak to win but too strong to be definitively defeated. This in turn would generate permanent conflict in a situation where instability had become the norm and was used by the leaderships of both blocs to hold together their supporters and keep them mobilised. But it could also be the result of a complete reorientation of the perspectives and objectives of the independence

movement in a way that allowed it to overcome its underlying weaknesses and its most contradictory aspects. This option, needless to say, was the least likely in the circumstances.

326.
Spread, build, make the Republic. Such has been the slogan of the movement after the fog of 27-O. With 'separation' and the 'Law against Law' now buried, 'make or build Republic' became the new strategic concept that obscured rather than illuminated the movement's own capacities, but now in a defensive mood of confusion and gridlock. Its meaning varied and was vague. Often it seemed to be synonymous with the implementation of effective measures or social laws. Although these were necessary, this led to confusion between the republican idea of building a political community and a framework for coexistence through the approval of laws and the implementation of concrete policies, and the proclamation of a new state after a process of institutional breakdown. One version of this slogan has remained within the perspective of the Procés (Junts x Catalunya and ERC), while another has had a voluntarist character (ANC and CUP). In the first case, it is an empty and rhetorical slogan that barely conceals the real disorientation or merely provides cover for symbolic actions aimed at maintaining the institutional tension that Junts x Catalunya needs to consolidate its project. In the second, it serves to express frustration with the government's actions and keep up the pressure for institutional ruptures, but without opening up a discussion on the limitations of the process begun in 2012 (ANC) or only partially doing so (CUP).

327.
In the short term, and in the absence of any plausible roadmap or agreement on one, the majority of the pro-independence forces seemed to be pinning everything on the remobilising effect (in Catalan society) and the re-legitimising effect

(in Catalonia, Spanish society and international public opinion) of the trials underway and the convictions. But it could also be a moment when all the contradictions exploded, when all the frustrations and dissatisfactions were expressed in electoral evasions or condensed in the streets. These were already evident on the anniversary of 1 October with the fracture between part of the movement and the government of the Generalitat as a result of the police crackdown by the *Mossos de Esquadra*. So, could there be a new momentum with no conclusive outcome and no long-term prospects?

328.
It is well known that there is no such thing as a vacuum in politics, and even less so in times of conflict. In a situation of confusion and lack of initiative, the yellow ribbon campaign in solidarity with political prisoners became the most visible daily expression of the independence movement and a day-to-day outlet for personal and collective solidarity. The ups and downs of the yellow ribbon summed up quite well the situation of the independence movement: mass support built on personal commitment and perseverance, but at the same time impotence and disorientation. Without realising it, the movement ended up engaged in a defensive battle against the reactionary forces that found in the yellow ribbon a lever for mobilising action and fomenting polarisation and social fracture. As an expression of solidarity, the yellow ribbon was a good initiative, but because it developed in a strategic vacuum, halfway between a disorderly retreat and a symbolic institutional drive forward, its defence became almost a goal in itself, rather than the cohesive symbol of a broader campaign. The debate over the ribbon replaced all other pending discussions.

329.
From within the pro-independence camp, the ERC has haltingly explored new perspectives. However, as victim of a gradualist

and social-democratic conception of social change and an institutionalist, parliamentary political practice, in the end it risks disorderly capitulation. The party has identified three decisive weaknesses of the independence movement: its dissociation of the proposal for a state of its own from any social demands, its inability to link support for a Catalan republic with the prospect of a Spanish republic and the end of the 1978 regime, and the need to forge alliances within Catalonia between independence supporters and those in favour of the right to self-determination. However, its electoralist and institutionalist conception of politics and its liberal-progressive programme (with classical social-democratic touches which are not very systematically expressed) prevent it from satisfactorily resolving the problems it correctly identifies. Reformist institutionalism acts as a strategic barrier that prevents it from entering fully into unexplored terrain.

330.
The path of strategic reformulation involves linking the pro-independence agenda to anti-austerity policies, arguing for a constituent process that would be compatible with both independence and a confederal outcome, and connecting the pro-independence perspective with that of the fall of the 1978 regime in the whole of the Spanish state. This triple turn is essential for the pressing twofold task now facing the independence movement: firstly, to create a majority political and social bloc between pro-independence supporters and those federalist sectors who are in favour of the right to decide and opposed to the 1978 regime; and secondly, to break out of the movement's isolation in the Spanish state as a whole, which is what opened the door to the repressive measures taken by Rajoy. Pressing on regardless vs. taking a step backwards to gain momentum is a false dilemma which conceals the alternative path of rethinking the movement's approach in order to embark on a new phase of political struggle.

331.
The problem of the independence movement goes far beyond the hackneyed expression of the need to 'broaden the social base'. What the movement, and its left wing in particular, needs is both a broadening and a reshaping of the project – a strategic reformulation leading to a wider political appeal. This fits very badly with Puigdemont's leadership of the independence movement, with the subsequent appointment of Quim Torra as his successor at the head of the Catalan government, and with an ANC that after October embodied more than anyone else the strategic crisis of the movement, remaining wedded to the founding paradigm of 'independence first, and then everything else'.

332.
The broadening of the movement must be thought of in terms of broadening its objectives. That means broadening its capacity to form alliances with those who are not pro-independence but who are opposed to the 1978 regime; broadening its proposals, abandoning independence pure and simple to embrace a social and democratic emergency plan; broadening its perspectives for rupture, developing a dialectic between centre and periphery and linking its own project to a change of regime. In short, it needs to renegotiate its own identity and not to entrench its most spurious founding characteristics. A Hegelian operation of strategic 'Aufhebung' or sublation, overcoming without negating? Why not.

333.
After completely subordinating itself to the Catalan government and the 'President' in the run-up to October and in its handling of the immediate aftermath, from March 2018 under the leadership of Elisenda Paluzie, the ANC seemed to take its distance, but on the basis of reasserting all its strategic limitations. Gaining independence from the Catalan

government and from the excessive institutionalisation of the Procés (particularly after 2015) was a positive step, but doing so on the basis of ratifying a failed strategy is a dead end. In reality, if the ANC wants Catalan independence, the first conclusion it should reach would be the need to break free from its initial paradigm. In other words, the independence strategy needs strategic independence from its own founding limitations. However, implementing a strategy of disconnection with one's own original hypotheses is not particularly easy. It requires a capacity for self-evaluation that is unusual in social and political organisations. On the contrary, the ANC's approach is one of reaffirmation without strategic reorientation.

334.

Nor have the CDRs ('Committees for the Defence of the Republic', previously 'Committees for the Defence of the Referendum') been able to bring about a change of dynamic. They were decisive on the eve of 1 October, when they partially outflanked the official structures (with which they had a relationship of collaboration and competition, inside and outside). Afterwards, however, they were unable to sustain an agenda of their own, for mass struggle from below, in a context where the brakes were being put on from above. As time went by, they began to lose strength and, from bodies of self-organisation on a large scale, in the classical mould of the popular power organisations that emerge in any moment of social and political upheaval, they turned into small nuclei of activists. In general, they tended to slide into an excessively avant-garde dynamic, although their specific realities have been very varied and there have been some remarkable local experiences, and in many cases they have retained significant legitimacy. In some ways they became refuges for a layer of discontented, militant activists. However, their response to the paralysis of the pro-independence parties has been to try to go 'all the way' without considering, or considering only partially, the overarching strategic problems. Their combative spirit combined with their lack of reorientation, in what we could call a policy of combative perseverance without strategic self-questioning.

335.
In the disarray after October, a whole current of liberal pro-independence thought emerged with its own voice, separate from PDECAT and Junts x Catalunya, which postulated an assertive pro-independence strategy. The initiative to organise primaries for a unitary pro-independence candidate in the city of Barcelona, launched by Jordi Graupera on 20 March 2018, was its main political expression. His proposal implied an attempt to outflank the political machinery of the independence movement, similar to that of Ada Colau when she launched (successfully) Guanyem Barcelona in June 2014. It reflected the dissatisfaction of many in the independence movement with the mess that followed 1 October and the image of impotence (and disunity) conveyed by Junts x Catalunya/PDECAT and the ERC. It implies a complete overhaul of the historical culture of Catalanism, judged timorous and impotent in the face of state coercion, in favour of an independence movement as uncomplicated as its 'true liberals' demeanour.[10]

336.
The 'true independence movement' led by Graupera should be analysed from two points of view: its relationship with a project for emancipation and its ability to correct the strategic limitations of the Procés. There is little doubt about the first question: this is a strictly neoliberal proposal, in the vein of Mas's 'government of the best' in 2010, based on a rhetoric of modernisation and competition. It is an unalloyed ideological ode to the values of North Americanised capitalism that seems a little out of date in the post-2008 world. Regarding the second question, although Graupera has had the merit of always pointing out the strategic fallacies of

the Procés (separation, Law against Law...) his alternative is purely subjective. It should be enough simply to change the leaders and put firm people like himself, who would not back down, in charge of the movement. But none of the movement's underlying problems are addressed, such as its middle-class social composition, its slim majority, the kind of alliances it needs, or its lack of any criticism of austerity policies. His calls for a courageous and tenacious stance barely conceal the strategic vacuity on which his proposal is based.[11]

337.
The new pro-independence current outside the political parties seemed to converge with the positions of the ANC itself, which, in its reaffirmation without reorientation, played with the idea of pressing on regardless and jumping straight into the electoral arena, in order to build a new genuinely pro-independence political party without the limitations of PDeCAT and the ERC. However, these limitations were not understood in relation to the weaknesses of the movement's founding strategy or its working practices. The temptation of trying to outflank electorally the pro-independence parties that 'failed' after 1 October, channelled the frustration of a part of the 'pro-independence people' towards a permanent search for solutions that had the curious merit of completely ignoring all the problems that explained October's defeat. It sought to explore new paths without taking stock of what had been achieved, or with only one-sided balance sheets, from which only self-deception, paralysis and individual opportunism could emerge.

338.
Whether or not it is actually able to overcome its own real limitations and strategic impasses, the independence movement has become a structural feature of Catalan society and a long-lasting mass movement that has substantially changed the

traditional objective of Catalanism in its various variants: the reform of Spain. It has developed solid roots, to use Gramscian jargon, in both 'civil society' and 'political society'. But it suffers from a triple underlying problem: a perverse dialectic between the social and the political, a highly mobilised but not very disruptive civil society, and important social, spatial and class biases in its support base.

339.
Firstly, the dialectic between the social and the political from 2012 to 2015 saw a growing subordination of the former to the latter. This allowed the political leaders of the Procés to move increasingly into the institutional sphere, at a time when this was dominated by moderate currents. And when this dynamic began to reverse, with the ANC distancing itself from the Govern (government), it did so without discussing the limitations of the social movement for independence, which had facilitated the errors in the political sphere. Consequently, the new autonomy of the social from the political appeared as a direct criticism of the parties and the Govern – but not as the result of a strategic reappraisal of the social movement itself. This merely opened the door to a new search for political shortcuts.

340.
Secondly, pro-independence 'civil society' has been solidly organised by the ANC (and to a lesser extent Òmnium), which was the real backbone of a movement with admirable perseverance and vitality. But it was lacking in 'punch' and was strategically armed with what we might call immaterial hypotheses, constituting a kind of strategic idealism that was ill-prepared to confront the material reality of the dominant power relations. Only between 20 September and 3 October, in the brief electrifying phase of the movement, did a really disruptive 'civil society' emerge, but it was one that was conditioned by the dynamics of the previous five years.

341.
Thirdly, pro-independence 'civil society' suffers from significant imbalances. In terms of class, it tilts towards the world of the middle classes (old and new), of public sector employees and white-collar workers with high levels of formal education. In social and spatial terms, it gravitates towards medium-sized cities, the centres of large cities, and small towns and villages. The age imbalance, however, is less marked. Although youth and young adults have played a decisive role in the movement, the data shows that the boom in support for independence after 2010 affected all age groups. The pro-independence turn of the Convergencia's traditional support base led to an exponential expansion of support for independence among the older population. In other words, it did not grow through the addition of a specific age cohort, but rather as the result of a specific socio-political situation.

Resistance

342.
'Thus, on the afternoon of the 20th, Jordi Cuixart addressed those present and demanded the release of all those detained. Despite calling for a peaceful mobilisation, he also invoked the determination shown during the civil war (using the expression "No pasarán!" – "They shall not pass"), and challenged the state to seize the material that had been prepared for the referendum and which had been hidden in different locations. He ended his speech by saying "today there are tens of thousands of us here, tomorrow there will be hundreds of thousands of us wherever we are needed ... Have no doubt that we will win our freedom."'[12] This paragraph from the Prosecutor's Conclusions sent to the Supreme Court on 2 November 2018, in which the charges against the pro- independence leaders were formulated, perfectly summarises the real nature of the political and ideological argument deployed against the independence movement and the true character of the 1978 Spanish state itself. A state which perceives the anti-fascist slogan 'No pasarán!' as a threat and not as a constituent part of its own identity.

343.
The relationship between repression and political and social protest is complex. The former can silence the latter or increase it. It depends on the political context in which it takes place, the nature of the measures taken and the social groups affected. The fact is, however, that for the first time in five years the independence movement was confronted with state repression that broke all the previous rules of the game. 'Repression is effective when it complements the impact of general policy measures that are themselves effective,' wrote Victor Serge in 1925.[13] The Spanish government is currently incapable of taking such effective measures, because it cannot even accept the legitimacy of the question raised by the independence movement, nor can it offer a credible reform of the state.

344.
The choice of repression is not enough in itself to put an end to the movement or to solve politically the issues that gave rise to it. It could inflict a serious short-term blow, and produce paralysis, disorientation and division, albeit at the cost of undermining the legitimacy of the Spanish state in Catalonia even further and, consequently, aggravating the long-term political problem it faces. It could put a definitive end to the October challenge and divert it into a protracted conflict that would be both functional and dysfunctional for the stability of the regime. Are we about to enter a phase of normalisation of a permanent conflict with no outcome, combining real confrontation and self-serving theatrics, which would become the main factor shaping Catalan and, to a large extent, Spanish politics? It is still too early to tell.

345.
It is well known that human societies have a very high capacity for adapting and normalising situations that are abnormal. Once the initial outrage had passed, the predictably long sentences handed down to the political prisoners would

become part of the everyday political landscape. Nonetheless, over time they would also become a headache for the Spanish state, which would have to manage the consequences of its own excesses and its inability to extricate itself from the state of political exceptionalism that it had itself helped to create. The short-sighted use of repression generates far-reaching consequences and making an obstinate stand in the present can feed a crisis in the future. The outcome would depend on the capacity of the independence movement and the entire anti-repressive bloc to combine reactive punch and political-strategic endurance.

346.
Every advance by a democratic movement provokes a polarising backlash from its opponents. Although it is obvious, it is always those who oppose from reactionary positions who are responsible for this polarisation. A democratic movement, therefore, should not be blamed for 'awakening' reaction. As its name suggests, this is a response to what is perceived as a threat of change. However, that fact does not absolve the independence movement of its strategic (ir)responsibilities, in so far as it never made a serious assessment of how to build itself and act in a way that would make things as difficult as possible for the reactionary forces. Many of its founding strategic fallacies offered a vulnerable flank which, at a critical moment, could be exploited by reactionary opponents. The same applies to the absence of politics from the 'forces of change' grouped in Catalunya en Comú–Podem, or their reduction of such politics to an institutional and media balancing act.

347.
The Catalan crisis released a spring that has been a fundamental part of Spanish nationalism throughout its history: the 'Schmittian' spectre of the enemy within, the anti-Spain. An anti-Spain with many historical incarnations and which now appeared in the form of Catalan 'separatism', but which,

once aroused, had an expansive reactionary logic that would progressively encompass ever wider social sectors and more political phenomena. It was but a small step from the criminalisation of Catalan 'separatism' to the criminalisation of Podemos and all kinds of dissent. The persecution of October led naturally to a hunt for the legacy of 15-M and its aftermath. Paradoxically, the independence movement has been simultaneously the main challenger to the 1978 regime and a scapegoat that facilitated a temporary institutional clampdown from above. This was as defensive as it was authoritarian and aggressive. The reactionary polarisation in response to the acceleration of the independence process in September–October favoured, in the short term, the most conservative forces in the Spanish state. It led to a closing of ranks among the pro-regime bloc and the entire state apparatus, under the hegemony of the most reactionary sectors.

348.
The tension between centre and periphery and the anti-Catalan (and anti-Basque) character of Spanish nationalism, whose fullest expression is to be found in its fight against the spectre of an anti-Spain, resemble to some extent, although not exactly, the role of contemporary xenophobia in other European countries. This does not mean that xenophobia and racism are not present in Spanish politics and society, but that they combine with the fight against the enemy within to make a spiral of exclusion. From this reactionary point of view, the homeland and the nation are not only being attacked by the foreigner, by the alien coming from outside, but above all by the permanent Catalan (or Basque) adversary coming from the domestic periphery. The expansive vocation of this reactionary message in the current historical context in fact encourages the turn towards xenophobia, which is an essential part of the neo-conservative turn by Casado's PP and of Ciudadanos' attempts to compete on the same terrain.

349.
The restorationist project of the PP and the state apparatus, supported by the mass media, which was activated during the October crisis, can be defined as a kind of 'resistance on the offensive'. 'Resistance' because it was incapable of taking on a reform from above, a 'passive revolution' in the Gramscian sense, which would partially integrate the demands of those who have been left outside the political framework of '78 (i.e. the supporters of Podemos and Catalan independence) and create a new distribution of political and institutional power and a new form of economic and social integration, together with a new and credible perspective for the future (half real, half imaginary), for most of the middle classes, the skilled workers and the qualified but precarious youth. 'Offensive' because it was and is very aggressive and authoritarian, cherishing the idea of taking advantage of the Catalan crisis to recentralise the entire structure of the Spanish state and isolate and undermine Podemos. But the very logic of this 'resistance on the offensive', now out of government and in opposition, will continue to deepen in the medium term the underlying reasons for the crisis of the political system set up in 1978.

350.
Using the permanent crisis of political legitimacy as a form of authoritarian governance is an expression of both strength (the ability to manage the crisis and to take advantage of its contradictions to build active support among a part of society) and weakness (the inability to stabilise a new social bloc and a new hegemony that would create a non-conflictual 'normality'). The impossibilities of the passive revolution are the still open possibilities of a democratising and transformational change. These possibilities, however, develop within a framework of reciprocal impotencies – not only the impotence of the passive revolution, but also the impotence of Catalan independence and the impotence of the 15-M and its aftermath, Unidos Podemos and the Comunes.

351.

Lacking a legitimating mark for his reign analogous to that given to his father by the defeat of the attempted coup on 23 February 1981, King Felipe VI's intervention in the October crisis may have bolstered in the short term the authoritarian response, but at the price of accelerating his own weakening as an institutional figure. It was a show of strength in the present, the cost of which was to curtail his authority in the future. A short-term intervention whose long-term consequences were not properly gauged. Is the King, then, the weak link in the regime? He is at least a figure whose repudiation unites all opponents of the '78 state'.

352.

The recriminations against the institutions and the various local initiatives against the King could open up a new arena for anti-monarchist republican engagement, and new opportunities for understanding in Catalonia between pro-independence supporters and opponents of the '78 regime, as well as a shared perspective between all of them and the Spanish republican movement. But for this to happen, Spanish republicanism must defend the right to self-determination and the legitimacy of the Catalan independence movement, while the latter must not ignore the crisis of the regime at the level of the Spanish state as a whole. If criticism of the monarchy can be a catalyst for the democratic radicalisation of part of society and for advancing an anti-regime agenda, it is also important that this does not imply a nostalgic glorification of the Republic and a fetishisation of that state form, which could lead to sterile efforts disconnected from a critique of the hard core of neoliberalism. Rather than setting our sights on the Republic as an institutional reality of the past, we should aim towards constituting new horizons based on a new kind of republicanism, one that is 'Indignant', rooted in 15 May and plurinational.

353.
At the level of the Spanish state, the authoritarian regression of the entire state apparatus and the political situation was patent. It left Unidos Podemos swimming against the tide as the only voice with a democratic approach, albeit with serious strategic limitations. The mismatch between this relative paralysis in the state as a whole and the Catalan process created a scissors effect that increasingly favoured divergence between the two realities and boosted reactionary forces. The authoritarian turn and the increasingly morbid social and political mood constituted a peculiarly Hispanic path towards the authoritarian backlash that prevailed across the European Union. It put an end to the relative exceptionalism of the Spanish experience after 15-M. We were Europeans once again, but this time not to celebrate naively the successes of neoliberal modernisation as in the eighties, but to join in the reactionary shift (albeit not without some counter-moves towards the left) that afflicts a good part of the Old Continent.

354.
It is impossible to tell what the final outcome of the crisis triggered by the Catalan October will be, but whatever happens, its impact will go far beyond Catalonia. Rajoy's attack on Catalan institutions, supported by the PSOE, marked an unprecedented escalation of repression and a major deterioration of democracy itself in the Spanish state. If the wheel of judicial repression continues to turn, as everything suggests it will, and if the post-Rajoy period does not bring a change in its sinister course, it will undoubtedly have ominous implications for the political model of the Spanish state as a whole and, more indirectly, of other European countries too. Its triumph will widen the scope of what is 'possible' for the powers that be, of what is officially 'acceptable' in the European context, of what can be 'done' in extreme circumstances. It will increase the level of structural cynicism among Europe's political establishment.

355.
If the legacy of the Catalan October is settled by repressive and authoritarian means, albeit slightly tempered after the fall of the PP, then other political crises, whatever their nature, will be dealt with in the same way. It will be another step on the road to authoritarianism and will further facilitate the implosion of democratic institutions across the continent, especially on its Mediterranean periphery, where they were blown apart by the economic 'shock doctrine'. In this respect, the Catalan crisis should be seen as part of the crisis of the parliamentary democratic model, under the prolonged impact of neoliberalism and austerity following the outbreak of the 2008 crisis. It cannot be understood in isolation from the general roll-back of democracy that was underway.

Splits on the Right

356.
The crisis of the PSOE marked the first phase of the Spanish political crisis. That of the PP was the second. The Ciudadanos operation launched in January 2015 provided both a change and a crutch for the two-party system while wresting from Podemos the monopoly on change. But its consolidation ultimately destabilised the right-wing camp as well. The PP had managed to resist in the 2015 and 2016 elections, in spite of everything. However, its decline intensified under the double impact of the Catalan crisis and a string of corruption scandals. The precipitating factor was the Catalan October that triggered an abrasive dynamic that trapped PP, which ended up suffering the friction that every clash generates, while Ciudadanos, on the one hand, and the far right of Vox, on the other, propagandistically capitalized on the situation.

357.
The election of Pablo Casado as the new leader of the PP represented in part a grassroots rebellion against the party establishment. It bears similarities to the re-election of Pedro Sánchez

at the head of the PSOE, but with the important difference that Casado had the support of heavyweights within the organisation and of the entire right-wing media and cultural apparatus. The pragmatic conservatism of Rajoy and Soraya succumbed to the neo-conservative revival promised by Casado. These were not times of routine or conventional politics and, between an electoral project aimed at assuring the stability of the state and a proposal for combat, the latter prevailed.

358.
His first mission was to halt the PP's decline and the draining of its traditional support base, to prevent the implosion of a party with an ageing electorate rooted in the less-educated social strata. Casado's project was, historically speaking, the second attempt by Spain's neo-conservatives to assert themselves; however, it could not simply try to reproduce the glory days of Aznar and opposition to Zapatero because the political and social context was very different. If we apply to it the overused term of populism, we could define it as neoconservatism with a populist form, whose aim was to recover its social roots in order to rebuild itself politically. Recovering the ground it had lost in the state and in the electoral arena implied an operation to remobilise and reinsert itself in society. This required a 'detour' into the social and cultural spheres in order to be politically and electorally reborn.

359.
In this strategy of 'neocon' revival, attacking the leaders and socio-cultural priorities of the left seemed like an inverted mirror to reinforce the credibility of its own project, as if showing daring in the face of the totems of the left were a barometer to measure the ambition of its own aims and to mobilise its troops for combat. As if the magnitude of the adversary were the measure of one's own: neocon pride asserted as a defiance of the left, in the search for strong adversaries against which to build oneself. The left was to

be fought more on the social and cultural terrain than on that of the economy, because that was where it seemed more credible as a threat and as a real adversary.

360.
Spanish nationalism, an unprecedented experiment in xenophobia that seeks to import the general dynamics existing in Europe into the Spanish state, and anti-feminism have been three of the basic pillars of the PP's neo-conservative turn. This last point involves more than just an attack on the specific achievements of feminism and the LGBT movement. Casado launched a frontal attack on all of their principles. It was a rebellion against feminism 'as a whole', a challenge that used the formula 'gender ideology', hitherto a preserve of the extreme right and widely deployed in several Eastern European countries, such as Hungary and Poland, to destroy all social explanations of the inequalities between men and women.[14]

361.
Casado's peculiarity is that he aims to merge traditional, right-wing conservatism with the logic of the extreme right which is on the rise in Europe, thereby prolonging the Spanish 'anomaly' that was due to the nature of the post-Franco political system and culture, and to the absence of an independent, extreme right-wing party. Only the incipient, but real, rise of Vox threatens this plan to unite the radicalised traditional right with the sociological and cultural far right within the PP. At the same time, the pro-Spanish liberalism of Ciudadanos prevents the PP from attracting more votes, and this makes it ultimately more vulnerable to a Vox that could grow even more if the PP does not clearly assert itself as the best tactical choice.

362.
Casado's ideological retooling aims to refloat the PP and reconstitute the neoconservative bloc in order to maintain a

system of two alternating parties. Revitalising this two-party system, however, demands a permanent tension between progressives and neoconservatives that excludes any interference in this binary clash, but which is based on an absolute pro-capitalist, neoliberal consensus and which does not call into question the conception of Spain, the form of its state or its basic social and cultural values. This tense bipartisanship, with no middle ground of consensus, is paradoxically a condition for the survival of the post-Franco political model itself. But it is also the cause of its own permanent instability, precisely because it cannot create such a false, pacifying 'consensus'. If Casado and Sánchez were to succeed in their respective projects, the new two-party system would be structurally unstable due to the shrinking social base of both parties, the background of economic uncertainty which impedes the consolidation of any political initiative, the lack of any final resolution of the Catalan question, and the permanent social and cultural tension that it requires to survive (against a backdrop of agreement on the economic model and its depoliticisation).

363.
Vox is the first significant, independent, organised expression of neo-fascism at the state level since the end of the Transition. Its main strength in the short term will be its ability to condition the agenda of the PP and Ciudadanos in a context in which the lack of an official anti-fascist culture in the Spanish political system makes a partial fusion with the conventional right easier. It also favours a rapid normalisation and acceptance of the extreme right, thereby smoothing its path, although this also partially undermines the subversive and rebellious posture it needs to succeed. In the case of Vox, this rebelliousness, faithful to the historical tradition of fascism and the far right in Spain, takes the form of a reactionary project that is highly traditionalist in nature.

364.

Growing out of the intensely reactionary political climate sponsored by the entire state structure (from the King to the big media groups) during the Catalan October, Vox would try to exploit the social resentment and the feeling of economic and socio-cultural vulnerability generated by the prolonged neoliberal transformation of society, exacerbated by the 'shock' of the last decade of crisis. The patriotic fervour whipped up against the Procés was decisive for the growth of Vox, but this would not have happened without the broader context of crisis, social devastation and cultural confusion caused by neoliberalism.

365.

Carried along by the Catalan crisis, Ciudadanos became the favourite option of the economic and financial powers that be, given Rajoy's loss of credibility in the months before his fall. Its project involves a combination of modernising, neoliberal renewal and fiscal prudence, a defence of Spanish nationalist identity, defined mainly as a reaction to the Catalan independence movement, and an exploitation of social resentments, which could include some gentle adjustments to habits and lifestyles, of a modern, liberal-competitive sort. This was clear during the 8 March women's strike, when Ciudadanos tried (not without contradictions and moments of absurdity) to distance itself from traditionalist, anti-feminist neoconservatism.

366.

The abrupt change of context following Pedro Sánchez's arrival in power disrupted the plans of Rivera's party, which in general has a limited capacity for real action apart from opportunistically taking advantage of favourable circumstances. Its own nationalist project (like most Spanish nationalism, as it happens) has been based more on presenting itself as a critical and polarising response to the Catalan independence movement than on any positive ability to develop a national perspective of its own or a social patriotism that does not depend on confrontation with an enemy within. They are more about reactive opportunism than the development of a plan for the future.

367.
If we apply the term 'populist' to Ciudadanos, we would have to consider that theirs is at once neoliberal, modernising, nationalist and anti-solidarity. It sells to the middle classes and to declassed workers the meritocratic dream of being a successful businessman or professional (in the image and likeness of the party's own leaders). It uses national identity as a mechanism for dissolving class antagonisms and exploits the frustration of the most disadvantaged in an unsympathetic sense to set them against other sectors of the oppressed. This last aspect is the most recent in Ciudadanos' politics and the most decisive in the medium term in the success or failure of its attempt to convert electoral and media support into a more far-reaching project of social and cultural hegemony.[15] However, the lack of local cadre and organised, grassroots support significantly complicates its progress in this direction.

368.
The orange party, in its leap from a Catalan organisation to a Spanish state-wide project, emerged as a party built on television sets and as a superficial, media-friendly, right-wing imitation of Podemos, but lacking the militant and activist dynamic that Pablo Iglesias's party had in its early days. It is weighed down by its founding weaknesses in terms of organisation and political culture. But it would certainly be a cruel paradox if, while Podemos has been hollowed out from below and consolidated an ever more electoral and media-oriented relationship with society, Ciudadanos were able to sink real roots on the ground.

An unexpected replacement

369.
The honeymoon period for the 'new' Pedro Sánchez, in terms of his desire for change and the scope of his proposals, was very short-lived. His victory in the PSOE primary elections in May 2017, against the entire party apparatus, the media and the financial powers, was indeed an unparalleled achievement. But although his triumph expressed an important and real underlying dynamic, a rebellion from below that demonstrated the scale of the party's unprecedented crisis, Sánchez himself was always an impostor. He had reinvented himself as a champion of the party's grassroots and a crusader for the values of the left in order to opportunistically channel the internal malaise in the organisation and regain the position of secretary general. Sánchez's new team never had a coherent plan to break with social-liberalism, but it did enjoy a relative autonomy from the economic and media powers and the state apparatus, which allowed it to move towards a future alliance with Podemos. It was confident that its discursive shift to the left would also reduce the space for Pablo Iglesias's party, which would ultimately be decisive for the no-confidence motion on 30 May and 1 June 2018.

370.
Faced with the 'Catalan crisis', however, Sánchez bowed to 'reasons of state'. This short-sighted and knee-jerk resort to reasons of state has been a mark of the Spanish political and financial elite in general, and especially its most right-wing faction, which is incapable of devising a viable plan for the state. The only response it had to the 'Catalan crisis' was an authoritarian one. It used it as a means to achieve temporary political cohesion and plaster over the cracks in the pillars of the political system, without tackling any of the causes that have weakened it. It was even incapable of designing a 'Lampedusian' reform from above, that would

'change everything in order to leave everything the same'.[16] The PSOE chained itself to a reactionary bloc in a subaltern manner, without being able to control it. This may have spared Sánchez from the media and financial pressure he would have suffered if he had shown the slightest hesitation, but this short-term peace of mind threatened to cloud his future. Acting as a 'statesman' when you don't control the process, the timetable or anything else doesn't usually pay off. Nor does competing with the right in implementing a policy of the 'iron fist'. For several months, Sánchez's PSOE was trapped in the reactionary climate that he himself helped to legitimise. This was alongside the rise of Ciudadanos, which had become the strategy of choice for the financial and media establishment to attempt to regenerate and restore the regime of 1978 in the face of the erosion of the PP and the stagnation of the PSOE.

371.
Surprises and plot twists are a characteristic feature of political crises. So just when Sánchez seemed cornered, the motion of censure changed things abruptly. This was not so much due to his own merits, but simply that he was in the right place at the right time. Crises operate in the realm of political representation, which has its own particular logic, although they are embedded in specific social and economic contexts, with certain relations of power, that define a given range of possible outcomes. One common feature is the inability of the ruling elite to unify and coordinate its interests around an overall solution that would avoid perpetually making the same mistakes and overcome the short-termism of decaying actors within the representative system. Entanglements are frequent and the one that led to Pedro Sánchez coming to power after the no-confidence motion was a classic. The end of an era, in fact.

372.
The Sánchez government was by no means a government of 'change', if we accord that word a strong and genuine meaning; rather, it was one of substitution, at once unstable and unexpected. It rested on the parliamentary logic of a representative system in crisis and not on an intervention by the state. Sánchez is a substitute who invited himself to the party and did not enjoy much sympathy among the political and financial elite or the state apparatus. They were betting on Rivera and Ciudadanos to channel the crisis of the regime. It was as if the PP's aggressive resistance and the spectre of a neo-restorationist threat from Ciudadanos had generated enough antibodies, not to provoke a breakdown of the regime, nor to compel a robust self-reform from above, but to activate the levers of an implausible, pleasant and non-traumatic way out of a prolonged institutional crisis. As if the PP's excesses in handling the Catalan October had unexpectedly boomeranged, propitiating a joint defensive manoeuvre by all those who were feeling asphyxiated.

373.
Sánchez's rise embodies an imperfect two-party system, one that has seemingly had its time and reflects both the depth of the political crisis and its limits. A PSOE government replaces a PP government, but in conditions of unprecedented weakness. The financial oligarchy, which was betting on Albert Rivera, agrees to lend support to Sánchez, as long as he complies with market orthodoxy and limits himself to easing the Catalan crisis without undertaking any complicated reforms. At the same time, its more centrist faction continues to support Ciudadanos as the neoliberal option for the future, while the more right-wing, neoconservative faction stands by Casado's project.

374.
Sánchez attempts to combine government action that adheres to the strictest neoliberal orthodoxy with complementary

measures that have a real or symbolic impact in the democratic and civic sphere and in the area of social policy that affects the specific groups he is trying to attract. In short, neoliberalism with social and sectoral palliatives, progressive values, along the lines of what Nancy Fraser has called 'progressive neoliberalism',[17] together with a de-escalation in authoritarian policies, but without any substantial changes. The key to its success or failure will lie precisely in its ability to make partial sectoral reforms visible and conceal its neoliberal core. To this end, it will seek a social and cultural polarisation with the 'neocon' right. In short, this is a 'business-friendly' project, seasoned with proposals that are closely connected with classic 'mainstream' progressive thinking. These tend to be as pompous as they are superficial, but no less necessary for all that. Beyond the initial gimmick of appointing the first ever government with more women than men, the truth is that Sánchez's government has declined to take any minimally audacious measures, and has backed away from any ground-breaking promises made beforehand.

375.
The consolidation of the Sánchez option, although unexpected, might in fact be the most audacious in terms of a faltering self-reform of the regime, since it would mean the definitive neutralisation of Podemos as an alternative and the deactivation of a disorientated Catalan independence movement. But it is far from clear that in the event that Sánchez manages to consolidate himself electorally (he'd only need between 25 and 30 per cent of the vote, a derisory figure for the good old days of the PSOE but sufficient in the current context) and to secure in the medium term a second government from a position of greater strength, he would actually be able to undertake any major operation to regenerate and restore the regime. This would require a courage that has so far been absent, both among the political class and in the more private circles of power. It would also

need a consensus among the media and intelligentsia that is currently elusive. The complexity of the strictly political and institutional dimension takes precedence over the weak material foundations for any consistent project of relegitimisation. But if, in the end, a successful state intervention of the left (and on the plurinational flank) were to take place, it would be quite unexpected and more or less accidental, and to a large extent the result of the strategic weaknesses of the regime's adversaries.

1   Pascal, Blaise, *Pensaments, Ara Llibres*, Barcelona, 2015, p. 176 [first edition in French *Pensées, 1670*].
2   Jaume Asens, 'Si hi ha urnes, jo aniré a votar al referèndum de l'1-o' (interview), *Crític*, 10 July 2017. Available in: www.elcritic.cat/actualitat/jaume-asens-si-hi-ha-urnes-jo-anire-a-votar-al-referendum-de-1-o-16652.
3   Noguera, Albert, 'Sobre las garantías del referéndum catalán', El diario.es, 5 September 2017. Available in: www.eldiario.es/contrapoder/garantias-referendum-catalan_6_683541658.html.
4   Gerardo Pisarello, '1–0: raons per mobilitzar-nos i votar', *Crític*, 5 September 2017. Available in: www.elcritic.cat/blogs/sentitcritic/2017/09/05/1-o-raons-per-mobilitzar-nos-i-votar/.
5   Purple is the official color of Podemos (Translator's note).
6   Karl Marx, op. cit., p. 135.

7   Daniel Bensaïd, *La discordance des temps*, Paris, Éditions de la Passion, 1995.
8   A synthesis of his thought can be seen in: Marc Font and Roger Palà, 'Què pensa Quim Torra? Els 18 articles més polèmics del nou president', *Crític*, 13 May 2018. Available in: www.elcritic.cat/reportatges/que-pensa-quim-torra-els-18-articles-mes-polemics-del-futur-president-22978.
9   Enric Juliana, 'Un teorema defectuoso', *La Vanguardia*, 23 December 2017. Available in: www.lavanguardia.com/politica/20171223/433826863380/elecciones-catalanas-teorema-defectuoso.html.
10 Jordi Graupera, 'Que siguin els últims', *El nacional*, 7 November 2017. Available in: www.elnacional.cat/ca/opinio/jordi-graupera-que-siguin-ultims_210429_102.html.
11 Jordi Graupera, 'El camí llarg', *El Nacional*, 14 January 2018. Available in: www.google.com/search?client=ubuntu&

channel=fs&q=graupera+el+cam%C3%AD+l larg&ie=utf-8&oe=utf-8.

12   *Conclusiones provisionales de la Fiscalía, Causa especial 3/20907/2017*, Secretaría 4, 2 November, 2018, pp. 84-85. Available in: www.ara.cat/2018/11/02/ Conclusiones_Provisionales_Tribunal_ Supremo_-2.pdf?hash=e0b7d578e15578f52 5537e0e4c4519c019d470ec.

13   Víctor Serge (1925), *What everyone should know about repression*, 1926. Available in: www.marxists.org/archive/serge/1926/ repression/index.htm.

14   Nuria Alabao, 'El giro ultra de Casado y la 'ideología de género'', *Ctxt*, 28 July 2018. Available in: ctxt.es/es/20180725/Firmas/ 20993/Nuria-Alabao-PP-Pablo-Casado-ideologia-de-genero.htm.

15   On this point, see: Nuria Alabao, 'El peligro 'populista' de C's está en Vallecas o El Raval', 29 May, 2018. Available in: ctxt.es/es/20180523/Firmas/ 19842/Cs-Ciudadanos-Madrid-Barcelona-csoa-ciudad-Nuria-Alabao.htm.

16   The phrase was used by Giuseppe Tomasi di Lampedusa in his classic novel, *The Leopard*, 1958. (Translator's note).

17   Nancy Fraser, 'The End of Progressive Neoliberalism', *Dissent*, 2 January 2017. Available in www.dissentmagazine.org/ online_articles/progressive-neoliberalism-reactionary-populism-nancy-fraser.

5
Strategic Spectres

376.
Catalan politics and the crisis of the 1978 regime is unfolding, and will unfold for an as yet undetermined time, under the impact of the spectres of October. Spectres that ran through October pointing to the possibilities of what could happen, and other spectres released after October by what finally did happen. Spectres that point to both a consummated past and a possible future. Spectres to be invoked by some, and exorcised by others. Spectres as hope for the future reappearance of unrealised possibilities, or as a nightmare about the return of threats dispelled. Spectres as a source of strategic maturity or as the revival of an endless and useless 'Procés-ism' version 2.0. Spectres that are self-absorbed or in fertile dialogue with the distant spectres of May 2011.

377.
A spectrologist par excellence, Derrida reminds us that the spectral is essentially untimely.[1] It unhinges contemporaneity from itself and blows up the linearity between past, present and future. The real October and the imaginary October thus merge in their balance sheets and in the impacts of their legacy. The potential October and the real October are in a state of tension with each other. October and its spectres haunt, in different ways, all sides – the 'pro-Procés' and 'non-Procés' independence movement, the non-independence left and also the restorationist forces. Each and every one of them is confronted with their own real weaknesses and their own particular spectres. They all

face a common challenge: to use the true spectres of October to ward off their own strategic fantasies.

378.

The spectre, Agamben remarks, is 'an intimately historical being' because it refers to a form of life that 'begins only when everything is over',[2] although, it should be pointed out, it is related to what has already happened or what could happen, and thus it breaks with temporality itself. It emerges from the past, reactivating a past event or a future promise, and interrogates our present, thereby destabilising the future. The events of September and October 2017 came to an end, releasing their own spectres, of what happened and of what could have been. It is impossible to ignore them. But the conflict in which the clash then took place is still there, albeit in a different form. The historicity of the spectre, seen in strategic terms, implies that 'when it is all over', a new stage begins that is indebted to the previous one, but not merely as an epiphenomenon of it. The spectre of the past yields lessons that, if not understood, can reduce present existence to a purely spectral condition.

379.

There is a danger that the independence movement and Catalunya en Comú–Podem could become spectres that inhabit the present like the living dead, but without even the capacity to interrogate the living. The unacknowledged collapse of their strategic hypotheses could turn them into inert zombies. Or leave them in a spectral condition that Agamben calls 'larval or dormant', which results from not accepting one's own situation and reduces the body inhabited by the spectral larva to a fictitious appearance of real life. Human on the outside, spectre on the inside. Avoiding this dismal condition requires strategically re-evaluating the past in the light of its spectres in order to change tomorrow through the struggles of today. The double political and social cycle that began in 2011 and 2012 needs to be revisited with an eye to the future. Spectral memory must not dissolve into the spectre of memory.

380.
How should we look back on the October Days? Being faithful to the event, as Badiou puts it, is essential to any robust perspective. Undoubtedly, the repentant radical, whether ex-communist or a veteran of 1968, is one of the saddest figures of all those who populate the universe of oppositional politics. Being faithful to 1 October 2017, however, does not mean foolishly repeating its virtues, or, worse still, glibly extolling its potential. Rather, it means developing a strategic reflection that reaches beyond its limitations and the founding fallacies of the independence movement and avoids reducing the real October to a sad spectral condition barely disguised by its mythologised aura.

381.
Memory always 'unfolds in the present, which determines its forms', recalls Enzo Traverso,[3] selecting what we want to remember and how. October 2017 is now in the past. But its historical fate is played out in a present that sets the parameters for how we recall it. What should we retain of the Catalan October, and for what purpose? The memory of October must be a strategic memory, distinct both from impotent nostalgia and from a sterile, idealised myth or a petrified, commemorative recollection. The memory of October has to be built out of the desire to learn from it and the knowledge acquired 'a posteriori'. Analysing October strategically leads us to a more mature reflection, which in turn allows us to return to it in a fresh way, and to grasp aspects that slipped under our radar at the time. Reading the past strategically allows us to orientate ourselves better in the present and help another future emerge.

382.

A creeping, commemorative petrification clouds every anniversary of October, and threatens its future memory. It uses the past to mask political impotence in the present, or as an alibi to justify abandoning objectives. 'Reclaiming tradition from the conformism that seeks to subjugate it',[4] in Benjamin's words, seems to be the pre-emptive formula for preserving the subversive character of its memory. This means not surrendering that memory to an institutionalisation that is as politically ineffectual as it is symbolically bombastic. It means not accepting the use of October as a means to domesticate the potential of the period from 20 September to 3 October, at the same time as it prevents us from thinking about its real limitations, hidden beneath the celebrations that are as solemn as they are empty.

383.

The spectre of petrified nostalgia must be exorcised by strategic thinking on the lookout for the spectres of unfulfilled possibilities and missed opportunities. Of forks in the road where the wrong path was chosen. Strategic balance is the condition, to return again to Marx's *18th Brumaire*, 'of magnifying the given task in the imagination, not recoiling from its solution in reality; of finding once more the spirit of revolution, not making its ghost walk again'.[5] That is, to imagine going as far as the eye can see, never giving up halfway, in order to rekindle the flame of political and social change and not its make-believe. This is certainly not compatible with unconditional faith in the Procés, including confused capitulation, rigid obstinacy or impotent passivity.

384.

October, with all its turmoil and paradoxes, appears to be a compulsory point of passage for any serious strategic learning. This is a learning process that is largely absent today, at least in the democratic camp and in the opposition to the 'democracy of Article 155'. The dilemma is crystal clear: either to settle for an October of barren, spectral strategic lessons or to embrace an October of fertile strategic spectres? (Re)thinking October therefore emerges as an unavoidable step towards relaunching, broadening and reformulating the content of a struggle against a regime that cannot yet claim victory at the risk of being undermined by its own peculiar spectres.

1 Jacques Derrida, 'Specters of Marx', *New Left Review*, May/June 1994.
2 Giorgio Agamben, *Desnudez*, Barcelona, Ed. Anagrama, 2001, pp. 53 and 54.
3 Enzo Traverso, *Le passé, modes d'emploi*, Paris, La Fabrique, 2005, p. 16.
4 Walter Benjamin, 'Tesis sobre el concepto de historia', *Iluminaciones*, Madrid, Ed. Taurus, 2018, pp. 309–10.
5 Karl Marx, op. cit.

6
Epilogue:
A Long Strategic Crisis

Several years later, how should 1 October 2017 be read? Victory or defeat? October ended in defeat, but it had moments of victory. If we take the metaphor of a race, the independence movement started strongly and was in the lead during the first half of the race, from 20 September to 3 October, but collapsed in the second half, being beaten at the finish line. The performance in the first half of the race shocked all and sundry and, undoubtedly, remains in the collective memory. So does the fragility shown by the state. But the defeat at the finish line is what counts in the end. There will always be the question of whether it lost because of its own weaknesses or because of the intrinsic strength of the adversary. In reality both dimensions are intertwined and combined.

Written relatively shortly after the referendum, in this book we pointed out then the need to think October with a strategic memory, overcoming both petrified nostalgia and amnesiac forgetfulness. Many years later, this is still even more necessary.

The outcomes that have mushroomed on 1 October are, logically, contradictory. Some interpretations read 1 October as a lost opportunity, as the result of erroneous decisions by the pro-independence leadership at decisive moments. Others emphasise the existence of an unfavourable correlation of forces with the state that could not be overcome. Even being opposing interpretations, often the basis for different political orientations, both readings have an aspect of truth and are two unavoidable positions. There is in fact feedback between the internal and external factors: the poor correlation of forces explains the hesitations and mistakes made at critical moments, while at the same time these further weakened the balance of forces.

However, the big problem with most of the readings of 1 October is that they tend to misrelate the failure of October with the foundational limits of the strategic hypotheses of the independence movement that emerged in 2012. These have already been analysed in the book, but they can be synthesised in the double disconnection of the independence claim with the criticism of austerity policies and of the Catalan republic project with a general rupture of the 1978 regime. In other words, the debate on 1 October cannot be dissociated from a broader strategic discussion.

In his analysis of the Dreyfus case, *Fascism and Americanism*, Gramsci introduces the distinction between *durata* (duration), that is, those normal periods in which a given social model is reproduced, and *fare epoca* (making epoch), those moments of change in which the continuity of social structures is broken.[1] I have previously[2] analysed the 15-M as a moment of disruption of the *durata* and of an unfulfilled opening, of the possibility of *fare epoca*. I think the same can be applied to 1 October. It did not 'make an epoch' in Gramsci's sense, but it opened the concrete possibility of doing so, which is in itself, a change in the situation and in the perception of the possible.

Lawfare[3]

The repressive action of the 20 September – 3 October period had its continuation in a long judicial-police process marked by the arbitrary use of law and force as a method of resolution of the political crisis. Adapting Clausewitz's famous phrase, as mentioned in the book, justice appeared as a form of continuation of politics by other means. And more specifically, it can also be added that judicial violence then appeared as the continuation of police violence by other means. A fully fledged judicial *squadrismo*.

The use of the legal apparatus for political purposes to strike at the independence movement is part of a broader process of institutional crisis. The judiciary has emerged in this process as a political actor dedicated to torpedo any decision of the Spanish parliament and the government that is opposed by the reactionary right. The Catalan crisis is both the main cause and the consequence of this dynamic of the conversion of the judicial apparatus into a reactionary political actor, in alliance with the political right and the conservative media circles.

The repressive strategy of the state consisted of a range of legal cases for which a total of 1,432 people were investigated.[4] As a whole these can be understood as a 'general case' against independence, if we return to the term used in 1940 by the Franco dictatorship to investigate the 'crimes' committed on the Republican side during the Civil War and which functioned as a mechanism to legitimise the coup of 1936 and Francoism.

At the centre of this strategy was the trial against the pro-independence leaders arrested in 2017, a political trial disguised as a legal trial, held in the first half of 2019. The entire legal process was based on the political and media fabrication of the narrative that 1 October was an attempted coup d'état and in legal terms a crime of rebellion – a crime that, moreover, in the Spanish penal code requires the existence of explicit organised violence.

By disregarding objective facts and distorting reality, the the goal of the judicial process was to politically neutralise the adversary, fabricating crimes ad hoc and using the law in an arbitrary and erroneous manner. In his classic text *On Crimes and Punishments* of 1764, Beccaria[5] pointed out that in this situation the judge becomes the 'enemy to the accused' and instead of carrying out what he called a 'true prosecution, for information' based on the impartial investigation of the facts, instead undertakes an 'offensive prosecution' whereby only a conviction, and not the truth, is sought. This dynamic of political fabrication of fictitious crimes culminated in the sentence of the Supreme Court of 14 October 2019, convicting nine pro-independence leaders for sedition (a crime one step lower than rebellion), with sentences ranging from 9 to 13 years in prison.

The most common term used to explain the judicial war against independence has been lawfare. Of military origin, the term was popularised by US Air Force colonel Charles Dunlap[6] who defined it as 'the use of law as a weapon of war'. The author would later reformulate this definition as a 'strategy of using – or misusing – law as a substitute for traditional military means to achieve an operational objective'. The use of the concept in the political arena became popular in Latin America, especially in Brazil and Argentina in 2017 and 2018 as a result of the political, media and judicial war against Presidents Dilma Rousseff, Ignacio Lula da Silva and Cristina Fernández. Transposed to the political arena, lawfare refers to a combination of the illegitimate use of the law and intense media warfare based on disinformation and lies. The judicial war has been both a contradictory expression of the political capacity of the state and its incapacity, of its powers and its weaknesses, and a synthesis of the magnitude of the political crisis. The result has been an outlaw state and judiciary whose concrete expression is a Supreme Court committing malfeasance, that is to say, a court that dictates sentences knowing that they are contrary to the law.

In the logic of lawfare, the law does not serve to set the rules of the game (more or less fair or democratic), but as an instrument of arbitrary combat. It establishes a combat justice, at the service of a combat nationalism, which activates the latent authoritarian impulses of all the institutional scaffolding of the state. The discretionary power is exercised in the name of the law, creating a policy outside the law but within the law. We have been witnessing a logic of exception dressed up in a pretended institutional and legal normality, but permanently betrayed by the very warlike and bellicose rhetoric of the powers of the state, political parties and the media.

Protracted strategic crisis

Faced with the threat of repression that loomed over them after 1 October and the symbolic proclamation of Catalan independence on 27 October, the pro-independence political leaders staged a personal and political disbandment, dividing between those who took the path of exile and those who faced arrest and the prospect of a long sentence. The choice between prison and exile was not the result of a calculated strategic decision, nor even a strategic fracture between the two major pro-independence parties, but the result of a spontaneous personal decision. In the best case, it was motivated by political considerations as to which was the most effective way to continue the political struggle, in the worst case by subjective considerations as to which way was the least hard on a personal and family level. As a result, both prison and exile, although they played an important role in undermining the credibility of the state by showing its authoritarian character, were always contaminated by tactical quarrels, lack of project and strategy, and personal and partisan interests.

On the domestic front, the attitude of the imprisoned leaders during the trial condensed all the limits of the pro-independence process opened in 2012. With the sole exception of Omnium Cultural leader Jordi Cuixart, the rest of those judged by the Supreme Court had a very low political profile during the trial, not very vindictive and submissive. They did not behave as would be expected of conscious political prisoners who embody a collective cause and who subordinate their personal fate to general political interests, but rather conveyed the impression that they were seeking to reduce their sentences as much as possible. Their strategy in the trial can be understood from a human point of view, but it is politically indefensible and constitutes another of the many irresponsible attitudes of the Procés leadership. The result, without a doubt, was politically devastating: it accentuated the loss of international credibility and, above all, disoriented and discouraged, once again, the pro-independence social base. This does not detract from the fact that an important part of it was emotionally and sentimentally sympathetic to the will of its leaders to get out of jail at any cost and remained electorally loyal.

On the foreign front, the leaders in exile, with Puigdemont at the head, gave the independence cause an important visibility and reaped notable political successes. However, theirs has been an exile where the lack of project and strategy could hardly be disguised with an excess of rhetoric, and where Puigdemont's electoral and political calculations have always presided over all movements. Moreover, the political function of the exile was destabilised by the overlapping of two roles of Puigdemont, that of president in exile and that of main leader of one of the pro-independence parties – that is, the confusion between the whole and the part at the same time.

As we wrote in the book, October 2017 meant the collapse of the mainstream strategic hypotheses of independentism. Since then, the situation only worsened, resulting in a growing internal polarisation within the pro-independence mainstream itself. In the book we already pointed out the limits of the major (though not the only) strategic orientations that crystallised after 2017 and that we now recall:

The first limit, represented by the ERC, was marked by a pragmatic turn towards negotiation with the PSOE and a bet that there would be a more transversal project that would penetrate the non-independence sectors of Catalan society. As we pointed out at the time, this strategy had the merit of considering many of the foundational strategic limits of the independence movement, but it deployed them in a completely pragmatic and institutionalist manner that undermined all its virtues and implied a de facto renunciation of its objectives. Initially, the ERC's turn was rewarded with important electoral growth. In a context of lack of prospects, it appeared before a section of the pro-independence voters and non-independence left-wing voters as a plausible option. After an initial push, the ERC collapsed electorally, faced with a double impossibility: first, to achieve clear advances on the national front in its negotiation with the PSOE, once the political and emotional success of the first anti-repressive measures such as the pardons to the pro-independence prisoners in 2021 had passed; and, on the social front, ERC's own social-liberal culture self-limited its ambitions at the head of the Generalitat. It is worth highlighting this second issue, often overlooked in conventional analyses of the ERC fiasco: the main Achilles' heel in its strategy to become the main Catalan party and steal the popular vote base from the PSC and the Comuns has been its inability to offer tangible and visible achievements in improving the daily lives of the bulk of the working and middle classes.

A second limit, embodied by Junts and Puigdemont, represents a policy of symbolic and rhetorical confrontation that avoids falling into a logic of normalised negotiation but does not have a real project of rupture either. Its main asset is the leadership of Puigdemont himself, popular enough to maintain an important social base without rival within independentism, but weak enough to generate a majority around him. Junts has maintained one of the most harmful and toxic aspects of the culture of the pro-independence process: the contrast between what is said in public and in private, between what is done and what is said. The result is a symbolic policy stuffed with gestures of rupture, compatible with the gradual resurrection of the old moderate and right-wing political culture of the Convergencia Democrática de Catalunya of Jordi Pujol.

The third major orientation, visibly embodied by the ANC (and also sustained by a myriad of opinion makers and small scattered collectives), is that of the 'permanent offensive'. It is based on a decontextualised voluntarism, alien to any analysis of the correlation of forces and the conjuncture. It represents a proposal of rupture in a vacuum, based (with some exceptions) on the reification of the movement's foundational strategic inconsistencies.

Only on the periphery of the independence movement, in the orbit of the CUP and in the extra-parliamentary left, have there been attempts, uneven and not always coinciding, to rethink strategies based on the outcome of the previous cycle. But what is certain is that for the most part, in the post-2017 phase, independentism was unable to overcome the two basic limits of the 2012–17 process: the dissociation of the proposal of the Catalan republic from criticism of austerity policies and the social question in general; second, the disconnection of the horizon of the Catalan republic from a general dynamic of rupture of the 1978 regime in all of the Spanish state, thus seeking democratic synergies throughout the state and a dialectic between the Catalan republic and the Spanish republic projects. Both questions are closely linked, since the sympathies of Catalan independence in the rest of the Spanish state are proportional to its left-wing content: the more Catalan independence appears as a progressive movement, associated with an anti-neoliberal, feminist agenda and the fight against climate change, the more democratic sympathies it has in the Spanish left-wing public opinion. The more it appears as a solely pro-independence movement, often with conservative leadership, the more isolated it is outside Catalonia.

As time went by, the endless prolongation of the strategic crisis has degenerated into a gradual decomposition and a growing disaffection of the social base of independentism towards the pro-independence parties and, to a lesser extent, towards the pro-independence social organisations themselves. The declining electoral evolution of independentism is a good example of this: the pro-independence parties achieved in the elections of 12 May 2024 their worst results since 2017: in total 1.36 million votes, representing 43 per cent. Comparisons with the 2017 and 2021 elections are complex, the former being an exceptional call just after 1 October when the Spanish government had already intervened in the Catalan administration, while the latter was still affected by the COVID. But the 2024 results certainly show a downward trend.

To a large extent the success of the independence movement, as we have already pointed out on several occasions, was based on the promise of a quick and easy victory. The expectation of triumph generated a permanent mobilisation and rapid growth of the movement. After 2017, the protracted crisis of expectations, coupled with internal divisions and the relative loss of credibility of pro-independence leaders, demobilised and discouraged a significant part of their social base. The independence proposal lost its appeal to the extent that it was no longer seen as a feasible concrete option.

In the book we wrote that 1 October was, using Gramsci's terms, an episode of 'big politics', but managed with a 'small politics' mentality, something constitutive of the whole process opened in 2012.[7] Following this reflection, the post-2017 period was further characterised by the absorption of the pro-independence dynamics by small politics – an increasingly naked small politics.

Complexities

The strategic limits of the independence movement have gone hand in hand with a social simplification. The growth of independence after 2012 generated some superficial illusions about Catalan society and overlooked its social and national complexities. Independentism never had a solid strategic policy towards those who did not join the bandwagon and moved between a triumphalist (and arrogant) 'they will adapt' or a resigned 'they are impossible to convince'. This orientation was useful for the pro-independence Right in the short term, although also harmful for it after the October battle, but it was always a long-term burden for the pro-independence Left, both social-democratic and radical. For its part, the Left that was not in favour of independence, represented by Iniciativa per Catalunya-Verds first, Podem later and Comuns finally, also abdicated from any serious attempt to articulate alliances between those who travelled inside and outside the pro-independence lane.

The social complexities that the independence movement had avoided exploded after the October shock with the combination of the repressive coup, the strategic collapse and the withering of the expectation of victory. October was the culmination of the rupture of the national consensus, surely precarious and imperfect, on which post-Franco Catalonia was based. This was intertwined with a crisis of social cohesion resulting from the long impact of the post-2008 crisis and a growing complexity of national identities and the linguistic reality of Catalan society as a result of the immigration boom between 2001 and 2007.

Suddenly, the failure to achieve a state of its own revealed weaknesses in the Catalan nation itself and, in particular, the fragile condition of the Catalan language. In the book we have already devoted a long section to the question of the Catalan language. However, the debate has mutated in recent years because of the decline in the social use of Catalan for several factors: first, a loss of roots among the youth; second, difficulty in being accessible in the digital world; and, third, the sociodemographic changes of Catalan society. In neoliberalised Catalonia, the relationship between Catalanness, the use of the Catalan language and the social upward mobility that it enjoyed during the immigration of Spanish origin and their children during the Franco regime and the Transition has been broken concerning the new foreign immigration. There are two factors for this: the economic crisis and the lack of expectations of social improvement, and the political crisis derived from the clash between the rampant hard-line Spanish nationalism that emerged in the second term of Aznar, and the independence process that reached its zenith in 2017. In short, the October boomerang exposed structural problems that the 2012–17 phase overlooked.

Faced with the loss of concrete expectations regarding independence, in the midst of a significant social weariness due to the degradation of the welfare model, and under the influence of a reactionary international cycle, the issue of immigration and xenophobia finally hit Catalan politics head on. After the failure of the double contradictory cycle of 15-M opened in 2011 and that of the Procés opened in 2012, a more conservative climate gradually emerged in the Catalan political debate. This, as is logical, has its own idiosyncrasies while showing resonances of the general international dynamics. The pro-independence far right emerged as a result of the uneasiness of a part of the conservative pro-independence social base. This was due to the long strategic decomposition after 2017 and a social and identity unease in the face of the demographic and socio-cultural transformations of contemporary Catalonia in a context of the welfare crisis. It should be noted that a study published in July 2024[8] shows that xenophobic attitudes are, however, a minority in Catalan society and that the growing media noise around immigration does not correspond to a significant xenophobic evolution of society, but to political strategies that seek to make room in a certain social and electoral niche.

The rise of the pro-independence, xenophobic and far-right Aliança Catalana party and its entry into the Catalan Parliament in the 12 May 2024 elections represents a significant transformation of the Catalan political landscape and the independence debate. It breaks the association between far right and Spanish nationalism that was usual in Catalan politics and modifies the terms of the Catalanism–Spanish nationalism axis. As usual in these cases, the most serious impact of the rise of the far right is not only its strength in itself, but its capacity to penetrate transversally into the social debate. Junts per Catalunya's flirtation with anti-immigration demagogy since December 2023, sufficiently explicit to be noticed but restrained enough to mark its distances with the far right, put the issue squarely at the centre of Catalan politics. Junts' policy is partly a reaction of fear at the rise of Aliança Catalana, although in reality it opens the terrain for it, and is also partly its own attempt to place a conservative agenda in the debate, believing that this may favour it in the long run.

Amnesty

The agreement for an Amnesty Law signed between Sanchez and the Catalan pro-independence forces in November 2023 (and finally unravelled in March 2024) can be considered a relevant victory for the independence movement. But it is a *sui generis* triumph. The amnesty is a victory born out of defeat. It came not as the culmination of an ascending movement, but as a result of its capacity to condition the governability of the state despite being in decline. Independentism succeeded in forcing an amnesty but without it being part of a broader and real agreement for a political solution to the conflict. It is not a key piece of a wider democratic strategy by the Spanish government, but an isolated element resulting from Sanchez's political needs.

The amnesty is, paradoxically, a point of departure and arrival for the PSOE. It is both an act and a process. It is a means and an end. It is not a starting point towards a global political solution, but an attempt to normalise political life and deactivate the conflict. Logically, for the PSOE a fundamental political solution could never be an agreement for a self-determination referendum, but a process of reform of the state that pivots around improvement of the funding of the Catalan self-government, the symbolic recognition of Catalonia as a nation and the protection of the Catalan language. But the PSOE's strategy consists rather in not having a strategic perspective of state reform, but in subordinating the reform of the state to its need of parliamentary stability and to a tactical tug-of-war with the pro-independence parties.

Support for amnesty and pacification is a minority position among the political elites of the state and the state apparatus itself. The approval of the Amnesty Law deepened even more the fracture between the elites, generating an internal failure in the governability of the state at a moment in which, paradoxically, the adversaries of the regime (Podemos and its spin-offs, and Catalan independentism) were deactivated, by the triple mechanism of integration–cooperation, repression and minoritisation.

The amnesty and the policy of normalisation is only the option of an executive power in a minority in the apparatus and structure of the state, supported by the legislative power in which three differentiated blocs converge out of interest. These three blocs are (a) the PSOE which opportunistically supports this path for its own electoral needs, (b) Sumar, Podemos and the other progressive (or peripheral nationalist) forces subordinated to PSOE whose programme revolves around pacification and détente, but not around the exercise of the right to self-determination, and (c) the Catalan pro-independence parties, ERC and Junts, which with diverse tactics support this path in the absence of other horizons.

Hence the structural fragility of the amnesty and the uncertainties about its effective application.

Perspectives

Many years after October 2017, the general situation is one of a crisis of strategy and expectations on the part of the pro-independence movement and a reduction of its social support base. The loss of the government of the Generalitat de Catalunya in 2024 is the culmination of this dynamic. This unfolds in the context of a general retreat of the left, whether pro-independence or not, anti-capitalist (CUP), alternative (Comuns) or moderate (ERC), and of the reconstruction of the PSC. Mortally wounded at the beginning of the double cycle of 15-M in 2011 and the independence process in 2012, the PSC arose from the ashes, absorbing part of the Spanish nationalist vote that had fled to Ciudadanos (reaching its zenith in 2017) and recovering the vote that had fled to the orbit of Podemos and the Comuns. The reborn PSC embodies a project of law and order. It has the least Catalanist profile in its history and embraces without nuances the continuity of social-liberal policies, and a development model based on services, tourism, low-paid labour and ecological predation.

The policy of the PSC in Catalonia raises 'consensus' and 'normalisation' as a banner after the shock of 2017 and the following repression. But theirs is the politics of consensus without prior debate, of forced consensus or consensus as the fruit of resignation and renunciation of any perspective of change. Their policy of renunciation is in reality the renunciation of politics. The PSC government in Catalonia symbolises a double pincer following the failure of the Indignados cycle and of the pro-independence cycle. Outside independentism, the unlimited subordination of the Comuns to the PSC testifies how far the Indignados cycle opened in 2011 has been left behind. Within the independence movement, the subordination of a minoritised ERC to the PSC, with its decision to invest Salvador Illa as President of the Generalitat, shows the dead end into which it ended up by going down the path of endless pragmatism.

In the Spanish state as a whole, the assault on the 'Regime of '78' represented by the double cycle Indignados–Podemos and the Catalan independence process did not succeed in overthrowing it. But in the end, it caused an irreparable fracture in its traditional ruling elite, destabilising the 'normal' functioning of the institutions. Besieged, deep tensions emerged between those who bunkered down in response to the external threat, those who understood the need to adapt and renew the rules of the game, and those who opted for an authoritarian stabilisation of the situation.

Since the Catalan October there has been a radicalisation of the Spanish right, marked since 2018 by the irruption of the far-right Vox party in competition-alliance with the PP, largely as an expression of a Spanish identity radicalisation regarding the Catalan independence 'threat'. Its emergence can be analysed as an extremist by-product of the very state-*squadrista* nationalism promoted on the occasion of the October 2017 crisis.[9] The sudden emergence of another even more far-right option in the European elections of May 2024, Se acabó la fiesta (SALF), is in turn another link in a chain of peripheral right-wing radicalisation that impacts on the entire conservative arc. The global radicalisation of the right, settled in a politics of permanent impeachment that does not accept the legitimacy of the opponent, short-circuits the normalised functioning of institutions and institutional turnover.

The violent and authoritarian resolution of the Catalan crisis precipitated a general degradation of democracy in the Spanish state as a whole, unleashing the ultras sectors in the political, judicial and media fields. Catalan pro-independence forces have been aware of this, but without drawing all the pertinent strategic conclusions such as the need to articulate its goal with the general rupture of the Regime of '78. The same is true for the Spanish left which, being a true victim of the democratic degradation, does not know how to articulate in its project the proposal of the Catalan independence movement, beyond merely defensive anti-repressive alliances.

Despite the right-wing radicalisation, the complexity of the Spanish political situation and the isolation of the PP due to its radicalisation facilitated the arrival of Sánchez in government in 2018, shortly before this book was published. First, following a motion of censure with the support of Podemos and the Basque and Catalan nationalists. Then, within the framework of a coalition government formed in January 2020 and renewed in 2023.

The coalition government of the PSOE, first with Unidas Podemos and then with the new Sumar project, can be summarised as novel in form but traditional in content. It expresses an anomaly in its form, but not in its programme, which is, fundamentally, that of a progressive stabilisation. It is a supervening and contradictory expression of the Spanish institutional crisis and of the destabilisation of the traditional forms of governance which, however, did not collapse. The PSOE can no longer rule alone, which shows its relative weakness, but it remains the central pillar, while the subaltern participation of Podemos, and later Sumar, in the government has acted as a mechanism of integration, co-optation and political deactivation. The old system of governance could not be restored, but the contending forces remained minorised and integrated. Forcing their way into government was Podemos' greatest political success, as well as the culmination of the abandonment of its founding objectives – a process that can be described by the concept of 'transformism' used by Gramsci[10] to refer to the adaptation of popular organisations to the agenda of the ruling classes. The current fight between Podemos and Sumar for the hegemony of the electoral space to the left of the PSOE does not represent a struggle based on substantially different strategic projects, but a struggle for the survival of the apparatuses in which, for reasons of self-interest, Podemos is raising a more leftist rhetoric.

Overall, the political situation in Catalonia and in the Spanish state is that of a general impasse. The double crisis of the Indignados cycle and the pro-independence cycle was partially deactivated, but the underlying problems that caused them remain unresolved. The progressive government of Sanchez represents a situation of unstable stability, without substantial transformations but without social or national attacks. In this situation the double challenge of the Catalan independence movement (and also of the Catalan left, pro-independence or not, and of the Spanish left) is to carry out patient and long-term work, based on overcoming the strategic limits of the previous phase, in order to be in better condition when it is necessary to change pace and move on to a new stage. The possibility of success or failure when the Spanish political situation hardens again will depend on the foundations consolidated in the current phase and on the degree of understanding of the limits of the previous one.

1   Antonio Gramsci, *Selections from the Prison Notebooks,* Lawrence & Wishart, 1971, p.256; (hereafter: SPN) Q14§76. Burgio and Filppini have developed more the analysis of *durata* and *fare epoca*: Alberto Burgio, *Gramsci. Il sistema in movimiento,* Derive Approdi, Roma, 2014; Michele Filippini, Using Gramsci: A New Approach, London, Pluto Press, 2017.
2   Josep Maria Antentas, "The 15M, Podemos and the Long Crisis in Spain: Gramscian Perspectives", *Journal of Iberian and Latin American Research* 28(3), 2022, pp. 365-380.
3   The remarks in this section are further elaborated in: Josep Maria Antentas, "Spain: The State, the Regime Crisis and the National Question", *Socialism & Democracy* 35(1), 2021, pp.51–78.
4   Òmnium Cultural sets at 4,200 the total number of people repressed in one way or another as a result of 1 October, including 1,432 investigated and 1,639 people victims of political violence on day 1. *Òmnium eleva a més de 4.200 les persones represaliades per defensar el dret a l'autodeterminació.* 15 July 2022. www.omnium.cat/ca/omnium-eleva-a-mes-de-4-200-les-persones-represaliades-per-defensar-el-dret-a-lautodeterminacio/
5   Cesare Beccaria, *On Crimes and Punishments.* New Brunswick: Transaction Publishers, 2009[1764], p. 16
6   Charles Dunlap, 'Does lawfare need an apologia?', *Case Western Reserve, Journal of International Law* 43 (2), 2010, p.122
7   Antonio Gramsci, *Cuadernos de la cárcel,* Tomo , México Ed. Era, 1999, p. 20. Q13 §5.
8   Oriol Bartomeus and Lucía Medina, *La immigració a Catalunya: un debat construït?,* ICPS, July 2024. www.icps.cat/archivos/Quaderns/quadern_juliol2024.pdf?noga=1
9   For more detail see: Josep Maria Antentas, 'Spain: The State, the Regime Crisis and the National Question', op. cit.
10 Gramsci, SPN, 58; Q19§24; Q8, §36

7
Political Chronology (2000–2024)

2000

FEBRUARY

- Serious xenophobic and racist riots in the Andalusian town of El Ejido following the murder of two people.

MARCH

- José María Aznar's PP is re-elected with an absolute majority in the general election of 12 March.

MAY

- Spanish army annual parade in Barcelona for the first time since 1981.

OCTOBER

- Mass demonstration against the National Hydrological Plan (PHN), which envisages a water transfer from the Ebro River, in Zaragoza. Beginning of a long and sustained struggle.

NOVEMBER

- ETA assassinates Ernest Lluch, former Catalan Socialist minister retired from political life and advocate of dialogue in the Basque Country.

2000

JANUARY–MARCH

- Lock-ins of immigrants 'without papers' in several Spanish cities in protest against the reform of the Law on Immigration. In Barcelona, important lock-in in the church of Santa María del Pi.
- The Spanish government announces the end of compulsory military service and the professionalisation of the armed forces.

FEBRUARY

- Mass demonstration against the National Hydrological Plan (PHN) in Barcelona.

MARCH

- Mass demonstration against the National Hydrological Plan (PHN) in Madrid.

JUNE

- Protests against the World Bank in Barcelona. Media scandal over police charges.

SEPTEMBER

- The President of the Basque Government announces a proposal to reform the Statute of Autonomy of the Basque Country, popularly known as the Ibarretxe Plan, which proposes to turn the Basque Country into a 'free associated state'.

NOVEMBER

- Student strikes against the Organic Law on Universities (LOU).

2002

MARCH

- Massive protest against the Hydrological Plan in Barcelona.
- Large mobilisation in Barcelona against the European Union summit.

APRIL

- Massive protest against the Hydrological Plan in Zaragoza.

JUNE

- General strike against the Aznar government's reform of unemployment benefits. The government will modify the most controversial aspects of its proposal, which will be approved in October.
- Mobilisation in Seville against the EU summit.

JULY

- Crisis between Spain and Morocco over the military eviction from Perejil Island occupied by the Moroccan gendarmerie.

NOVEMBER AND DECEMBER

- 13 November. The Greek single-hull tanker Prestige, loaded with 77,000 tonnes of fuel oil, sinks off the coast of Galicia. An oil slick spreads rapidly and reaches the coast at the beginning of December.
- Mass mobilisation in Santiago de Compostela called by the Plataforma Nunca Mais (Never Again Platform) set up to demand environmental, legal and political accountability for the disaster.

2003

FEBRUARY–MARCH

- Mass protests against the Iraq war. 15 February date of the largest mobilisation. Widespread public opposition to the war.
- Aznar participates with Bush, Blair and Durao Barroso in the Azores Summit where an ultimatum is issued to Saddam Hussein.
- The Supreme Court outlaws Herri Batasuna, Euskal Herritarrok and Batasuna, the political brands of the nationalist left in the Basque Country.
- Large demonstration by the Nunca Mais platform in Madrid to protest the incompetent management of the Prestige disaster by the Spanish and Galician governments.

NOVEMBER

- Victory of the Partit Socialista de Catalunya (PSC) in the Catalan elections. Pasqual Maragall is proclaimed president at the head of a progressive coalition government with Esquerra Republicana de Catalunya (ERC) and Iniciativa per Catalunya Verds (ICV). End of Jordi Pujol's long conservative nationalist presidency (1980–2003).
- Beginning of the process of reforming the Statute of Autonomy of Catalonia.

2004

MARCH

- 11 March. Islamist attacks at Atocha station (Madrid). The PP government tries to attribute them to the Basque organisation ETA.

- March 13. Spontaneous demonstrations outside PP headquarters to demand the truth about the attacks.
- 14th March. Victory of Rodríguez Zapatero's PSOE in the general elections as a reaction to the PP's lies about the attacks.

APRIL

- Zapatero announces the immediate withdrawal of Spanish troops from Iraq.
- Congress approves the modification of the 2001 National Hydrological Plan Law (PHN) and the repeal of the Ebro water transfer.

2005

FEBRUARY

- Referendum on the Treaty establishing a Constitution for Europe. Victory for 'Yes' by 77 per cent, but only 41 per cent turnout.
- The Spanish Congress rejects the Ibarretxe Plan.

JULY

- The law authorising same-sex marriage is passed.

SEPTEMBER

- The Catalan Parliament approves the reform of the Statute of Autonomy with the support of all parties except the Popular Party.
- Five people are killed by Moroccan and Spanish police action during an attempted mass jumping of the Ceuta fence.

NOVEMBER

- Massive right-wing mobilisation in Madrid against the Organic Law on Education (LOE) of Zapatero's government.

2006

JANUARY

- The PP announces a campaign to collect signatures throughout Spain against the Catalan Statute of Autonomy. It will eventually obtain 4,020,000 signatures.

FEBRUARY

- Demonstration in Barcelona against the Spanish Congress' cuts to the Statute approved by the Catalan Parliament. Slogan: 'We are a nation and we have the right to decide.'
- First revelations in the press of alleged irregularities by Iñaki Urdangarin, Duke of Palma and husband of the Infanta Elena, at the head of the Nóos company.

MARCH

- ETA, after three years without fatal attacks, announces a permanent ceasefire.
- The Spanish Congress of Deputies approves a trimmed-down version of the draft reform of the Statute approved by the Parliament of Catalonia.

MAY

- V de Vivienda is born, a movement in favour of the right to housing that will organise actions during 2006 and 2007.

JUNE

- The new Statute of Catalonia is ratified in a referendum with 74 per cent of votes in favour, but only 48.8 per cent turnout.

JULY

- The PP files an appeal against Catalan Statute before the Constitutional Court.

NOVEMBER

- Elections to the Catalan Parliament. José Montilla, PSC candidate, elected president at the head of a new coalition government with ERC and ICV. The anti-Catalanist Ciudadanos party enters Parliament with 3 deputies and 3 per cent of the vote.

DECEMBER

- ETA breaks the ceasefire with an attack at Madrid's Barajas airport T-4, killing two people.

2007

FEBRUARY

- The new Statute of Autonomy of Andalusia is approved in a referendum.

DECEMBER

- Peak of the Spanish real estate bubble that began in the late 1990s. Beginning of a turning point.

2008

FEBRUARY

- Protests by teachers and students against the new Catalan Education Law (LEC).

MARCH

- General elections. Zapatero re-elected president.

NOVEMBER

- Student protests against the Bologna Plan in all Spain.

DECEMBER

- The year ends with a historic fall in the stock market: 40 per cent of the IBEX35 index.
- Unemployment rises to 13.9 per cent.

2009

FEBRUARY

- Opening of an investigation at the Audiencia Nacional into an alleged corruption scandal involving businessmen with links to the PP. This is the beginning of the Gurtel case, one of the most important corruption scandals of the period.
- Founding assembly of the Platform of People Affected by Mortgages (PAH) in Barcelona.

MARCH

- Student protests against Bologna throughout Spain. In Barcelona, the demonstration ends in serious clashes with the police. Crisis in the Catalan Department of the Interior over police action: Councillor Joan Saura dismisses the political head of the Catalan police, Rafael Olmos, although he defends the work of the officers.
- Protests by teachers and students against the Llei d'Educació de Catalunya (LEC) in Catalonia.
- Right-wing demonstration in Madrid to demand a halt to the Zapatero government's reform of the abortion law.

MAY

- General strike in Euskadi called by nationalist unions.

JUNE AND JULY

- Luis Bárcenas resigns as treasurer of the PP due to the fact that he is under investigation by the Supreme Court in the Gürtel case.
- Approval of the Ley d'Ensenyament de Catalunya (LEC) by the Catalan Parliament. ICV and the trade unions oppose it.
- The Spanish government announces the creation of the Fund for Orderly Bank Restructuring (FROB) to deal with possible banking problems.

AUGUST

- Iñaki Urdangarin and his wife, the Infanta Cristina, move to Washington to live.

SEPTEMBER

- Citizens' referendum ('consulta') in the town of Arenys de Munt (population 9,191) on independence for Catalonia. 96.2 per cent of the votes cast (41 per cent turnout) are for 'Yes' to independence. Great media impact of the action and strong hostility from the Spanish government. Beginning of a process of local consultations on independence.
- Félix Millet, former president of the Fundació Orfeó-Català Palau de la Música, a prestigious cultural institution, confesses to having stolen at least 3.3 million euros from the institution. Beginning of the Palau case, one of the biggest corruption scandals in Catalonia.

OCTOBER

- Large right-wing anti-abortion demonstration in Madrid.

DECEMBER

- Manifesto 'In defence of Internet rights' in protest at the inclusion in the Zapatero government's draft bill on sustainable economy of amendments relating to freedom of expression, information and access to culture on the Internet. It is the beginning of a long series of protests against the so-called 'Ley Sinde' that will last until 2011.
- First wave of local referendums ('consultas') for independence in Catalonia, held in 167 municipalities.
- Unemployment reaches 18.8 per cent.

2010

FEBRUARY

- Second wave of local referendums ('consultas') for independence in Catalonia, held in 80 municipalities.
- The Spanish public debt risk premium rises above 100 points.

MARCH

- Zapatero government announces deep cuts in response to the deteriorating economic situation and the demands of the European Union. Decisive turning point.

APRIL

- Third wave of local referendums ('consultas') for independence in Catalonia, held in 211 municipalities.
- The official unemployment rate in Spain reaches 20 per cent.

MAY

- The Bank of Spain intervenes in CajaSur.

JUNE

- Fourth wave of local referendums ('consultas') for independence in Catalonia, held in 48 municipalities.
- Constitutional Court ruling on the Statute of Catalonia: 14 articles are declared unconstitutional, 23 articles and 4 provisions are subject to reinterpretation, and it is remarked that the preamble declaring Catalonia a nation has no legal validity.

JULY

- Massive demonstration in Barcelona, with the participation of President Montilla of the PSC, under the slogan 'We are a Nation. We decide.'

SEPTEMBER

- General strike against the labour reform promoted by the Zapatero government.

NOVEMBER

- Elections to the Catalan Parliament. Artur Mas, candidate of Convergència i Unió (CiU), is elected president. He announces a 'government of the best' with a neoliberal accent and the aim of achieving a 'fiscal pact' with the Spanish government to improve Catalonia's financing.
- The year closes with Spain's public debt at 60.1 per cent of GDP, one tenth of a percentage point above the limit set in the EU stability pact.

2011

JANUARY

- ETA announces a 'permanent, general and internationally verifiable' ceasefire.

- Agreement between the Spanish government, the CCOO and UGT trade unions and employers on pension reform. Retirement is progressively delayed from 65 to 67 years of age.
- General strike in Euskadi called by nationalist unions.
- General strike in Galicia called by the nationalist union CIG.

FEBRUARY

- Approval of the so-called 'Sinde Law' on freedom of expression, information and access to culture on the Internet.

MARCH

- The PAH, together with other social organisations, begins the process of a Popular Legislative Initiative to change the mortgage law. 500,000 signatures are required.

APRIL

- Demonstration in Madrid by Juventud sin Futuro (JSF) with the slogan 'Without a home, without a job, without a pension. Youth without fear. Reclaiming our future. This is just the beginning.'
- First mobilisations against the Catalan government's health care cuts.
- Fifth wave of local referendums ('consultas') for independence in Catalonia: the consultation is held in Barcelona city.
- Conferència Nacional per l'Estat Propi in Barcelona. The process of setting up the Assemblea Nacional Catalana (ANC) begins.
- The unemployment rate stands at 21.3 per cent.

MAY

- Trade union demonstration against the cuts in Barcelona.

- 15th May. Mobilisation in many cities in Spain called by Democracia Real Ya! under the slogan 'We are not commodities in the hands of politicians and bankers!' At night an acampada begins in Puerta del Sol (Madrid). Beginning of the Indignados movement.
- Municipal and regional elections. The Indignados movement does not yet have an impact on the results. Conservative nationalist candidate Xavier Trías wins in Barcelona, putting an end to 32 years of PSC mayoralty.
- Attempted police eviction of the encampment in Plaça Catalunya (27 May).

JUNE

- 15 June. The Indignados surround the Catalan Parliament during the debate on the budget. President Mas enters the Parliament by helicopter.
- 19th June. A day of demonstrations in many Spanish cities called by the Indignados movement.
- The encampments in the squares are gradually dismantled.

JULY

- The Bank of Spain intervenes in the Caja de Ahorros del Mediterráneo.

SEPTEMBER

- The National High Court (Audiencia Nacional) sentences Arnaldo Otegi, leader and coordinator of the nationalist left wing, to ten years in prison for membership of ETA.
- Demonstrations throughout Spain called by the PAH under the slogan 'For the right to decent housing: retroactive dation in payment, Stop evictions and social renting now.'
- Start of the green tide against cuts in education in Madrid.
- Progressive appearance of 'Mareas' (tides) against cuts in multiple sectors, with health and education at the forefront, active until 2013.

- The Spanish government nationalises CatalunyaCaixa, Novacaixagalicia and Unnim.

OCTOBER

- Global day of mobilisations promoted by the indignados under the slogan United for a Global Change.
- ETA announces the 'definitive cessation of its armed activity'.

NOVEMBER

- Final media explosion of the Urdangarín case with the police raid on the offices linked to the Nóos Institute. Anticorruption investigates the Duke of Palma for alleged crimes of false documentation, prevarication, fraud against the Administration and embezzlement of public funds.
- The risk premium on Spanish sovereign debt reaches 458 points.
- General elections. Victory by absolute majority for the PP. Mariano Rajoy becomes President.

DECEMBER

- Urdangarín is legally accused and removed from the official activities of the royal family, which is forced to dissociate itself from the scandal.
- Unemployment rate reaches almost 23 per cent.

2012

FEBRUARY

- 'Valencian Spring': strong student mobilisations against cuts (and later against repression) in Valencia.

MARCH

- Official creation of the Assemblea Nacional Catalana (ANC) in Barcelona.

APRIL

- The PAH starts collecting signatures for the ILP.
- King Juan Carlos I suffers a serious hunting accident in Botswana. The elephant hunt takes place at the worst moment of the economic crisis. Serious deterioration of his image and acceleration of his decline. On leaving the hospital in Madrid where he had been repatriated, he says: 'I'm very sorry; I made a mistake and it won't happen again.'
- Unemployment reaches 24.44 per cent, the highest level since the crisis began.

MAY

- General strike by the education sector at all stages (from nursery school to university) in defence of public education and against the Rajoy government's reforms.
- Rodrigo Rato (former finance minister in the Aznar government and director of the IMF) resigns as president of Bankia and falsely assures that the bank is solvent. This is the beginning of Spain's biggest banking crisis.
- The government nationalises Bankia, whose deficit reaches 24 000 million euros.
- Bankia's board of directors asks for a bail-out of 19,000 million euros, the largest in the history of Spain.
- The risk premium reaches 539 points.
- Mining strike in Asturias and Leon in protest at the reduction of public aid to the coal sector.

JUNE AND JULY

- Finance Minister Luis de Guindos announces that Spain will receive an EU bailout of 100,000 million euros to clean up the banking system.
- The 15MpaRato collective files a lawsuit against Rodrigo Rato and the board of directors of Bankia.
- Rajoy's government announces a very strong austerity plan before Congress.
- The risk premium exceeds 600 points.

SEPTEMBER

- 11th September. First mass demonstration for independence called by the ANC under the slogan 'Catalonia, new State of Europe'. All forecasts are exceeded. A few days later, Artur Mas calls early elections, promising a referendum on self-determination.
- 25 September. Mobilisation 'surround the congress' in Madrid.

NOVEMBER AND DECEMBER

- 14th November. General strike against Rajoy's policy of cuts. In Barcelona a police rubber ball bursts the eye of a demonstrator, Ester Quintana, generating a big media debate.
- Marea Blanca (White tide) in Madrid against the cuts of the regional government.
- Elections to the Catalan Parliament. Conservative nationalist Artur Mas wins, but fails in his bid for an absolute majority, losing seats to ERC. The pro-independence and anti-capitalist Candidatura d'Unitat Popular (CUP) enters parliament with 3 per cent of the vote and 3 deputies.
- The year closes with a record unemployment rate of 26 per cent (5,965,400 people).
- Spain is the EU country with the highest public deficit (10.6 per cent of GDP including the bank bail-out).

POLITICAL CHRONOLOGY

2013

JANUARY

- The so-called 'Bárcenas papers' are published, an alleged accounting notebook of the former PP treasurer in which undeclared payments to party leaders and officials appear.

FEBRUARY

- Ada Colau, spokesperson for the PAH, appears in the Spanish Congress as an invited guest in the Economy Commission. Her intervention criticising the banks and announcing that she will point her finger at the MPs who oppose the PAH has great media repercussions.
- The PAH announces that it has obtained 1,402,854 signatures in support of the ILP. The PP does not dare to block it and it is admitted for processing in Congress on a day of mobilisations. A poll puts support for the ILP at 87 per cent.

MARCH AND APRIL

- The PAH carries out an *escraches* campaign against the MPs who oppose the approval of the ILP.
- The PAH withdraws its bill as it has been modified in Congress, at the initiative of the PP, in a direction contrary to its objectives.
- The Infanta Cristina is summoned to testify as a suspect in the Nóos case.

MAY

- General strike in Euskadi called by nationalist unions.

JUNE

- Former PP treasurer Luis Barcenas is unconditionally imprisoned.

SEPTEMBER

- 11 September. 'Via Catalana para la Independència' (Catalan Way for Independence): 400 km human chain across Catalonia.
- Strike and massive demonstration in the Balearic Islands in defence of the Catalan language and against the language policy of the PP regional government.

OCTOBER

- General strike of the educational community against the Organic Law for the Improvement of Educational Quality (LOMCE) of the PP government. In Catalonia also strike against the Catalan Education Law (LEC), in a climate of generalised protest against cuts in public and state-subsidised education.

DECEMBER

- The Catalan Parliament approves a ban on the use of rubber balls by the Catalan police from April 2014.
- The Spanish government approves a pension reform law that decouples the rise in pensions from inflation.
- The 'black cards' scandal erupts: Caja Madrid executives used opaque credit cards (without fiscal control) for personal expenses.
- The Law on Savings Banks and Banking Foundations is passed, under which the former savings banks will disappear.

2014

JANUARY

- Public launch of Podemos.
- The risk premium of Spanish public debt falls below 200 points for the first time since April 2011.

- Demonstrations and riots in the working-class neighbourhood of Gamonal in the city of Burgos in protest at the announcement of municipal works that would reduce free parking spaces.

FEBRUARY

- Infanta Elena testifies before the judge.

MARCH

- March of Dignity: mobilisations against cuts and austerity policies culminate in a large demonstration in Madrid.

APRIL

- The Spanish Congress rejects (299 votes against and 47 in favour) the proposal for an agreed referendum on the independence of Catalonia.

MAY

- European elections. Strong erosion of PP and PSOE which, despite being the two most voted parties, only account for 49 per cent of the votes. Podemos emerges: 8 per cent and 5 deputies.

JUNE

- Abdication of Juan Carlos I to alleviate the decline of the Crown.
- Massive mobilisations in the Canary Islands against the demonstration against oil prospecting by Repsol. The regional government does not support the prospecting. In January 2015 Repsol will desist.
- The government sells 49 per cent of AENA, the company that manages the airports. It is the biggest privatisation in 16 years.

JULY

- The PAH announces an ILP in Catalonia.
- Pedro Sánchez is elected Secretary General of the PSOE.
- The former conservative nationalist president of Catalonia, Jordi Pujol, publicly admits to having hidden money abroad for 34 years from the Treasury, which he claims to be an inheritance from his father. Major political scandal.

SEPTEMBER

- 11 September. Mass mobilisation in favour of independence. Demonstration in the form of a 'V' for 'Vote'.
- The President of Catalonia Artur Mas signs the decree calling for the referendum ('consulta') on the independence of Catalonia to be held on 9 November. The question is twofold: 'Do you want Catalonia to become a state? If yes, do you want it to be an independent state?'

OCTOBER AND NOVEMBER

- Founding congress of Podemos in Vistalegre (Madrid). The theses defended by Iglesias and Errejón clearly prevail.
- The Constitutional Court bans the 9-N referendum ('consulta'). The Catalan government announces a Plan B: the organisation of a 'process of citizen participation' that includes a ballot box vote. The formal organisation of the referendum will be carried out by several non-governmental organisations.
- 9 November. 2.3 million votes in the participatory process. 80.76 per cent in favour of independence.

2015

JANUARY

- Large demonstration, 'March for Change', organised by Podemos in Madrid.
- Some polls place Podemos as the leading party.
- Beginning of media promotion of Ciudadanos, a liberal nationalist Spanish party, until then based only in Catalonia, as a 'right-wing Podemos'.

MARCH

- The Organic Law on Citizen Security, popularly known as the Gag Law, is passed.

MAY

- Jordi Sánchez is elected head of the ANC to replace Carme Forcadell.
- Municipal and regional elections. Victory of the so-called 'candidatures for change' (left-wing alliances in which Podemos participates) in key cities (Madrid, Barcelona, Zaragoza, A Coruña, Cádiz ...).

JUNE

- Official break-up of Convergencia i Unió (CiU), a coalition created in 1978, due to strategic differences over independence: Convergencia (CDC) opts for the sovereigntist path and Unió (UDC) for a regionalist path.
- Junts pel Sí is created, an alliance between CDC and ERC, with the support of personalities, to contest the elections to the Catalan Parliament as a 'unitary' pro-independence list.

JULY

- The Catalan Parliament approves the ILP presented by the PAH almost unanimously. The law approved in

Catalonia will serve as inspiration for the PAH to present similar proposals to other regional parliaments.

SEPTEMBER

- 11 September. New mass mobilisation for Catalan independence.
- 27 September. Elections to the Catalan Parliament. Considered 'plebiscitary' on independence. Victory for Junts pel Sí. Together with the CUP, the pro-independence movement has an absolute majority of MPs, but not 50 per cent of the votes. Ciudadanos first opposition force.

DECEMBER

- General elections. Victory for the PP but with weak results (123 deputies, 28 per cent). Very poor result for the PSOE (90 deputies, 22 per cent), although it manages to stay ahead of Podemos (69 deputies, 20 per cent). Ciudadanos fourth force (40 deputies, 14 per cent). Fragmentation of parliament. In Catalonia, the coalition En Comú Podem, sponsored by Podemos and Ada Colau, is the most voted force.

2016

JANUARY

- Artur Mas, after realising that he does not have the support of the CUP, steps aside and resigns his candidacy. Carles Puigdemont, from the same party as Mas, is proclaimed President of Catalonia.

FEBRUARY

- The Nóos trial begins with Iñaki Urdangarín and the Infanta Cristina de Borbón as the main protagonists.

- A team of puppeteers is arrested and remanded in custody for five days, in application of the Gag Law, accused of extolling terrorism during the performance of a play in Madrid. They are finally acquitted.

MARCH

- Arnaldo Otegi is released from prison.
- Abrupt political and personal rift between Iglesias and Errejón.
- Publication of false defamatory information against Podemos. Beginning of a long media dirty war against the party.

APRIL

- The Spanish government suspends most of the content of the Catalan ILP promoted by the PAH with an appeal to the Constitutional Court, which implies the precautionary suspension of the law.

JUNE

- General elections. Elections are repeated after half a year of political deadlock and the impossibility of forming a new government. The PP wins again (137 seats), the PSOE falls to 85 but maintains second place, and Unidas Podemos (coalition between Podemos and Izquierda Unidad), with 71 seats, fails to overtake the PSOE. In Catalonia, the coalition En Comú Podem, sponsored by Podemos and Ada Colau, is the most voted force.

JULY

- A woman denounces a gang rape during the Sanfermines fiestas in Pamplona. This is the beginning of the 'La Manda' case, which will have wide social repercussions in the coming years.

SEPTEMBER

- Puigdemont announces before the Catalan Parliament the holding of a referendum on Catalan independence within a year, with or without the agreement of the state.
- Birth of the Partit Demòcrata de Catalunya (PDeCAT) as a re-foundation of Convergència Democràtica de Catalunya (CDC) with the aim of distancing itself from its regionalist past and corruption scandals.
- Internal coup in the PSOE against Pedro Sánchez, led by the old guard around the former president Felipe Gonzalez and the territorial leaders led by the Andalusian president Susana Díaz. Sánchez resigns after four days of internal chaos. The new PSOE helps Rajoy's investiture as president.

2017

FEBRUARY

- The former Catalan president Artur Mas and three other ministers of his government are sentenced for disobedience in the wake of 9-N, leading to their disqualification for between half a year and a year and a month.
- Second Podemos congress in Vistalegre. Iglesias' list (56 per cent) wins over Errejón (37 per cent). Anticapitalistas obtains 9 per cent.
- Sentence in the Nóos case. Urdangarín sentenced to six years and three months in prison for prevarication, embezzlement, fraud, influence peddling and two tax offences. Acquittal of the Infanta Cristina.
- The former presidents of Bankia, Rodrigo Rato, and Caja Madrid, Miguel Blesa, sentenced to 4 and 6 years in prison for the 'black' credit card scandal.

MARCH

- Start of the Palau case trial. Millet denounces 'irregular financing' of CDC.
- 8th March. Feminist mobilisations within the framework of the International Women's Strike. Reinvigoration of March 8th.

MAY

- Pedro Sanchez wins the PSOE primary elections against the PSOE apparatus. He is proclaimed new Secretary General in June.
- The Sindicat d'Inquilins (Tenants Union) is born in Catalonia, inspired by organisations in other countries and dedicated to defending people living in rented accommodation.

JUNE

- President Puigdemont announces that the referendum on self-determination for Catalonia will be held on 1 October with the following question: 'Do you want Catalonia to be an independent state in the form of a republic?'
- Banco Popular, almost bankrupt due to toxic real estate assets, is expropriated by the European Union.

JULY

- Mariano Rajoy testifies before the Audiencia Nacional and denies knowledge of the economic affairs related to the Gürtel plot.

AUGUST

- Islamist attack on the Ramblas in Barcelona. Catalan President Puigdemont, Mayor Ada Colau, Spanish President Rajoy and King Felipe VI take part in the demonstration to condemn the attack, in an institutional climate that is rarefied by the imminence of 1 October.

SEPTEMBER

- The Bank of Spain considers at least 75 per cent of the bank bail-out to be irrecoverable.
- 6–7 September. The Catalan Parliament approves the Referendum Law, which gives legal cover to 1-O, and the Transitory Laws, which regulate an eventual independence process. Official call for 1-O. Maximum institutional tension.
- 11 September. New mass demonstration for independence.
- 20 September. Police search the headquarters of the Catalan government's Ministry of Economy. Spontaneous protests against this move.

OCTOBER AND NOVEMBER

- 1 October. Holding of the independence referendum. 2,300 polling stations in operation and widespread social mobilisation to defend them. Police charge polling stations.
- 3 October. General strike ('National stoppage') in Catalonia in support of the referendum and against police violence. Peak of the mobilisation.
- 8 October. Major demonstration in Barcelona against independence.
- 10 October. The pro-independence parties agree on a declaration of independence. Puigdemont temporarily suspends the declaration, calling for international mediation and negotiations.
- 16 October. Jordi Sánchez and Jordi Cuixart, leaders of the ANC and Òmnium Culural, are charged with sedition and as organisers of the 20-s protests and imprisoned.
- 27 October. The Catalan Parliament votes on a declaration of independence. The Catalan government makes no attempt to implement it. The Spanish government announces the application of Article 155 whereby the Catalan administration is suspended and directly controlled

by the Spanish government. Rajoy announces the dissolution of the Catalan parliament and the call for Catalan elections on 21 December.
- Puigdemont and part of the Catalan government go into exile. Vice-president Oriol Junqueras and other members of the government stay behind and are imprisoned.

DECEMBER

- Parliamentary elections. New pro-independence majority. Junts per Catalunya led by Puigdemont is slightly ahead of ERC. Ciudadanos is the most voted force.

2018

JANUARY

- Sentence in the Palau case. Felix Millet convicted. Irregular financing of CDC is accredited.

MARCH

- Massive 8th March in the framework of the World Women's Strike. Milestone for feminism in Spain.
- Puigdemont announces the formation in exile of the Council for the Republic, a private body that will work for the internationalisation of Catalonia's independence process.

APRIL

- The members of 'La Manada', a group of five men accused of sexual assault in 2016, are acquitted of rape and convicted of sexual abuse. Feminist protests break out in several cities.
- The German justice system releases Carles Puigdemont, who had been arrested a few days earlier, and refuses to extradite him to Spain.

MAY AND JUNE

- Rapper Valtònyc goes into exile in Brussels in view of his imminent imprisonment for glorifying terrorism and offences against the King, among others.
- ETA announces by letter that it is 'completely dissolving all its structures' and that it is closing 'its historical cycle and its function'.
- Quim Torra, Puigdemont's proposed candidate in view of his inability to be invested, is appointed president of the Generalitat.
- Sentence in the Gürtel case. The ringleader of the plot, Correa, sentenced to 51 years. The ex-treasurer of the PP, Bárcenas, is sentenced to 33 years, and the PP is condemned as a legal entity.
- The sentence leads to a motion of censure against Mariano Rajoy. Sánchez is sworn in as president with the support of the PSOE, United Podemos, and several Catalan and Basque nationalist parties.
- The Supreme Court upholds Urdangarín's conviction, although the sentence is reduced by five months to five years and ten months.

JULY

- Pablo Casado is elected president of the PP at the 19th National Congress. He embodies a young neocon generation indebted to Aznar.

SEPTEMBER

- September 11. New large pro-independence demonstration.

OCTOBER

- Pro-independence demonstrations on the anniversary of 1 October.
- The far-right Vox party, then extra-parliamentary, holds a high-profile event in Vistalegre, attended by 10,000 people.

NOVEMBER

- The European Court of Human Rights (ECHR) rules that the rights of Arnaldo Otegi and other defendants were violated in the National High Court (Audiencia Nacional) trial in which they were convicted.

DECEMBER

- Elections in Andalusia. The PSOE wins but experiences a strong setback in its historic stronghold and does not have a majority to form a government. Vox bursts into parliament with force for the first time: 11 per cent and 12 deputies.

2019

JANUARY

- Errejón announces his departure from Podemos to create a new platform for the May municipal and regional elections in Madrid.
- PP candidate Juanma Moreno is sworn in as Andalusian president at the head of a coalition government with Ciudadanos, and with the external support of Vox. End of forty years of uninterrupted PSOE government in Andalusia.
- The Spanish government agrees to withdraw the appeal of unconstitutionality on the Catalan ILP promoted by the PAH.

FEBRUARY

- Youth mobilisations against climate change organised by Fridays for Future.
- Demonstration in Plaza Colón in Madrid called by the PP, Ciudadanos and Vox against Sánchez's alleged concessions to Catalan independence. Photo of the

leaders of the three parties, Casado, Rivera and Abascal. The demonstration represents the public legitimisation of Vox.
- The trial begins in the Supreme Court against the Catalan political leaders imprisoned for 1 October.

MARCH

- New massive feminist mobilisation on the occasion of the international women's strike.
- Important demonstration of the 'España vaciada' ('Empty Spain') in Madrid, organised by groups from rural and abandoned areas. The issue of 'Empty Spain' will be part of the political debate in the following years with the creation of some local/provincial parties with some electoral success.

APRIL

- General elections. The PSOE wins, but needs the support of Podemos to have a majority in Congress. Long and unsuccessful negotiations between the two parties, as Sánchez does not accept Iglesias' proposal to form a coalition government.

MAY

- Municipal and regional elections. The main 'mayors of change' elected in 2015 are defeated. Kichi, mayor of Podemos and member of Anticapitalistas, revalidates his victory in Cadiz. Ada Colau comes second in Barcelona but wins a majority of votes in the council to be re-elected.
- In the European elections, the list headed by former president Puigdemont wins in Catalonia.

JUNE

- The Supreme Court rectifies the sentence in the 'La Manda' case and convicts its members of sexual assault.

SEPTEMBER

- Another big youth protest and climate strike called by Fridays for Future.

OCTOBER

- The Supreme Court announces sentences against Catalan pro-independence leaders. Sentences range from 9 to 13 years in prison for the crimes of sedition, disobedience and embezzlement of public funds.
- Protests against the sentence break out in Catalonia. Mass march to El Prat airport and occupation of T-1 for a few hours. Local rallies, roadblocks and student strike. The 'Marches for Freedom' tour various parts of Catalonia. Demonstrations and night-time clashes with the police in Barcelona last several days.

NOVEMBER

- General elections. The PSOE wins again. PSOE and Unidas Podemos quickly announce a coalition government. It is the first since the Transition. Más País, Errejón's project, fails and gets only one deputy. Ciudadanos collapses. Resignation of its leader Albert Rivera and the beginning of the party's unstoppable decline.

2020

JANUARY

- Sánchez is sworn in as president.
- The exiled Catalan ex-president, Carles Puigdemont, is authorised to apply for his MEP status.
- General strike in Euskadi called by nationalist unions.

MARCH

- 8th March. New large-scale feminist mobilisations.
- 14th March. Declaration of a state of alarm to manage the spread of COVID-19. General confinement of the population.

MAY

- Start of indefinite strike at Nissan in Barcelona due to the threat of closure of its factory in Barcelona.

JUNE

- End of the state of alarm. End of general lockdown, but maintenance of some restrictions on face-to-face activities, mandatory face masks, and other measures.

JULY

- The investigation of the trial against the Pujol family ends. The judge finds evidence of crimes against the whole family for belonging to a criminal organisation or illicit association, money laundering, fraud against the Public Treasury and forgery of documents.
- The Supreme Court overturns the 2011 conviction of Arnaldo Otegi and other Basque pro-independence leaders.

AUGUST

- King Juan Carlos I, emeritus, with mounting judicial problems and hit by increasing journalistic revelations about corruption scandals, leaves Spain.

SEPTEMBER

- The Cumbre Vieja volcano on the island of La Palma (Canary Islands) erupts. Volcanic activity continues until December 25.
- The Audiencia Nacional acquits Rodrigo Rato and the other defendants in the Bankia bankruptcy.

- The President of the Catalan government, Quim Torra, is suspended from office by the Supreme Court for a crime of disobedience.
- Agreement between the unions and Nissan management in Barcelona that, to a large extent, accepts the company's plans.

OCTOBER

- New media revelations about the opaque business dealings of the emeritus Juan Carlos I.
- Second state of alarm. Some restrictions on face-to-face activities.

NOVEMBER AND DECEMBER

- The media scandal surrounding the emeritus king continues. Juan Carlos I files a tax return with the Treasury to regularise his tax situation.

2021

FEBRUARY

- Elections in Catalonia. The PSC is the leading force, but the three pro-independence parties have an absolute majority and 52 per cent of the votes (but with a turnout of only 51 per cent). ERC is ahead of Junts by the slimmest of margins. Vox enters the Catalan parliament for the first time.
- Demonstrations and riots in Barcelona in protest at the imprisonment of the rapper Pablo Hassel on charges of apologising for terrorism.

MAY

- Pere Aragonès of Esquerra Republicana de Catalunya (ERC) becomes president of the Generalitat after

lengthy negotiations with Junts per Catalunya, with the CUP voting in favour.
- Regional elections in Madrid. Wide victory for Díaz Ayuso's PP, with a hard right-wing and populist discourse. Más Madrid (the party created by Errejón), headed by Mónica García, second force, ahead of PSOE. Bad results for Iglesias, candidate for Podemos. He announces that he is resigning and leaving politics.

JUNE

- The government, amid opposition from the right, grants a partial pardon to the pro-independence leaders imprisoned for 1 October. Their disqualification is maintained.

JULY

- Corinna Larsen, Juan Carlos I's mistress, denounces the emeritus king for harassment before the High Court of Justice in England.

SEPTEMBER

- The Public Prosecutor's Office of the Supreme Court affirms that Juan Carlos I hid commissions in tax havens.
- New mobilisation for independence on 11 September after 2020 was suspended due to the pandemic.

OCTOBER

- Otegi apologises to ETA victims: 'We feel your pain. It should never have happened.'

DECEMBER

- Start of the vaccination campaign by COVID.

2022

JANUARY

- The High Court of Justice of Catalonia reaffirms its ruling on 25 per cent of classes in Spanish in schools and gives the government of Catalonia two months to implement it.

FEBRUARY

- Labour reform approved by the Spanish government, with the agreement of employers and trade unions.
- Regional elections in Castile and Leon. New victory for the PP. A coalition government is formed and Vox enters a regional government for the first time, with its leader as vice-president.
- Express defenestration of PP president Pablo Casado after a confrontation with Díaz Ayuso, the regional president of the Community of Madrid, also from the PP.

MARCH

- Protests by transport drivers, promoted outside the sector's official federations, over the cost of energy.
- The Public Prosecutor's Office closes the investigations into Juan Carlos I, freeing him from criminal prosecution.
- Agreement of the European Council to allow Spain and Portugal to limit the price of gas.
- The Spanish government aligns itself with Morocco in the conflict over Western Sahara.

APRIL

- Alberto Nuñez Feijoo is elected new president of the PP. More conciliatory and less neocon public profile than Casado.

- Citizen Lab and the *New Yorker* reveal that Spain spied on more than 60 pro-independence leaders, including the Catalan president and his predecessors, with the Pegasus Spyware program.
- The government approves a very limited Royal Decree on transparency of the Royal Household that does not oblige Felipe VI to publish his assets.

MAY AND JUNE

- The director of the National Intelligence Centre (CNI), Paz Esteban, is dismissed over the Pegasus scandal. PP and PSOE block any investigation of the case in Congress.
- Teachers mobilise in Catalonia to protest against the change in the school calendar and the lack of teachers.
- Regional elections in Andalusia. Historic absolute majority for the PP. Vox stagnates for the first time (13.46 per cent). Adelante Andalucía, the coalition led by Teresa Rodríguez (Anticapitalistas and former regional secretary of Podemos) manages to enter parliament (4.58 per cent, 2 deputies).
- At least 23 dead in a massive attempt by sub-Saharan immigrants to jump the Melilla fence. Sánchez justifies police violence by Moroccan authorities.
- NATO summit in Madrid focused on the consequences of Russia's invasion of Ukraine.

JULY

- New revelations certify the dirty war against Podemos orchestrated by the PP government, sectors of the police and the media, with the dissemination of false information.
- The Spanish Congress approves the Law of Democratic Memory.
- Year-on-year inflation reaches 10.8 per cent, the highest since 1984.

AUGUST

- The UN Human Rights Committee rules that Spain 'violated the political rights' of former members of the Government and Parliament of Catalonia by suspending them from their public functions before being sentenced in 2019.
- The Law of Integral Guarantee of Sexual Freedom, known as the 'only yes is yes' law, is passed.

SEPTEMBER AND OCTOBER

- Major pro-independence demonstration on 11 September. A clear divorce between the Catalan National Assembly (ANC), which proposes a declaration of independence in 2023, and President Pere Aragonès, of the ERC, and threatens a citizens' list outside the parties in the next elections.
- Fifth anniversary of the referendum of 1 October marked by a climate of division between pro-independence forces.
- Josep Costa, ex-vice-president of the Parliament, stands up, in a gesture with wide media repercussions, to the court in the trial of the former Bureau of the Parliament of Catalonia for disobedience.
- Junts per Catalunya decides to leave the Catalan government, which is now formed exclusively by ERC.

NOVEMBER

- The High Court of Justice of Catalonia acquits the former president of the Parliament of Catalonia Roger Torrent and three other pro-independence members of the Chamber's board of the crime of disobedience to the Constitutional Court for having allowed the debate and approval of a resolution on the right of self-determination of Catalonia and another against the monarchy.

DECEMBER

- The Spanish Congress approves the suppression of the crime of sedition, the modification of that of embezzlement, which affects the Catalan pro-independence leaders, and the change in the method of election of the magistrates of the Constitutional Court. Atmosphere of great tension between PSOE and PP and between the Spanish government and the most conservative sector of the judiciary.
- The year closes as the warmest in the history of Spain since meteorological records have been kept.

2023

FEBRUARY

- Approval of the Law for the real and effective equality of trans people and for the guarantee of LGTBI rights, better known as Trans Law.
- The Supreme Court maintains the disqualification of four pro-independence leaders convicted for 1 October (Oriol Junqueras, Raül Romeva, Jordi Turull and Dolors Bassa) despite the change in the Penal Code regarding embezzlement. Five others ceased to be disqualified because they were not convicted at the time for this crime (Forcadell, Forn, Rull, Sànchez and Cuixart).

MARCH

- Vox presents a failed motion of censure in the Spanish Congress.
- The former Minister of Education Clara Ponsatí returns to Catalonia after five years of exile. Brief detention and release.
- Laura Borras, former president of the Parliament of Catalonia, is sentenced to four and a half years in prison

and 13 years of disqualification for false documentation and administrative malfeasance. The offences are not related to the independence process. In June her seat in the Parliament of Catalonia is removed.

MAY

- The Brazilian soccer player Vinicius Júnior is the target of racist insults in a match between Valencia C.F. and Real Madrid. The case has wide international repercussions.

AUGUST

- As a result of the negotiations between PSOE and Junts, the party of the ex-president Puigdemont, the Spanish government starts the formal procedures to apply for official status forf the Catalan language in the European Union. It is the beginning of a long series of procedures still unresolved.
- 20 August. Victory of the Spanish women's national team in the World Cup. A scandal breaks out when the president of the Royal Spanish Football Federation (RFEF), Luis Rubiales, kisses the national team player Jenni Hermoso without her consent. After bullying the player and statements against feminism, and protests from all the players, Rubiales ends up resigning from his post two weeks later.

SEPTEMBER

- The Congress approves the processing of the reform of the Chamber's regulations which will allow the elected members to use the co-official languages recognised in their respective Statutes of Autonomy, i.e., Catalan, Basque and Galician.

NOVEMBER

- The PSOE reaches an agreement with ERC, first, and with Junts, later, for the investiture of Pedro Sánchez.

The agreement with Junts includes an amnesty law.
- Maximum radicalisation of the right-wing Spanish nationalist protests.
- 17 November. Sánchez is invested president of the government.
- 30 November. Feminist General Strike in Euskadi. Significant follow-up in education.
- Data from the Meteorological Service of Catalonia show that the country is suffering the worst drought in its history, with a precipitation deficit that has been dragging on since autumn 2020. In the following months the drought will worsen.

DECEMBER

- Five years of blockage of the renewal of the General Council of the Judiciary (CGPJ), due to the refusal of the PP to reach an agreement with the PSOE.
- Podemos leaves the Sumar coalition, dissatisfied with the secondary role to which it has been relegated within the coalition led by Yolanda Díaz.
- The year closes with a more moderate inflation rate of 3.1 per cent.

2024

JANUARY

- The Ministry of Labour and the unions, with the opposition of the employers, agree to increase the minimum wage by 5 per cent.

FEBRUARY

- A corruption case related to the payment of commissions for the public purchase of masks during the COVID-19 pandemic breaks out, with Koldo García

Isaguirre, former advisor to the ex-minister of Pedro Sánchez's government, José Luis Ábalos, at its centre.
- Start of regional mobilisations in Madrid in public education.
- Catalan government tightens water use restrictions as drought worsens.

MARCH

- The Catalan Parliament rejects the budget presented by the government of Pere Aragonès of ERC.

APRIL

- April 25th. After media and judicial attacks on his wife, Pedro Sánchez announces in a public letter that he is giving himself five days to reflect on his continuity as president of the government. After the deadline he announces that he will remain in office.
- Rainy month in Catalonia, alleviating the drought and the emergency measures dictated by the Catalan government.

MAY

- 12th May. Elections to the Catalan Parliament. Victory of the PSC. Junts, led by Carles Puigemont still in exile, comes second. Collapse of the party of president Pere Aragonès, ERC. Overall, very bad results for the pro-independence parties, which blame the demobilisation of voters. Entry into Parliament of the Catalan Alliance party (*Aliança Catalana*), a far-right xenophobic pro-independence formation.
- Encampments break out in several universities in solidarity with Gaza and in favour of the rupture of relations with Israel. Under student pressure the University of Barcelona (UB) approves the rupture of scientific and academic collaboration with Israel.
- Teachers strike in the País Valencià in defence of the Catalan language and against the policies of the

conservative Spanish nationalist regional government.
- Regional protests in defence of public health and public education against the right-wing government of Isabel Díaz Ayuso in the region of Madrid.
- Protests in Mallorca against mass tourism and in defence of the right to housing.
- The Spanish government recognises the Palestinian state.
- 30 May. The Spanish Congress passes the Amnesty Law.

JUNE

- 9 June. Victory for the PP in the European elections (34 per cent) but the PSOE remains close (30.2 per cent). Vox rises to 9 per cent. Emergence of a new far-right party, Se acabó la Fiesta (4.59 per cent), led by a far-right YouTuber. Sumar (4.65 per cent) and Podemos (3.28 per cent) achieve similar results in their mutual battle for electoral hegemony on the left. In Catalonia, the socialist party, PSC (30 per cent), wins by a wide margin.
- The amnesty law comes into force after its publication in the Official State Gazette. An uncertain period begins in which the judiciary will try to boycott the enforcement of the law.

AUGUST

- 8 August. Salvador Illa, PSC candidate, is invested president of the Generalitat de Catalunya, with the votes of his party, ERC and Comuns. A few days before, ERC activists had approved in an internal referendum the pre-agreement with the PSC. Carles Puigdemont makes a fleeting reappearance in public in Barcelona and returns immediately afterwards to exile in Brussels. The judicial battle for the application of the amnesty continues, given the manoeuvres of the judiciary to hinder its implementation, particularly in cases such as that of Puigdemont.

Glossary of Organisations

Alianza Catalana (Catalan Alliance)
Pro-independence, far-right and xenophobic political party founded in 2020. In 2023 it won the mayoralty of the town of Ripoll and in May 2024 it entered the Catalan Parliament with two members and 3.78% of the votes.

Anticapitalistas (Anticapitalists)
Revolutionary, feminist, ecosocialist and internationalist political organisation. Among its best-known leaders are Teresa Rodríguez and Miguel Urban. Anticapitalistas played a decisive role in the creation of Podemos in 2014, and maintained a line of opposition to Iglesias until its official exit from Podemos in February 2020 (although since 2017 its participation in Podemos was basically reduced to the region of Andalusia where it held the party leadership). Its partner organisation in Catalonia is Anticapitalistes, which in 2014 participated in the creation of Podem in Catalonia and in 2015 of En Comú Podem (the Catalan alliance between Podemos, the Greens and Ada Colau). It supported the referendum of 1 October 2017.

Assemblea Nacional Catalana (ANC, Catalan National Assembly)
Organisation formally set up in May 2012, following a process that began in April 2011. It was the organiser of the pro-independence demonstration of 11 September 2012 that started the so-called 'Process'. Between 2012 and 2017 it was the main social organisation of the pro-independence movement.

After 2017 it defended the need to move towards another confrontation with the state and to make Catalonia's independence effective. In 2022 it consummated its divorce from the dialogue strategy promoted by the Catalan government led by Esquerra Republicana de Catalunya (ERC) and threatened the possibility of promoting a 'civic list' outside parties in the next elections to the Catalan Parliament.

Candidatura d'Unitat Popular (CUP, People's Unity Candidacy)

Catalan pro-independence and anti-capitalist political party. After being successful in municipal elections in 2007 and, especially, in 2011, it entered the Catalan Parliament for the first time in 2012 with 3 deputies. Between 2015 and 2017 its 10 deputies were necessary to guarantee a pro-independence majority in the Parliament. Since then, it critically supported the Catalan government, sustaining it in exchange for its commitment to the independence referendum. In 2015, their refusal to elect Artur Mas as president, marked by his policy of social cuts, forced him to withdraw and propose Carles Puigdemont, from his own party, as a candidate for the presidency, obtaining the support of the CUP. Since 2017, CUP has gradually distanced itself from the pro-independence government of the Generalitat, headed first by Quim Torra (until 2021) and then by Pere Aragonés.

Catalunya en Comú (Catalonia in Common)

See En comú Podem.

Ciutadans/Ciudadanos (Citizens)

Liberal party founded in 2006 in Catalonia with a marked anti-Catalanist discourse and opposed to language immersion in Catalan in Catalan schools. Since late 2014 its leader Albert Rivera began to be promoted in the media throughout Spain as a liberal alternative to Podemos. In the Catalan elections of December 2017, after the referendum of 1 October, it became the leading electoral force, but was unable to form a government in the face of the majority pro-independence bloc. Caught between the PP and the far-right Vox, the party went into crisis during 2019 and Albert Ribera resigned as president after the poor results in the general elections of November 2019, being replaced by Inés Arrimadas. Since then, the party has been on a path of decomposition, disappearing from almost all regional parliaments where elections have been held.

Comisiones Obreras
(CCOO, Workers Commissions)
Main trade union confederation in Spain and Catalonia. Traditionally linked to the communist party, since the 1990s it evolved towards social-liberal positions. Its Catalan branch had a low profile during the pro-independence 'Process' that began in 2012. It did not support the referendum of 1 October, nor the state repression against pro-independence leaders and the intervention of the Catalan administration through Article 155 in October 2017.

Comunes (or Comuns or Els comuns)
See En comú Podem.

Confederación Española de Derechas Autónomas
(CEDA, Spanish Confederation of Autonomous Rights)
Spanish coalition of Catholic and right-wing parties formed in 1933 during the Second Republic as an alternative to the Republican left and the labour movement. After the 1933 elections it supported the government of the conservative Republican Alejandro Lerroux.

Confederación Nacional del Trabajo
(CNT, National Confederation of Labour)
Trade union confederation founded in Barcelona in 1910 and inspired by anarcho-syndicalism. Its epicentre was Catalonia.

It developed rapidly in Barcelona during the years of the First World War and the post-war period, with Salvador Seguí as its main leader, in a climate of strong labour unrest and employer violence. Outlawed during the Primo de Rivera dictatorship between 1923 and 1930, in the period of the Second Republic, it became the most important trade union force in Catalonia and Spain. It was instrumental in the early stages of the Civil War and in the revolutionary collectivisations. During the anti-Franco period it did not play a relevant role and did not manage to rebuild itself satisfactorily in the Transition, although anarcho-syndicalism became an important current among militant minority trade unionists.

Convergència Democràtica de Catalunya (CDC, Democratic Convergence of Catalonia)
Centre-right Catalan nationalist party created in 1974 by Jordi Pujol. In 1978 it formed an electoral alliance with the small Christian-Democratic party Unió Democràtica de Catalunya (UDC). It governed Catalonia between 1980 and 2003, under the leadership of Jordi Pujol, and again between 2010 and 2015 under the leadership of Artur Mas and Carles Puigdemont (2015–17). With gradualist and moderate origins, it embraced a more sovereigntist discourse from the early 2000s and became de facto pro-independence from 2012 onwards. In 2016 it re-founded itself under the name Partit Demòcrata Europeu Català (PDeCAT), in order to shed its regionalist past and the burden of accumulated corruption scandals.

Convergencia i Unió (CiU, Convergence and Union)
Centre-right nationalist coalition between Convergència Democràtica de Catalunya (CDC) and Unió Democràtica de Catalunya (UDC) created in 1978. It governed Catalonia between 1980 and 2003 and 2010 and 2015. Dissolved in 2015 due to differences between CDC and UDC over Catalan independence.

Crida per la República (National Call for the Republic)
Short-lived pro-independence movement and organisation launched by Carles Puigdemont in 2018. It was dissolved in 2020 when Puigdemont and his team backed Junts per Catalunya.

En comú podem (ECP, Together We Can)
Electoral coalition created in 2015 between Podem (the Catalan branch of Podemos), ICV (Greens) and Barcelona en Comú, the local party of Barcelona Mayor Ada Colau, a former housing activist who successfully jumped into politics in May 2015, winning the local elections in Barcelona. It is the Catalan branch of Unidas Podemos.

Esquerra Republicana de Catalunya (ERC, Republican Left of Catalonia)
Progressive Catalanist political party created in 1931, becoming the main party in Catalonia during the Second Republic. Of republican, federalist tradition and defender of the right to self-determination, it assumed explicitly pro-independence positions from 1989 onwards, absorbing an important part of the radical pro-independence youth activism developed in the 1980s, which opted for an institutional stance. Under the leadership of Josep Lluís Carod-Rovira, between 2003 and 2010, it was part of the Catalan government within the framework of a tripartite government led by the Socialist Party of Catalonia (PSC) and also formed by Iniciativa per Catalunya Verds (ICV). From 2012, under the leadership of Oriol Junqueras, it became the second party in the pro-independence movement, after Convergencia Democràtica de Catalunya (CDC), collaborating and competing with the latter. It formed part of Junts per Catalunya, a short-lived coalition created with CDC for the 2015 Catalan elections, becoming part of the Catalan government with CDC in the process leading up to 1 October. In the Catalan elections of 2021 it became the leading pro-independence force, with its candidate

Pere Aragonés being sworn in as president of the Generalitat. Between 2012 and 2017 it was perceived by an important part of the pro-independence movement as a party that, given its trajectory, had a firmer commitment to independence than CDC. After 2017, under the leadership of its imprisoned leader Oriol Junqueras, it made a sharp turnaround in its strategy, advocating the need for a dialogue with the state to achieve amnesty and an agreed referendum on independence.

Estat Català (Catalan State)
Catalan Republican Party founded in 1922 by Francesc Macià. In 1931 it participated in the creation of Esquerra Republicana de Catalunya (ERC), with Macià becoming president of the restored Generalitat de Catalunya.

Iniciativa per Catalunya Verds (ICV, Initiative for Catalonia Greens)
Catalan Green party that emerged in the 1990s as a re-foundation of the heirs of Eurocommunism. Until 1997 it was the Catalan organisation linked to Izquierda Unida in Spain, and since then it has functioned as a Catalan party without a Spanish reference. Between 2003 and 2010 it was part of the Catalan government as a minority partner in a tripartite government formed with the Partit Socialista de Catalunya (PSC) and Esquerra Republicana de Catalunya (ERC). An advocate of the right to self-determination, but not independence, it opposed the independence process that began in 2012 and did not support the 1 October referendum, although it considered it a legitimate but non-binding protest activity. In 2015 it allied with Podem and Ada Colau, a former activist who would be elected mayor of Barcelona.

Izquierda Unida (IU, United Left)
Coalition created in 1986 by the Communist Party of Spain (PCE). In 2016 it allied with Podemos to form Unidas Podemos. Its most prominent public figure is Alberto Garzón.

Junts pel sí (Together for Yes)
Electoral coalition formed in 2015 between Convergència Democràtica de Catalunya (CDC) and Esquerra Republicana de Catalunya (ERC), and some independent personalities, which won the Catalan elections, but without an absolute majority. It was not repeated for 2017 elections.

Junts per Catalunya (Together for Catalonia)
Party promoted by the Catalan president-in-exile Carles Puigdemont for the 2017 Catalan elections, which he won. After Puigdemont could not be invested as president of the Catalan government, it was Quim Torra, an independent elected deputy in its ranks, who would become president. In the 2021 elections, led by Laura Borràs, it came in second place, becoming part of a coalition government with Esquerra Republicana de Catalunya (ERC). In October 2022, by internal referendum, its militants (winning by 55% to 45%) decided to abandon the government with ERC and move to the opposition, criticising the dialogue strategy of ERC.

Lliga Regionalista (Regionalist League)
Regionalist Catalan party founded in 1901, which became one of the main political forces in Catalonia and the main representative of conservative Catalanism in the first decades of the 20th century.

Mossos d'Esquadra
Official police force of the Generalitat de Catalunya created in 1983. It performs the ordinary functions of citizen security, administrative police, judicial police, intervention and community policing. In 2017, the force gained a lot of media attention for its handling of the Islamist terrorist attacks in Barcelona in August. During the 1 October referendum it maintained a calculated balance between not preventing the referendum from being held but at

the same time not openly disobeying any orders from the Spanish administration so as not to incur any illegality.

Omnium Cultural
Organisation founded in 1961 to promote Catalan language and culture. After the beginning of the pro-independence 'Process' in 2012, it played a growing role in alliance with the Assemblea Nacional Catalana (ANC). After the election of Jordi Cuixart in December 2015 as its president, the organisation shifted towards a more transversal and inclusive line, seeking to appeal to sectors that are not pro-independence but defenders of Catalonia's right to self-determination. It deepened this line in the aftermath of 1 October referendum.

Partido Popular (PP, Popular Party)
The main right-wing party in Spain. It governed the country between 1996 and 2004 under José María Aznar and then between 2011 and 2018 under Mariano Rajoy. It stands for an aggressive and exclusionary Spanish nationalism and defends a hard-line authoritarian approach to Catalan independence. In June 2018 it elected Pablo Casado as president, an exponent of a neocon line that was in tune with Aznar's legacy and distanced from Rajoy's pragmatism. Following an internal rebellion in February 2022, Casado was replaced by the more pragmatic Nuñez Feijoo, after a period of poor electoral results (with some regional exceptions such as Galicia and Madrid) in the face of the growing rise of Vox.

Partido Comunista de España
(PCE, Communist Party of Spain)
Created in 1921. It played a prominent role in anti-Francoism. After the first general elections in 1977 it became the main force to the left of PSOE. Since 1986 it has been the driving force behind the Izquierda Unida federation, which in 2016 allied with Podemos.

Partit Demòcrata Europeu Català
(PDeCAT, Catalan European Democratic Party)
Pro-independence centre-right party created in 2016 as part of a failed process of refounding Convergència Democràtica de Catalunya (CDC). At the end of 2017, it joined the Junts per Catalunya candidacy led by President Carles Puigdemont in exile. It broke with Junts in the Catalan elections of 2021, in which it ran on a gradualist and moderate programme with respect to independence and openly neoliberal. It did not win any MPs.

Partit Obrer d'Unificació Marxista
(POUM, Workers Party of Marxist Unification)
Non-Stalinist heterodox Marxist party founded in 1935 as a result of the unification of the Bloc Obrer i Camperol (BOC), led by Joaquim Maurin, and Andreu Nin's Izquierda Comunista (IC). Of all Spain, it was in Catalonia where it was most established. In the civil war it was repressed by PSUC and Stalinism and its Republican allies, and Andreu Nin was assassinated. During Franco's regime, its former members followed different paths. Joaquim Maurin, exiled in the United States, stayed away from politics and evolved towards more moderate positions. The POUM did not manage to rebuild itself satisfactorily after the end of Franco's regime.

Partit Socialista d'Alliberament Nacional
(PSAN, Socialist Party of National Liberation)
Marxist pro-independence party created in 1968 under the influence of the Third World movements of the time, which would become the pioneering organisation of Catalan revolutionary pro-independence currents.

Partit Socialista de Catalunya
(PSC, Catalan Socialist Party)
Catalan organisation federated with PSOE. From the 'Transition' to 2010 it was the second largest party in Catalonia.

It governed the city of Barcelona from 1979 to 2011, with Pasqual Maragall as its most prominent mayor (1982–1997). Between 2003 and 2010 it headed the government of Catalonia in a coalition with Esquerra Republicana de Catalunya (ERC) and Iniciativa per Catalunya Verds (ICV) under the presidencies of Pasqual Maragall (2003–2006) and José Montilla (2006–2010). After a strong period of electoral crisis, under the impact of the 15-M movement in 2011 and the independence process, it once again asserted itself as a central force in Catalonia, winning the regional elections of 2021, although without being able to form a government. Strongly opposed to independence, it defended the suspension of the Catalan government in 2017 with the application of Article 155, although its position has been more Catalanist than that of the PSOE.

Partido Socialista Obrero Español (PSOE, Spanish Socialist Workers' Party)

Founded in 1879. After playing an irrelevant role in the struggle against Francoism, it managed to become a central force during the Transition. It governed Spain between 1982 and 1996, under the presidency of Felipe González, between 2004 and 2011, under the leadership of José Luís Rodríguez Zapatero and, since 2018, with Pedro Sánchez at the helm. Opposed to Catalan independence and a main pillar of the 1978 regime.

Partit Socialista Unificat de Catalunya (PSUC, Unified Socialist Party of Catalonia)

Catalan communist party created in July 1936 as a result of the merger between the Unió Socialista de Catalunya, the Partit Comunista de Catalunya, the Partit Català Proletari and the Federació Catalana del PSOE. It was an independent Catalan party and a full member of the Third International, with a sovereign relationship with its Spanish referent, the Communist Party of Spain (PCE). It played a decisive role in anti-Francoism, aligned itself with Eurocommunism in the 1970s, and became the third force in the first elections to the Catalan parliament with 18% of the vote. It suffered a serious internal crisis in 1981 and in 1986 sponsored the coalition Iniciativa per Catalunya, with other small forces. In the mid-1990s it dissolved within Iniciativa per Catalunya, which was to become a green party, Iniciativa per Catalunya Verds (ICV).

Podemos
Party launched in January 2014 for the European elections in May 2014. Its emergence revolutionised the Spanish political map. Born with a rebellious profile, it quickly evolved towards institutionalisation and moderation of its proposals. In 2020, as part of a broader coalition with Izquierda Unida called Unidas Podemos, it entered government in coalition with PSOE. Its main leader was Pablo Iglesias (who resigned from his responsibilities in May 2021) and, the second, until his break with Iglesias in 2016, Íñigo Errejón. At its founding core was Anticapitalistas, an organisation that until its formal departure from Podemos in February 2020 represented a line of opposition to Iglesias and Errejón.

Tsunami Democràtic (Democratic Tsunami)
Movement that emerged in October 2019 to promote mobilisations against the conviction of pro-independence leaders for sedition. With a clandestine structure, without a visible leadership, it organised mobilisations through social media, apps and other online media. Its first and main action was the call for a mass march to occupy T-1 at El Prat Airport. After some relevant actions, it lost momentum and, likely decimated by state repression, disappeared.

Unió Democràtica de Catalunya (UDC, Democratic Union of Catalonia)
Christian-Democratic party founded in 1931. In 1978 it formed a coalition with Convergència Democràtica de Catalunya

(CDC), called Convergència i Unió (CiU), which led the Generalitat de Catalunya from 1980–2003 and 2010–2015. In 2015 it broke its alliance with CDC by opposing the pro-independence process, suffering a major internal split from those in favour of pursuing the pro-independence path. It stood alone in the Catalan and Spanish elections of 2015 without obtaining any deputies. The failure led to the resignation of its historic leader Josep Antoni Duran i Lleida, first, and the dissolution of the party, later, beset by debts.

Unió Federal Nacionalista Republicana
(UFNR, Republican Nationalist Federal Union)
Catalan political party founded in 1910 as an alliance between republicans, federalists and Catalan nationalists. After its initial success it soon went into decline, a victim of its great internal heterogeneity.

Unión General de Trabajadores
(UGT, Workers General Union)
Second largest trade union confederation in Spain and Catalonia, with a social-democratic orientation. Its Catalan branch had a low profile during the pro-independence 'Process' that began in 2012. It did not support the 1 October referendum, nor the state repression against pro-independence leaders and the intervention of the Catalan administration through Article 155 in October 2017.

Unidas Podemos (UP, Together We Can)
Electoral coalition between Podemos and Izquierda Unida created in 2016.

Unió Socialista de Catalunya
(USC, Catalan Socialist Union)
Catalan reformist socialist political party created in 1923 as a Catalanist split from the Catalan Federation of the PSOE.

In 1936 it was one of the founding organisations of the Partit Socialista Unificat de Catlaunya (PSUC) affiliated to the Third International.

Vox
Far-right party that burst onto the Spanish political scene in 2018, entering a regional parliament for the first time, the Andalusian one. In the 2019 general elections it became the third most voted force, behind PSOE and PP. Reactionary Spanish nationalism, along with xenophobia and anti-feminism, has been its main hallmark.

Acronyms

ANC	Assemblea Nacional Catalana
CCOO	Comisiones Obreras
CEDA	Confederación Española de Derechas Autónomas
CDC	Convergència Democràtica de Catalunya
CiU	Convergencia i Unió
CNT	Confederación Nacional del Trabajo
CUP	Candidatura d'Unitat Popular
ECP	En Comú Podem
ERC	Esquerra Republicana de Catalunya
ICV	Iniciativa per Catalunya Verds
IU	Izquierda Unida
PP	Partido Popular
PCE	Partido Comunista de España
PDeCAT	Partit Demòcrata Europeu Català
POUM	Partit Obrer d'Unificació Marxista
PSAN	Partit Socialista d'Alliberament Nacional
PSC	Partit Socialista de Catalunya
PSOE	Partido Socialista Obrero Español
PSUC	Partit Socialista Unificat de Catalunya
UDC	Unió Democràtica de Catalunya
UFNR	Unió Federal Nacionalista Republicana
UGT	Unión General de Trabajadores
UP	Unidas Podemos
USC	Unió Socialista de Catalunya

About the publishers

RESISTANCE BOOKS is a radical publisher of internationalist, ecosocialist, and feminist books. Resistance Books publishes books in collaboration with the International Institute for Research and Education (iire.org), and the Fourth International (fourth.international). For further information, including a full list of titles available and how to order them, go to the Resistance Books website.

info@resistancebooks.org
www.resistancebooks.org

THE INTERNATIONAL INSTITUTE FOR RESEARCH AND EDUCATION is a centre for the development of critical thought and the exchange of experiences and ideas between people engaged in their struggles. Since 1982, when the Institute opened in Amsterdam, it has organized courses for progressive forces around the world which deal with all subjects related to the emancipation of the oppressed and exploited. The iire provides activists and academics opportunities for research and education in three locations: Amsterdam, Islamabad and Manila. The iire publishes *Notebooks for Study and Research* in several languages. They focus on contemporary political debates, as well as themes of historical and theoretical importance.

iire@iire.org
www.iire.org

Recent books in this series

Palestine and Marxism
Joseph Daher, £10,
ISBN: 9781872242231

Internationalism or Russification -
A study in the Soviet Nationalities Problem
Ivan Dzyuba, £17,
ISBN: 9780902869189

The Well-Dressed Revolutionary -
The Odyssey of Michel Pablo
Hall Greenland, £18,
ISBN: 9780902869103

Hope and Marxism - Historical and Theoretical Essays
Ernest Mandel, £15,
ISBN 9780902869417

Marxists against Stalinism
Ernest Mandel and Chris Harman,
preface by Paul Le Blanc, £15,
ISBN: 9780902869578

Introduction to Marxist Theory- Selected Writings
Ernest Mandel, introduction by Ian Parker,
ISBN: 9780902869653

Critique of Modern Barbarism - Essays on Fascism,
Anti-Semitism and the Use of History
Enzo Traverso, £17,
ISBN: 9780902869820

www.ingramcontent.com/pod-product-compliance
Lightning Source LLC
Chambersburg PA
CBHW030253100526
44590CB00012B/389